D0071270

THE RIGHT TALK

THE RIGHT TALK

HOW CONSERVATIVES TRANSFORMED THE GREAT SOCIETY INTO THE ECONOMIC SOCIETY

MARK A. SMITH

PRINCETON UNIVERSITY PRESS

Princeton and Oxford

MARY M. STRIBLING LIBRARY

Copyright © 2007 by Princeton University Press
Published by Princeton University Press, 41 William Street,
Princeton, New Jersey 08540
In the United Kingdom: Princeton University Press, 3 Market Place,
Woodstock, Oxfordshire OX20 1SY
All Rights Reserved

Library of Congress Cataloging-in-Publication Data

Smith, Mark A. (Mark Alan), 1970–
The right talk : how conservatives transformed the Great Society
into the economic society / Mark A. Smith.
p. cm.
Includes bibliographical references and index.
ISBN-13: 978-0-691-13017-0 (cloth : alk. paper)
ISBN-10: 0-691-13017-5 (cloth : alk. paper)
1. Conservatism—United States.   2. United States—Politics and government.   3. United States—Economic conditions.   4. Rhetoric—Political
aspects—United States.   I. Title.
JC573.2.U6S6434 2007
320.520973—dc22   2006100280

British Library Cataloging-in-Publication Data is available

This book has been composed in Palatino

Printed on acid-free paper. ∞

press.princeton.edu

Printed in the United States of America

1 3 5 7 9 10 8 6 4 2

JC
573.2
.U6
S65
2007

FOR MOM AND DAD,

who let me find my own way

CONTENTS

THE RIGHT TALK

ONE

Introduction

In 1954 a brash and brilliant twenty-eight-year-old began planning a bold literary venture. As the future editor and initial publisher of *National Review*, William F. Buckley, Jr., worked tirelessly to secure financing and assemble a talented group of writers. The inaugural issue dated November 19, 1955, showcased the magazine as a forum where conservative ideas would be explained, refined, and applied to problems and politics at home and abroad. In Buckley's first "Publisher's Statement" describing purposes and goals, the budding intellectual icon noted that *National Review* "stands athwart history, yelling Stop, at a time when no one is inclined to do so, or to have much patience with those who so urge it."[1] Buckley left no doubt that he felt profound regret and even despair over America's recent past and distasteful present.

Having seen the political ground shift underneath them during the two previous decades, conservatives of the 1950s could point to a long list of grievances. To begin, the international power and prestige of the Soviet Union seemed to be rising rather than falling. The USSR had gained the enmity of a wide range of Americans, with conservatives at the front of the line, by failing to respect private property, prohibiting the exercise of civil liberties, centralizing all political authority in the state, and spreading communism to other nations. The Communist grip on Eastern Europe tightened after Soviet tanks crushed a nascent rebellion in Hungary in 1956. Pursued by both Democratic and Republican

administrations, the American foreign policy featuring contain-
ment over confrontation looked morally weak and geopolitically
ineffective to the intellectuals collected under *National Review*'s
masthead.

Politics in America had also witnessed a revolution on matters of domestic policy. Whereas business owners and managers
once enjoyed a high degree of insulation from the federal government, now they faced many forms of intervention. Government agencies, most of them created during the Depression, regulated prices and restricted competition in industries such as
banking, insurance, airlines, trucking, and radio and television
broadcasting. With workers demanding a seat at the bargaining
table, managerial autonomy also eroded due to internal challenges. Boosted by formal recognition from the federal government and the establishment of fair labor-management practices,
union membership nearly tripled from only 12% of the workforce in 1930 to 33% by the time *National Review* first hit the newsstands.[2]

The entrenchment of unions as a seemingly permanent fix-
ture on the industrial landscape coincided with a major growth
in the welfare state. Moving slowly but systematically, policymakers enacted and expanded programs to provide benefits to an
ever-growing body of citizens. Social Security, which initially
reached only a minority of the labor force, broadened as law-
makers regularly absorbed new categories of workers into the
system and on several occasions voted to increase benefit levels.
At roughly the same time that Buckley criticized "the intransi-
gence of the Liberals, who run this country," Congress added dis-
ability coverage to the retirement system. Unemployment insurance, which just a few decades earlier was a patchwork network
that did not exist at all in many states, had recently attained per-
manence and stability, and public housing—though only a modest program in budgetary terms—was following the same upward trajectory. The various components of the welfare state
received financing from payroll taxes, corporation taxes, and excise taxes, but the most rapidly increasing source of revenue
in the postwar years was the steeply progressive federal income

tax. Although few people paid at the top marginal rate, the tax symbolized a concrete government commitment to equality that threatened cherished conservative values.

Perhaps worst of all from the perspective of conservatives, who saw the danger of not just a string of painful defeats but the prospect of unconditional surrender, the scope of the national debate had narrowed when important leaders from the Republican party sought to accommodate the New Deal rather than overturn it. The moderate Dwight Eisenhower prevailed at the 1952 Republican convention, disappointing backers of Robert Taft who hoped that the Ohio senator would be the standard-bearer for turning back the clock. Buckley's opening issue of *National Review* signaled a last-ditch stand and even foreshadowed a counterattack by praising the independence and free thinking of the "conservatives who have not made their peace with the New Deal." After promising from the outset that the magazine would offer principled criticism of Eisenhower's policies and programs, *National Review* later declined to endorse the president's reelection bid in 1956.[3] Not until Barry Goldwater's candidacy in 1964 could the conservative journal give an enthusiastic endorsement to a presidential nominee.[4]

The resounding failure of Goldwater's candidacy and the steady stream of policies abhorrent to the right forced *National Review* and its ideological brethren to continue their defensive posture. The most prominent political movements of the 1950s and 1960s, the struggles for civil rights and voting rights, overcame opposition from traditional bases of conservatism: southern legislators and adherents of states' rights elsewhere in the nation. Despite their former opposition to the Supreme Court's 1954 decision in *Brown v. Board of Education*, Buckley and other conservatives eventually looked back with approval on federal involvement in overturning Jim Crow laws.[5] On other matters, however, many of the policy legacies of the 1960s remained controversial into the twenty-first century. Federal court decisions protected the rights of the accused, required a higher wall of separation between church and state, and enforced a one-person, one-vote rule for the drawing of district boundaries. A hard-fought political battle ended in 1965 when Congress passed legislation creating Medicare and Medicaid, positioning the federal government as a major player in the financing of health care. More generally, the Great Society called for a War on Poverty that would be won through job training programs and community development initiatives.

At the same time, government activities directly affecting business proliferated, and the era of largely unregulated capitalism receded further into the past. The issue of environmental protection burst onto the national scene, sparking laws covering air pollution, water pollution, waste disposal, land use, pesticide control, wilderness set-asides, and the treatment of endangered species. Consumer protection also became a prominent issue and led to government efforts regulating pharmaceuticals, automobile safety, lending practices, and coal mines. Parallel legislation brought worker health and safety, overseen by the Occupational Safety and Health Administration, under the umbrella of federal regulation. By the early 1970s regulatory agencies were intervening in the day-to-day affairs of business to a degree never before seen in peacetime. Nearly two decades after *National Review*'s inception, public policy had become considerably less aligned with conservative principles and Buckley was still largely reduced to "yelling Stop." Unknown at the time, however, the nadir had been reached, and conservatives would soon move from reacting to unpalatable political developments to creating favorable ones.

The Right Turn in American Politics

By comparison with the period spanning the New Deal through the Great Society, the country moved sharply to the right in the decades after the mid-1970s. One indicator of the political success of the right has been the amount of scholarly and journalistic attention it has attracted. After stimulating only a limited set of book-length treatments in the 1980s, the right saw the list expand dramatically in the following two decades.[6] Writers carefully, systematically, and in many cases sympathetically probed the roots of modern conservatism in the organizations, issues, leaders, and intellectual currents of the 1950s and 1960s.[7] Other informative books traced conservatism as a political force over long periods of up to a half-century.[8] Some well-researched works focused primarily on the strategies, institutions, and politicians of relatively recent times.[9]

The academic and popular writers investigated the nation's new political alignments, beginning with campaigns and elections. The Republican party grew more reliably conservative as its liberal and progressive wing that once included figures such as Earl Warren, Robert La Follette, Nelson Rockefeller, and William Scranton virtually vanished. In the ultimate barometer of a party's effectiveness, the more ideologically cohesive Republicans increased their vote totals. The GOP had stood as the clear minority party from 1932 to 1979, winning only four of the twelve presidential elections. Republicans of that era controlled on average only 39% and 38% of the seats in the House of Representatives and the Senate, respectively.[10] From 1980 to 2005, by contrast, Republicans prevailed in five of the seven presidential races and attained majorities in the House for twelve years and the Senate for eighteen years. Even after the decisive midterm elections of 2006, which gave Democrats narrow majorities of 53% in the House and 51% in the Senate, the GOP remained in a far stronger position than it had been a few decades earlier. In 2007 Republicans held thirty-one more seats in the House and eleven more seats in the Senate than they averaged from 1932 to 1979.

Many policy changes followed from the Republicans' thirty-plus years of ascent from the minority party into a status of being competitive with, and sometimes stronger than, Democrats. Revisions to policy were especially noteworthy in the area of taxation. During the recent period of Republican dominance at the presidential level, the top marginal income-tax bracket dropped drastically from 70% in 1980 to 35% in 2006. Other taxes disproportionately paid by high earners, such as levies on capital gains, dividends, and estates, have either fallen significantly or stand ready to be eliminated entirely. Meanwhile, taxes with a greater incidence at the bottom and the middle of the income spectrum, particularly payroll taxes, sales taxes, property taxes, and excise taxes, have increased over time. When federal, state, and local taxes are put together, the progressivity that formerly character-ized the tax system has been vastly weakened.[11]

The transformations achieved in regulatory policies were equally dramatic. Aided in some instances by coalitions drawn from several places in the ideological spectrum, deregulation of prices and entry conditions swept across the industries of air-lines, banking, utilities, natural gas, telecommunications, finan-cial services, and broadcast media. Consumer and environmen-tal regulation remains robust, but the resources allocated to enforcing the laws have generally declined. Inspections of food processing plants, for example, fell sharply in the 1980s and 1990s.[12] Even though President George W. Bush led few success-ful legislative cutbacks of environmental protection, his two administrations used executive orders and agency discretion to implement a variety of rollbacks, exemptions, and reductions in enforcement.[13] Meanwhile, attempts failed in the 1990s and 2000s to enact new regulations to address global warming and repetitive-stress injuries in the workplace.

Labor regulations, too, have moved in a conservative direc-tion. Administrative rulings and appointments to the National Labor Relations Board have combined to impose additional hur-dles on union organizing and maintenance. Corrected for infla-tion, the minimum wage shrank by nearly 40% in real terms from 1968 to the end of George W. Bush's first administration. In 2004 the Labor Department initiated procedures to exempt the em-ployers of eight million workers, by one estimate, from the re-quirement of time-and-a-half pay for overtime.[14] Despite the im-portant exception of the Americans with Disabilities Act, an expensive effort to require accommodations for the disabled, the hand of the federal government now touches business much more lightly than was the case in the 1970s.

The welfare state has also retrenched in some areas even though its cutbacks were not as extensive as those covering gov-ernment regulation. In the mid-1970, workers who lost their jobs were eligible for up to fifteen months of benefits from unemployment insurance; thirty years later the figure stood at six months even as the average monthly benefits, adjusted for inflation, had dropped by 10%.[15] An important government priority in the 1970s, job training now receives only a fraction of the spending levels previously allocated and reaches far fewer beneficiaries.[16] Many programs affecting low-income Americans, such as food stamps and public housing, have seen similar restrictions on the scope and generosity of coverage. The real value of average benefits from Aid to Families with Dependent Children fell by more than half from the mid-1970s to 1996, when Congress terminated the program as a federal entitlement.[17] The newer state-run programs under Temporary Aid for Needy Families include lifetime limits, strictly enforced work provisions, and other requirements.

Other conservative attempts to dismantle the welfare state have been less successful. After some changes in 1983, Social Security persisted in its previous form. George W. Bush advocated the partial or full privatization of Social Security during his presidential campaigns in 2000 and 2004, but when he revisited the issue in 2005 he faced the immense challenge of selling the public on the concept of personal accounts instead of guaranteed benefits. In a political environment where most programs targeted at the poor have shrunk, the Earned Income Tax Credit—a wage subsidy for low-income workers—greatly increased through legislation enacted in 1990 and 1993. Spending and programs for special education grew dramatically in recent decades, and states expanded the scope of Medicaid throughout the 1990s. Medicare added a prescription drug benefit in 2006, provided by private insurers working outside of Medicare, that initially attracted opposition from hard-core liberals and conservatives alike, albeit for different reasons. Overall, one can say that several parts of the welfare state moved rightward, a few elements moved leftward, and other components either remained roughly stable or else changed in directions difficult to categorize.

Conservatives' desires for changes on cultural and social issues have not fared as well. Outside of crime control, where sentencing laws are stronger, law enforcement receives larger shares of government budgets, and prisons lock up many more people, the policies pushed by significant segments of the conservative coalition have failed to advance very far. Affirmative action, for example, has been curtailed but continues in public and private institutions. Christian fundamentalists and evangelicals, the most important constituency for a cultural politics of the right, have relatively little to show for a thirty-year political mobilization that included a well-known allegiance to the Republican party. Despite the enactment of some restrictions, for example, abortions remain legal nationwide in the early and middle parts of a pregnancy. Reinstating organized group prayer in public schools, a central component of the Christian right's agenda in the 1970s, is barely mentioned anymore; nor are once-prominent calls for restoring traditional gender roles in society. The public has become more accepting of homosexuality, not less, a development reflected in the passage of nondiscrimination laws and the provision of same-sex benefits by many employers.

To the extent that summarizing across disparate areas is possible, from taxation to abortion, from the welfare state to school prayer, conservatives made major strides in translating electoral power into policymaking power, but the process remains far from complete. Thus, *turning right* is an appropriate metaphor to describe what has happened in the last three decades. Certain policy areas did undergo remarkable upheavals, and yet a thoroughgoing and comprehensive transformation has not yet occurred. If a young conservative writer were to launch a journal of opinion in the early part of the twenty-first century and assess the political terrain, she would express a vastly different charge to her followers than did William F. Buckley, Jr. Today she might write that the magazine would "stand atop history, yelling Go, at a time when so many are inclined to do so."

Education and the Economy

A puzzling question of the period from the mid-1970s forward is why conservative swings in policy materialized only in certain areas. When an electoral majority passes and implements many of its preferred policies but fails to win across-the-board changes, one wonders what accounts for the differences. Some leverage for understanding the seemingly irregular pattern of the right's policy victories can be gained from what appears at first to be an unlikely source: the relationships among education, money, and employment. An examination of these linkages in the minds of young people and policymakers will provide clues to the broader landscape of American politics that this book seeks to explain. Indeed, to comprehend the forces that caused an extensive albeit incomplete shift to the right in public policy, there is no better place to begin than the widespread recasting of education to emphasize its economic consequences.

A long-running survey of college freshmen documents the heightening of economic motivations by inquiring about, among other things, students' attachments to different objectives. Responses to the vast majority of goals, ranging from "raising a family" to "becoming accomplished in one of the performing arts" to "becoming an authority in my field," have fluctuated by no more than a few percentage points over the life of the survey. One goal stands out, however, because of its increasing prominence. A life where one is "very well off financially" has been deemed "essential" or "very important" by a growing proportion of students. After remaining flat from 1966 to 1972 at about 40%, the relevant figure jumped to 63% by 1980 and 73% by 2000.[18] While this question certainly measures materialist and consumerist desires, answers to it also reflect the economic futures young adults believe they will encounter. In a world of uncertain job prospects and overwhelming debt for much of the population, it makes good sense to give more importance to money.[19]

The motivations of money and employment emerge well before entry into higher education and, in fact, represent driving rationales for many young men and women to attend college in the first place. At the dawn of the twenty-first century, *Frontline* broadcast a program about the SAT and its centrality to college admissions. The show profiled several students from when they prepared to take the test to waiting anxiously afterward for the results. Most of the students and parents simply assumed the desirability of a college education without stating any concrete reasons. Nevertheless, insights into the underpinnings of contemporary American politics can be gleaned from those who did discuss their intentions, which were always defined in terms of upward mobility, job opportunities, and financial success. An earnest and forthright high school senior said flatly, "I feel that if I went to Berkeley, then, you know, I'd probably have a better chance of getting a good job so I can lead a decent life." One father stated that he wanted "something better for my son, to use his brain in a career that he would do better than what I have right now." Another parent expressed the common sentiment that "you can either work your tail off in high school and college, or you can spend your life in a series of jobs that involve name tags, hairnets, and the phrase, 'Would you like fries with that.'"[20]

Careers and vocations, it should be noted, have always been central to considerations of college specifically and education generally. Still, over the centuries worldwide and even in the more limited span of American history, education has been valued for other reasons. Thomas Jefferson believed that freedom and democracy could not exist without well-informed citizens who understood the historical, philosophical, and practical foundations of their system of government and the issues it faced. Contemporary theorists working in a Jeffersonian spirit see schools as places where students can learn the democratic norms of civility, tolerance for dissenting views, and the importance of public participation in the political life of local and national communities.[21] Besides this civic justification, widely expressed goals for schools have often included the value of knowledge for its own sake, the transmission of a nation's culture, and the personal development and self-fulfillment of students.[22]

Although these other aspirations persist in the minds of many teachers and administrators, public discussion on the purposes of education focuses on preparing graduates for the workforce—a fact that helps explain the nationwide growth of policies based on testing and accountability. The initiation, development, and maturation of high-stakes testing was the most noteworthy reform in education policy since 1980. In the 1980s and 1990s, most states implemented testing procedures intended to measure student learning in a core group of subjects. The No Child Left Behind Act of 2001 intensified these trends, requiring elaborate standardized tests whose results determine rewards and punishments. Aggregated by individual classrooms and schools, scores on the tests attract wide publicity and increasingly guide the funding and curriculum decisions of federal, state, and local policymakers.

Controversy continues about the desirability of these methods of measurement and assessment, with a backlash from many teachers and parents emerging in the first decade of the twenty-first century. In one respect, though, debates over whether standardized tests facilitate student learning represent second-order questions that rest on a prior assumption. The reasons why we should care about educational achievement are the first-order questions, for which the answers are often simply assumed but sometimes spelled out. When the policymakers who create, oversee, and enforce the testing regimes explain why educational achievement must be demanded and expected, the reasons usually relate to jobs and the economy. The relevance of standardized testing for this book, then, lies not in whether it shifts policy to the left or the right—liberals and conservatives can be found on all sides of the debate—but in the broadly shared assumption that the education system, however it is designed, should meet the economic needs of students and the nation.

The Economic Side of Political Struggles

The recasting of political discussions and students' behavior around the economic impact of education is merely the tip of the political iceberg. Immensely important in their own right, public perceptions of the purposes of education also illustrate a widespread trend in American politics. This book will document that for many domestic policies, the attention paid to financial consequences has increased substantially. The same criteria used for understanding education were applied outside the school-house door; from the welfare state to taxation, from transportation to regulation, political debates revolve more heavily around implications for employment, wages, and growth than was the case just a few decades ago. To be sure, other concerns regularly rise on the national agenda and spark news coverage, political conflicts, and the interest of citizens. During the 2006 midterm elections, for example, voters expressed their dissatisfaction with the continuing war in Iraq, congressional corruption tied to lobbyist Jack Abramoff, and Representative Mark Foley's email entreaties to young male pages in the House of Representatives. The fact that other matters galvanize the nation at various times notwithstanding, this book will show that parties and politicians in recent times have devoted widespread and enduring attention to the economic dimensions of many different issues.

With economic considerations becoming the coin of the realm in a range of debates over public policy, we now take them for granted. Few people pause to reflect when presidents, governors, state legislators, and school board members announce that the primary mission of schools is to prepare graduates for the workforce of the twenty-first century, and nothing seems unusual when similar economic arguments are marshaled in other policy areas. Rather than being natural and inevitable, however, these ways of thinking and speaking reflect specific processes that unfolded at a particular time in American political history. In responding to the information and opportunities available to them, a variety of participants in politics and public affairs elevated the economic basis over other potential criteria for decision making. Stressing this factor seemed to be just common sense to both citizens and political leaders, but alternative touchstones could have been envisioned.

Does the increased attention paid to the economic aspects of issues help explain the rightward turn in public policy? On first glance, it might seem that anxiety about job stability and financial security would push policy to the left rather than the right, for that was the result when similar conditions emerged in previous eras. Most notably, the industrial and agricultural collapse during the Depression forced conservatives to the sidelines of the nation's politics. While controversy has long raged about whether the New Deal represented a social democratic push or else saved capitalism from itself, there can be no question that it overturned the noninterventionist, small-government sentiment prevalent in the 1920s. During the Depression, it was the liberals who controlled the terms of political debate and the conservatives who appeared bereft of ideas.

Then and into the succeeding decades, conservative thinkers and politicians often tried to move the spotlight away from economic matters and toward other values and goals. Russell Kirk, one of the most prominent conservative intellectuals of the 1950s and 1960s, later wrote: "The great line of division in modern politics . . . lies between all those who believe in some sort of transcendent moral order, on one side, and on the other side all those who take this ephemeral existence of ours for the be-all and end-all—to be devoted chiefly to producing and consuming."[23] The eternal moral questions, Kirk believed, should be exalted over transient struggles regarding employment and acquisition. Barry Goldwater expressed similar sentiments in chiding his adversaries:

> The root difference between the Conservatives and the Liberals of today is that Conservatives take account of the *whole* man, while the Liberals tend to look only at the material side of man's nature. The Conservative believes that man is, in part, an economic, an animal creature; but that he is also a spiritual creature with spiritual needs and spiritual desires. What is more, these needs and desires reflect the *superior* side of man's nature, and thus take precedence over his economic wants.[24]

One of the cardinal rules of politics is that the losing side attempts to realign the bases on which decisions rest, seeking different means of assessing issues that will lead participants to revise their positions.[25] Goldwater sensed, accurately, that the nation's concentration on the economic dimensions of issues during and after the Depression placed the right at a disadvantage. Popular support for the traditional prescription of low taxes, minimal regulation of business, and as few social programs as possible had sunk alongside Herbert Hoover's once-sterling reputation. With conservatives from the 1930s to the 1960s failing to gain much traction on claims that their policies would deliver prosperity, a shrewd observer could easily conclude that their proposals would not be implemented unless and until other criteria were brought into play. Thus Goldwater was well served in striving to move the national dialogue beyond economic subjects.

The patterns surprisingly reversed themselves beginning in the 1970s as conservatives began triumphing on bread-and-butter matters involving taxes, government regulation, and certain social programs. Conservative revisions to laws and executive actions in the last quarter-century occurred disproportionately on issues associated with the economy. These policy changes were intertwined with a new style of communication: Instead of attempting to move the national agenda away from economic priorities, the evidence in this book reveals, the right's leading spokespersons did just the opposite. In speeches, party platforms, campaign advertisements, and journals of opinion, the economy attracted a far higher profile from the 1970s forward. On issues such as taxation, labor, regulation, energy, education, the environment, government spending, and international trade, conservatives consistently stated that their policies would lead the country to prosperity.

The trend whereby conservatives emphasize the economic effects they expect from their policy initiatives does not easily square with a common interpretation of contemporary American politics. Articulated and publicized most thoroughly by Thomas Frank's *What's the Matter with Kansas*, this perspective holds that Republicans have continually played a game of bait and switch.[26] Over several election cycles, the party's candidates supposedly constructed their campaign themes mainly around social and cultural issues such as abortion, homosexuality, crime, drugs, permissive sexual behavior, and religious expression in public life. The GOP's stands on moral traditionalism are believed to have yielded a harvest of voters acting against their economic self-interest, who would have chosen Democrats had the campaign environment not made culture its centerpiece. The Democrats, meanwhile, failed to redirect people's attention to the economic concerns on which the party has consistently held a clear advantage in the electorate. After winning office, the narrative continues, conservative politicians implemented a policy agenda that differed greatly from what they had promised the electorate. With the public's gaze diverted elsewhere, the GOP made far-reaching legislative and administrative decisions on the very economic issues it downplayed during campaigns.

As is often the case, the conventional wisdom contains elements of truth. A thorough and systematic investigation would probably find the Republicans' cultural stands to have attracted some voters while repelling others but, in the net total, to have strengthened the party's electoral appeal over the last three decades. I argue in this book, however, that the rest of the bait-and-switch account completely misses the tidal waves that have crashed over American politics. Contradicting the usual story, intellectuals and politicians on the right have not bypassed the material dimensions of public life during campaigns and policy debates. Far from concealing their economic plans for fear of voters' disapproval, Republicans repeatedly highlighted that program on the expectation that a jobs-and-growth message would resonate with the electorate. Furthermore, I will demonstrate, Democrats did not cede the economic terrain but instead paralleled Republicans in shifting the discussion of jobs, incomes, and growth to the forefront of their rhetoric. Although certain presidential elections revolved around different themes, especially terrorism and Iraq in 2004 and crime, race, and patriotism in 1988, this was the typical pattern from the early 1970s to the present. The same phenomenon occurred during the equally important intervals between elections; when mobilizing support from colleagues and constituents to pass legislation, political leaders increasingly pointed to the potential economic benefits of their policies. In the day-to-day course of governing, American politics became more, not less, oriented around the economy and the issues that define it.

Besides misunderstanding the emphases of campaigns and

legislative deliberations, prevailing interpretations of American politics err in determining who held the advantage. Contrary to the standard belief, economic issues normally provided an electoral asset to the Republicans, not the Democrats. The election of 1992, commonly remembered as proving that Democrats would win if only the public focused on the economy, was the exception rather than the rule. In six of the eight presidential elections from 1976 to 2004, Republicans benefited from public perceptions on which party would be better for the economy. The GOP's triumphs carried far beyond elections and into policymaking. Republican ideas were frequently enacted into policy in the last quarter-century, at least in areas defined and debated in economic terms.

Of course, previous scholars have explored in depth the most important reason why Republicans expanded their electoral support over a period of several decades.[27] The issue of race burst onto national politics in the 1950s and 1960s, splintering the Democratic party and eventually bringing white southerners into the Republican fold. As late as 1960, Republicans won only 6% of the seats in the House of Representatives from the states of the former Confederacy; by 2006 the corresponding figure was dramatically higher at 59%. In the 1990s and 2000s, the South provided most of the GOP leadership at the national level, including Newt Gingrich, Trent Lott, Tom Delay, Bill Frist, and George W. Bush. A strong base of white southerners almost guarantees Republicans a significant number of electoral votes in every presidential election.

Because close observers of American politics already appreciate the long-term effects of race on the electoral fortunes of the two parties, little could be gained by rehashing old storylines in this book. In a later chapter I present data indicating that economic concerns added to the electoral appeal of the GOP over a thirty-year period, but my primary analyses focus on rhetoric and policy rather than voting. The typical beliefs of scholars and journalists notwithstanding, economic questions in the last few decades have expanded, not retracted, in their amount of space on the public agenda. As illustrated by the issue of education, campaigns and legislative deliberations have continually stressed the economic facets of many political controversies. In addition to tracing the impact on the parties and domestic policies, I will explain the emergence and persistence of this economically based rhetoric.

This book, then, undertakes the challenge of explaining *how, why, and with what effects American politics became reoriented around economic interpretations of issues.* Even the biggest revolutions can begin with an initial spark, and the story told here is no different. The impetus for political change came from a climate of economic insecurity that spread across the population in the early 1970s and intensified in the succeeding decades. Much broader than the conventional connotation of a "weak economy" and lasting long after the oil crises subsided, economic insecurity in the 1980s, 1990s, and 2000s included such matters as downsizing, international competition, slow wage growth, personal debt and bankruptcy, and weakened health and pension coverage. Under the different context for politics created by economic insecurity, new policy directions resulted from the interaction of political rhetoric, the programs advocated by the two major parties, and the public's reaction to the options and arguments offered to it. Following the rise of economic insecurity, conservative intellectuals revived old ideas such as supply-side economics and opposition to government regulation. Publicized through a recently created network of intellectual institutions, those ideas soon commanded widespread attention.

The argument of the book continues by documenting that both parties converged on one potential response to the new-found context: using the available means of communication to make the economy a higher priority than it had been in the early post–World War II decades. From there, however, the strategies of the parties departed. Drawing on collaborative intellectual and organizational support, Republicans largely maintained their policy positions over time and reframed them by giving an economic cast to stances formerly defended on other grounds. The Democrats instead repositioned by abandoning some of their previous stands and adopting different ones, an evolution capped by the embrace of deficit reduction as the core of the party's economic program. Democrats in earlier eras stood ready and willing to fund new programs, but since the early 1980s the party's presidential candidates have been severely constrained by their commitments to fiscal responsibility.

The flow of American politics in recent decades can thus be summarized by a basic fact: *With some exceptions, Republicans and their ideological allies changed their arguments while Democrats changed their positions.* Disarmingly simple in its essence, this contrast is complex in both its origins and its implications. Besides charting the course of this development, in later chapters I will explain its consequences for policy and elections. When combined with the more effective advocacy of the GOP, the subsequent repositioning of Democrats pushed policy to the right in areas rhetorically linked to the economy. Even if the parties' respective electoral fortunes had remained fixed, policy still would have moved in a conservative direction. Electoral battles did not stay constant, though, and the Republicans' greater success at the ballot box—aided by the public's usually favorable perception of the party on economic matters—multiplied and deepened the policy changes from the 1970s through the opening years of the twenty-first century.

The Plan of the Book

To guide the rest of the book, chapter 2 elaborates a theoretical model of the role of rhetoric in the processes leading to the formation of policy. By carrying the effects of ideas and interests, rhetoric serves as a unifying concept for the study of politics. The chapter joins together the behavioral study of framing with central principles from the humanistic study of rhetoric, particularly the need to view speakers and writers in relation to their audiences. In articulating the book's contribution to theory building about politics, chapter 2 places rhetoric at the center of analysis. Working with this theoretical framework, chapter 3 then documents the opportunity beginning in the early 1970s that would stimulate political and rhetorical innovation up to the present. Widespread insecurity made Americans amenable to thinking about issues in economic terms, thereby encouraging political actors to construct their rhetoric in corresponding ways.

Seeing the development of rhetoric to be dependent on congenial ideas that have been clearly and cogently expressed, chapter 4 examines the conservatives' establishment of an intellectual infrastructure in journals of opinion and think tanks. In chapter 5 I follow up by analyzing a half-century's worth of publications by public intellectuals holding a conservative orientation. Accurately perceiving the external context, conservative thinkers and writers altered their rhetoric to accentuate the prosperity they expected their policies to create. Chapter 6 then contrasts the rhetoric of Barry Goldwater and Ronald Reagan, along with Republican governors, in the priorities expressed and reasons given in support of their proposals. For Goldwater and the governors of his era, economic consequences stood relatively low on the stated priority list and did not provide the main justification for conservative policies. President Reagan's rhetorical legacy, borrowed by other political leaders from his party, was to identify economic quantities as the leading criteria by which to judge a range of domestic policies.

Chapter 7 investigates the Democratic party's stances that reacted to—and were constrained by—the actions that the Republicans took. The choice of Republican leaders beginning with Reagan to offer tax cuts, and the response of Democrats in attaching significance to the budget deficit, gave the GOP a straightforward economic message and mitigated the potential for an effective Democratic challenge. With Republicans actively pursuing their goals on taxation, deregulation, and welfare state retrenchment and the Democrats making deficit reduction the central component of their economic program, public policy turned to the right. Chapter 8 documents the corresponding advantages Republicans acquired in the courts of public opinion and election outcomes. A more positive image of Republicans as stewards of the economy, the assembled data reveal, yielded sizable dividends in presidential elections. In the concluding chapter I address the present and future of American politics by considering what might happen to redirect current trends. Given the likelihood that economic insecurity will persist or even intensify, American politics will continue to be marked by the widespread use of an economic lens for examining, discussing, and deciding political questions.

TWO

The Role of Rhetoric in the Formation of Policy

In a fully rational world, one could explain policy changes according to the virtues of the specific proposals that initiated them. With political programs rising and falling according to their verifiable merits, citizens and political leaders would simply choose the best course of action after evaluating contending alternatives through experience, observation, or reason. When applied to recent American history, this possibility implies that conservative initiatives became adopted into law because they were shown to serve the public interest. People who define themselves as conservatives might be tempted to embrace such an explanation. Of course, the corollary is that when the conservative agenda stalled, the plans must have collapsed from the weight of their own shortcomings—an account liberals might find appealing.

Seemingly attractive on the surface, explanations based on policies' objective characteristics invariably strip from politics all of the, well, politics. Disputes about the public good are the essence of political life, for there would be no purpose for collective decision making were there no differences among citizens needing to be resolved. Even within the mind of a single person, limitations of logic restrict one's ability to explain the fate of programmatic initiatives based on their inherent desirability. People from any group, regardless of their ideological dispositions or deeply held values, could find abundant examples—both now and at any previous point in time—of policies they find foolish, counterproductive, or immoral. If they were to attribute the enactment of policies they endorse to the embodied merits obvious to all, the policies to which they object would need a similarly charitable explanation; otherwise the analysis would create self-serving distinctions unconvincing to anyone else.

Building upon a rich tradition in the study of public policy, this book rejects the view that policy proposals are formulated and chosen according to a rational, systematic procedure that uncovers their intrinsic worth.[1] Instead, the following chapters will advance a *political* story that takes seriously the need, in any pluralistic society, for a vision of the public good to attract broad approval (though not necessarily the assent of a majority) before being written into law. A political explanation of the shifting policies of government must address advocacy and argumentation in the public realm, individual and group determination of interests and preferences, and the connection between political leaders and mass publics. A policy agenda could pass all conceivable tests of merit and still languish unfulfilled unless advocates effectively justify it and build a coalition of supporters.

As a necessary first step toward explaining why political issues came to be understood through economic interpretations, this chapter introduces a model of the role of rhetoric in the formation of policy. Particular emphasis falls on the concept of framing, a tool that politicians and other policy participants use to achieve their goals. The behavioral study of framing, an approach that focuses on effects, is fused here with the humanistic study of rhetoric, an approach that grounds its research within specific contexts. Successful rhetoric, my model implies, leads to new policies by expanding the size of the supporting coalition. Policy revisions also occur when political actors alter their positions, a course they follow only when available rhetoric, developed within the constraints of the context, cannot sustain the political viability of previously stated positions. Flexible in its application and potentially addressing a wide range of cases, my model of rhetorical construction and consequences will be presented in the current chapter in general terms. In later chapters, I will add considerable specificity to explain how conservatives used greater attention to economic matters to move policy to the right.

Interests, Ideas, and Preferences

At the most basic level, explaining policy choices requires understanding the preferences of political elites, especially those who wield formal authority over policy. No consideration of elites' preferences, in turn, can ignore their underlying interests because political actors often—perhaps usually—behave in ways they believe will advance their self-interests. These interests can sometimes be discovered quickly and easily, such as when manufacturers of products losing market share to imports perceive the benefits of tariffs. An interest-based account would also accurately predict that religious minorities would be the strongest advocates of separating church and state, for their faiths could easily be overrun if government subsidized or supported the dominant religion.[2] For politicians and parties, the need to win election and reelection is a fundamental and undeniable interest. At the same time, electoral motives are too general to translate in a straightforward way into all the stands that candidates and officeholders take.[3] Like clay not fully molded into shape, interests need assistance to acquire their structure and form.

According to many scholars, ideas represent the means through which interests come to be defined. "Long dormant in the study of politics," political scientist Robert Lieberman observes, "ideas have staged a remarkable comeback in the social sciences."[4] A potentially expansive concept, ideas include both ideologies, which simplify the overwhelming complexity of political life, and intellectual frameworks such as Keynesianism and supply-side economics applicable to particular policy domains.[5] Ideas can also encompass values like equal opportunity, traditional morality, limited government, individualism, and egalitarianism, which organize the more specific elements of a political orientation.[6] Alternatively, ideas about cause and effect, often based on scientific principles, findings, and theories, can help political actors determine which policies will further their objectives.[7]

Both individual scholars and theoretical paradigms differ in the relative emphases given to interests and ideas. Many theoretical disputes in political science and sociology revolve around which variable is most important, the causally prior one that determines the other. Still, most researchers—when pressed—would admit some analytic usefulness of the factor falling outside the center of their preferred paradigm.[8] Indeed, a prominent line of research rejects both the need and the possibility of treating interests and ideas as separate and competing explanations of policy decisions.[9] Following a similar approach, I focus here on the joint effect of interests and ideas, working in tandem, to form another key concept: elite preferences.

Whereas interests and ideas are quite general, preferences—the product of their interaction—are more concrete and focused. Being a step closer to actual policy, preferences contain programmatic content that describes the goals of political actors. Examples of preferences include support for progressive taxation, gun control, environmental protection, and helping the uninsured acquire health coverage. Formed through codetermining interests and ideas, preferences direct the actions of political leaders. Studying how preferences get channeled into policy, however, requires additional investigation.

The Place of Rhetoric in Politics

Whatever their origins, preferences are publicly expressed through rhetoric. In contemporary societies rhetoric has acquired a negative connotation of vacuous, insincere, flowery, or bombastic language deployed by smooth-talking manipulators. When preserved in its older and venerable meanings derived from its golden age in classical Greece and Rome, the term simply refers to verbal and nonverbal means of persuasion such as logical arguments, emotional appeals, personal credibility, presentation of evidence, and the language, organization, and delivery of speeches. Much of modern rhetorical theory and criticism has moved in different directions, such as Kenneth Burke's "symbolic inducement to attitude and action" and new understandings of rhetoric as constituting or reconstituting audiences rather than responding to those already existing.[10] Still, classical rhetoric's preoccupation with the strategies, qualities, and techniques in messages remains central to rhetorical studies. Almost all contemporary scholars of rhetoric focus on messages that, whether written, oral, visual, or some combination thereof, influence audiences. The conception of rhetoric that Aristotle proposed—the faculty of discovering the available means of persuasion in a given case—continues to be useful for explaining political developments.

Several approaches to the analysis of politics feature rhetoric as a centerpiece. Most obviously, scholars in the interdisciplinary study of political communication hold that political processes and outcomes hinge on the words and other symbols used by individuals, groups, and the mass media. The field of policy studies, too, incorporates rhetoric when examining the impact of shared evaluations of policy targets and how conditions prevailing in society become defined as public problems.[11] Within the study of social movements, sociological research parallels communication scholarship in stressing the capacity of discourse and language to affect the emergence, effectiveness, and decline of movements.[12] Finally, the constructivist paradigm in international relations and comparative politics views interests not as exogenous but rather as the product of rhetorical processes that build identities and norms.[13]

Not all fields and schools of political analysis study rhetoric to learn how politics is conducted, who wins and loses, and what policies are adopted. The causal effects of rhetoric are usually downplayed within materialist and rationalist theories including Marxism, realism, and especially rational choice. The most common approach to rhetoric taken in research based on rational choice is simply to ignore it. In academic disciplines a concept garners more respect by being attacked or serving as a foil than by being overlooked entirely, for in the former cases the re-searcher at least acknowledges its importance as a hypothetical possibility. When rational-choice scholars do explicitly reference ideas generally and rhetoric specifically, they typically view them merely as "hooks" that actors use for their preferences—hooks that do not contribute independent effects on policy outcomes.[14] Although it might make for interesting reading, within rational choice a rich description of the rhetoric that various participants employ is superfluous in explaining the results of the struggle.

A closer examination, however, reveals that studying rhet-oric is entirely compatible with the logic of rational choice. The rational-choice paradigm typically grounds preferences in self-interest, but in a pluralistic society actors must give reasons and justifications for their behavior.[15] One can hardly build a coalition, attracting support from previously apathetic or disapproving on-lookers, by saying that a policy should be adopted "because it benefits me." Political candidates who forthrightly confessed to the electorate that they chose their stands on the issues accord-ing to self-interest would soon be checking the want ads for a new career. Even if outside observers conclude that self-interest determines preferences, the actual participants continually ad-vance public-spirited arguments to attract others to their causes. Once scholars acknowledge that fact, it becomes crucial to study the publicly articulated rationales, for good ones enhance the chance of success while poor ones increase the likelihood of fail-ure. A theoretical account based on self-interested behavior must address the origins and consequences of rhetoric in order to ex-plain political outcomes accurately.

There is a second reason why making rhetoric a focal point of investigation is consistent with the assumptions of rational choice. The daily activities of interest groups, politicians, parties, social movements, and op-ed writers often revolve around an at-tempt to influence audiences through rhetoric. Lobbyists spend much of their time forming and honing messages to be conveyed directly to policymakers or indirectly to them through other po-litical elites, the media, or the public at large. Seeking to create fa-vorable visions and versions of themselves and their plans, politicians conduct polls, form focus groups, and hire political consultants. Political leaders often admit that the purpose of those activities is to find the best language, arguments, and personae for advocating their qualifications and policy stances.[16] It is no surprise that strategies of communication occupy continual attention in the White House and represent a defining aspect of the modern presidency.[17]

Political actors would not expend so much effort if their public address had only minimal effects on colleagues, other policymakers, and the citizenry at large. If one assumes, following rational choice, that political actors can best assess their own interests and that they weigh costs and benefits before deciding on optimal strategies, it would be *irrational* to spend so much time, money, and energy devising and delivering rhetorical messages that were not crucial for achieving desired ends. Even under the assumption that rhetoric is merely instrumental, then, people who work in politics for a living clearly believe it to be consequential for political struggles. Viewing rhetoric as a powerful tool, even a weapon, does not relieve the political analyst of the need to explore its creation and evolution and its workings with audiences. To do otherwise would be like assessing the resolution of wars without considering which side wields the more powerful swords, guns, tanks, or aircraft. True, the weaponry may not have constituted the underlying cause of armed conflict, but its use and effectiveness are surely important in determining the victor.

Perhaps it was just such thinking that led political scientist William Riker, at the end of his long and productive career, to study rhetoric within the framework of rational choice. Recognizing that who wins and loses in politics depends on which aspect of an issue provides the primary basis of evaluation, Riker proposed that legislators can change decision-making settings and thus make their preferred outcomes more likely by controlling the dimensions of a conflict through rhetoric.[18] The model of rhetorical construction I present here departs from a purely rational-choice perspective by holding, as described earlier, that preferences are not simply a function of interests but also embody ideas. Because rhetoric plays a critical role in the processes of determining interests and developing ideas, and because the resulting preferences cannot be communicated to others until they are formalized through written, visual, or oral means, rhetoric's place in politics goes beyond the purely instrumental aspects deployed by political elites. Rhetoric is intertwined with interests and ideas and should not be seen only as a downstream variable through which foundational concepts are expressed. Prior to the formation of preferences, political actors use rhetoric to understand and interpret the surrounding world.

The model I describe in this chapter finds common ground with rational choice, however, in holding that *once their preferences have been formed*, political participants seek to defend them in the most persuasive manner. At this point rhetoric becomes an intervening variable, carefully crafted by politicians and political leaders to be as attractive as possible to constituents, bureaucrats, and other political elites.[19] Yet as an intervening variable that carries considerable force, rhetoric—along with its strategic deployment—helps explain who wins and loses in struggles over policy. The strategic use of rhetoric need not be conscious: Experienced politicians, who have given more speeches, held more meetings with other policymakers, and spoken with more constituents than they can count, will often behave instinctively in marshaling the most effective arguments and appeals for the positions they are taking.

Rhetoric provides the connection, then, between preferences and policy choices. Political actors' preferences cannot be the direct cause of policy, for politics is a social enterprise that rests on interpersonal communication as well as messages transmitted through the mass media. Preferences must be publicly presented, advocated, and defended through rhetoric to gain influence with other actors. Rhetoric thus represents the currency of politics, in that everything important passes through it. With words and other symbolic acts, campaigns are conducted, coalitions are mobilized, and policies are enacted. That is not to say that rhetoric is some kind of disembodied force, an "unmoved mover" that appears out of thin air to drive the political system. Instead, I assert in this chapter that the exact opposite is true: Rhetoric expresses actors' preferences but also adjusts to the context from which it emerges.

My model of the place of rhetoric in politics can be clarified through a schematic diagram, and figure 2.1 maps the relationships among the main variables. Interests and ideas, as the figure depicts, combine to form the preferences of elites. Those preferences subsequently affect the decisions elites make when they gain policymaking power, but only after getting filtered through rhetoric. Rhetoric lies in the middle of the diagram, with the many arrows coming to and flowing from it capturing symbolically its importance to the policy process. A visual representation of this book's theoretical aim, figure 2.1 places rhetoric at the center of analysis. Note that rhetoric not only carries and conveys elite preferences but also reflects the social context and public opinion. These contributors to rhetoric are described in detail later in the chapter.

As seen in figure 2.1, rhetoric feeds into policy by affecting the size of the supporting coalition. During campaigns for public office, candidates attempt to assemble a winning coalition of disparate individuals and groups. After elections are over, the day-to-day course of governing continues to depend on coalition building because in most political systems, and especially in America's, no political actors hold unilateral control over policy decisions. Within the Madisonian institutions of the United States, opportunities abound to block policies through legislative committees, bicameral disagreements, executive vetoes, and bureaucratic delays. To gain lasting policy innovations, political actors must offer rhetoric, both during elections and while governing, to build coalitions sufficiently large to overcome potential opposition. Moreover, the availability of persuasive rhetoric determines whether preferences can be publicly stated or else must be modified or abandoned. Without the ability to find convincing messages for mass and elite audiences, politicians may be forced to soft-pedal their preferences or discard them entirely. A coali-

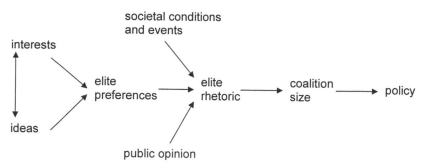

Figure 2.1. A Model of the Policy Process

tion can more easily achieve its policy aims when actors who otherwise might have stood on the other side have changed their positions.

Framing and Its Effects

The insights my model yields can be seen by examining one particular kind of rhetoric, namely framing, which has guided scholarship in political communication. Participants in policy debates such as politicians, journalists, researchers, activists, and interest groups create frames designed to simplify controversies that invariably encompass multiple dimensions. The process of framing distills the subject by highlighting a limited number of elements, thereby providing a means of grasping it. A typical frame may contain condensing symbols, narrative storylines, or references to other political events that capture what a controversy is really about.

Considerable differences exist across studies in how framing is defined, probably an inevitable outcome given the sprawling literatures in communication, social psychology, linguistics, political science, and sociology that invoke the concept. For the purposes of this book, I work with a common though not universally accepted definition that stresses the selective presentation by a communication source of certain aspects of an issue, problem, or event.[20] Through that selection process, the source fashions a lens through which to view the larger matter and implicitly pushes competing ways of understanding to the side. The process of framing, frequently studied when news coverage adopts one frame over another, is important to politics because it can affect mass perceptions and determine which candidates and policies will gain significant backing.

A growing literature shows that frames constructed by elites affect public opinion, and recent studies have begun to specify the conditions under which framing is successful.[21] Much of the work addresses race, where one finds, for example, that Americans are more likely to embrace affirmative action if it is framed as compensation for an institution's past discrimination.[22] Many scholars point to accessibility as the psychological mechanism that induces framing effects. Because citizens do not attend to all aspects of issues simultaneously, framing can shape public opinion by determining which considerations are most easily recalled and retrieved from people's memories.[23] The impact of framing also could result from altering the importance of beliefs. By implying that one factor is more relevant to the issue than another, framing can change opinions by shifting the weights citizens ascribe to particular beliefs.[24]

The research program in political communication on the effects of framing has grown in part because it can employ standard behavioral approaches. Researchers tend to study phenomena that can be addressed with available methodologies, and framing can easily be treated as an independent variable helping to form individuals' political attitudes. The content of news stories or any other means of communication, for example, can be experimentally altered to assess how people respond to alternative frames.[25] Frames can also be unobtrusively embedded in surveys through changes in question wording that combine experimental control with the advantage of representative samples.[26] With randomly selected respondents receiving different frames, variations in answers can then be explained by the frame that was presented.

The ease with which certain aspects of framing can be explored with experiments and surveys contrasts with the difficulty of answering questions not as suited to systematic measurement. The quantitative study of framing thus has devoted little consideration to the creation, production, and dissemination of frames. In a major assessment of research in political communication and public opinion, the effects of framing on public opinion received extensive discussion, but framing as a dependent variable merited not a single sentence—undoubtedly because there simply was not much behavioral literature to review.[27] The concluding chapter of an edited volume on framing within the study of mass communication acknowledges: "There has not been much of an effort to examine the origins of frames, or the factors that determine which frames will dominate the various channels of communication through which they flow."[28] Studying the origins of frames can be done within social science, as this book demonstrates, but any such examination requires careful attention to the developmental processes through which frames emerge and persist.

The Origins of Elite Framing

The limitations of the behavioral research are offset by one of the strengths of the humanistic study of communication known most often as "public address" or simply "rhetoric." Although scholars of rhetoric have sought to explain effects, perhaps their most characteristic contributions have involved, along with analyzing the internal workings of texts, efforts to locate communication within specific occasions and situations that help to account for the reception of messages among audiences. Influential rhetorical theorists hold that argumentation unfolds before a particular audience, anticipated by a speaker who chooses forms of evidence consistent with its predispositions.[29] More generally, within departments of communication, the dominant tradition within the humanistic study of rhetoric abides by the principle that the meaning and impact of texts can best be gleaned by reading them within the historical moments and interpretive communities from which they arose.[30] Investigating the background and circumstances of the speaker, occasion, and audience is a mainstay within traditional rhetorical analysis.[31]

Among scholars of presidential rhetoric, the humanistic emphasis on context has been folded into social science approaches and data in a manner parallel to that proposed here, as a few examples make clear. Presidents give speeches to gain backing for their programs, scholars widely agree, but throughout the nineteenth century presidents operated within the context of constitutional norms that viewed direct communication with the public as inappropriate.[32] Televised advertisements in modern times sometimes attack opposing candidates yet are careful to remain within the context provided by public values and expectations.[33] Sophisticated works on framing by the news media take a similar approach in combining analyses of elite and mass politics, seeing frames as the product of interactions among political leaders, news organizations, and cultural assumptions.[34]

This view of a fluid, mutual relationship between "text and context" has also found a home within the sociological study of framing.[35] The sociological approach considers not only how frames influence recipients but also the ways people, organizations, and institutions produce frames in the first place. By integrating the humanistic and sociological attention to context into the behavioral study of framing, one can illuminate processes that are hidden when viewed solely from any single perspective. It is for this reason that context, defined here to include public opinion on the one hand and societal conditions and events on the other, joins rhetoric as a key feature of the model of rhetoric and policy in figure 2.1.[36] An important question that remains asks precisely how the context affects the rhetorical strategies of political actors, the subject I address next.

Framing and Mass Audiences: Public Opinion as the Context

Rhetoric and framing are central to mass politics because current and prospective voters often serve as either the proximate or the ultimate target of communication strategies. No party or politician can thrive without an electoral base, and so gaining and maintaining public approval will always represent an essential goal. This public support contributes to policy change both directly, by bringing new officeholders to power, and indirectly, by setting limits on legislative and executive enactments. In contrast to the incremental adjustments to policy that commonly occur without public participation or even awareness, major changes involve a far stronger public role.[37] The ideological direction of government does not shift without large numbers of people noticing it, so any explanation of long-term, large-scale movements in policy must take public opinion into account.

Scholars of political communication have properly viewed framing as a tool for managing and sometimes manipulating public opinion, but the unstated assumption is that political elites control the emergence of frames. Certainly, current and aspiring leaders do assemble frames by intentionally choosing the words, phrases, reasons, and appeals they believe will attract support for themselves and their policy proposals. Yet while politicians exercise discretion in devising frames, they are not free from constraints. They cannot simply construct any rationale they want for a position, for they depend on approval from constituents to win or continue in office. In striving to strike chords that resonate broadly, politicians assess the kinds of frames that will and will not appeal to the public.

During the 1960 presidential election, for example, John F. Kennedy knowingly stressed issues on which public opinion polls indicated that Americans viewed him positively. The Kennedy campaign developed a strategy to make those issues salient in his public address, expecting them to be weighted more highly when voters reached their overall evaluations of the candidate. Although such a method of campaigning would be second nature today and had been done unconsciously since time immemorial, Kennedy and his advisers were innovative in conducting the necessary polls and explicitly articulating the approach. The available evidence, based on an analysis of surveys the campaign commissioned, shows that Kennedy's hopes were fulfilled.[38] Thus the perceptions and priorities of citizens affected the campaign's strategy and messages, which in turn looped back to affect public opinion.

Fully understanding the political importance of framing requires considering the two-way street of mutual interaction and influence among elites and mass publics. The common understanding of framing as a top-down, elite-driven process should be replaced with a more complex view whereby the beliefs and experiences of citizens affect what will resonate with them. Sensing available opportunities, politicians frame their rhetoric to reflect and then shape public opinion. Analyzing this interactive dynamic can help to unify not only political science but also the study of political history, which is often split between those who focus on "high politics" and those addressing culture and pressure "from below." The relationships between them mean that neither should be examined without considering the other, for elite politics emerges from the shadow of mass politics and vice versa.

All political advocates want to construct appealing frames, but their success is far from assured. A common strategy among political leaders is to introduce a new aspect of an issue to upset the existing alignment of positions, giving an alternative outcome a greater likelihood of victory.[39] Because political elites cannot guarantee the success of these issue redefinitions, the advantage in framing goes to those who can tap into previously existing sentiments. Influencing fundamental values or even instilling new attitudes is difficult, so political actors can more readily capitalize on what is already present in the culture.[40] Through framing, policy participants attempt to activate values, attitudes, and beliefs that advance their cause while directing people's attention away from those that, were they brought to the surface and explicitly linked to policy issues, would pull in the opposite direction.[41]

Framing and Mass Audiences: Societal Conditions
and Events as the Context

Besides regularly assessing public opinion, one crucial part of the context, politicians monitor the conditions and events prominent in people's minds. Politicians want to know citizens' awareness and perceptions of the contemporary circumstances that can form the basis of policy initiatives and the rhetoric used to advocate them. At various historical moments the salient circumstances might include immigration, industrialization, religious revivals and awakenings, wars and other foreign policy conflicts, technological changes, suburbanization, the aging of the population, and the entry of more women into the paid labor force. These conditions are best considered not as givens but rather as offering a range of possibilities for ascribing meaning to them. Within the pool of plausible interpretations, political actors struggle over who holds the best one, for those who define the problem gain the upper hand in choosing the solution.

Which conditions resonate with the public will be determined not only by people's own experiences but also by the information they encounter and absorb from the news media. From everything that could be reported, the news media select a limited number of stories and angles based on organizational pressures, operating procedures, and journalistic conventions of what counts as newsworthy.[42] Economic incentives, especially the profit motive and the competition among media outlets for viewers, listeners, and readers, create systematic influences on the production of the news. To make the news interesting to potential consumers, journalists emphasize dramatic, fragmented, and personalized stories and angles while downplaying the analytical, historical, and institutional dimensions.[43] The importance of this mediated version of reality is most pronounced with issues, such as foreign affairs, that are remote from people's daily lives.[44] When coverage focuses on a particular matter, news organizations draw attention to it while unintentionally pushing other potential stories to the background. By covering certain conditions or events and portraying them in specific ways, the news media thus supplement the experiences of citizens and establish pegs upon which politicians can hang their persuasive messages.

Patterns of news coverage are invariably connected with the changing allocation of attention in society. One of the most important and influential advances in the scholarly study of politics has come from linking changes in preferences to changes in attention. Politics cannot be fully grasped without considering the effects of attention shifting from one issue to another and from one to another aspect of any given issue.[45] Attention to certain problems in society instead of others helps determine what kinds of rhetoric resonate with people, thereby advantaging some proposals and disadvantaging others. Policy initiatives that could be favorably presented to the public in one period, with certain circumstances and news coverage as the backdrop, might not be sellable at another point when public and media attention have moved on to something else. Policy participants are more likely to embrace a proposal when they can defend it rhetorically using a touchstone made salient through both people's experiences and media coverage. Meanwhile, the additional individuals or organizations necessary for a winning coalition may be gained if new criteria, currently prominent because of changing political, economic, or social conditions, govern the decision.

Contemporary conditions and media coverage therefore offer an ever-shifting array of possibilities that allow politicians' rhetoric to evolve considerably faster than the preferences, usually stable over time, it is marshaled to support. Through their rhetorical "presentation of self" to voters, politicians strive to cultivate a reputation for orderly, predictable, and principled stands that will guide their behavior in office.[46] Because political opponents point to flip-flopping to attack a candidate's integrity and trustworthiness, switching positions is normally an inadvisable practice. Among members of Congress, stable preferences are implied by the consistency over many years of the placement of their roll-call votes on an ideological scale.[47] Elected officials pursuing a personal vision of the public interest, though, still must be able to explain their behavior to constituents should the need arise.[48]

Whatever actually motivates their decisions, officeholders seek convincing justifications that can win public acquiescence or approval.

It is here that the payoff from recognizing the relationship between context and rhetoric becomes most clear. Rhetoric is not just an intermediary between preferences and policy. Instead, rhetoric also draws from and responds to the context; the context determines whether preferences can be successfully defended through rhetoric, or whether they must be downplayed when it comes to announcing positions for public consumption. Although political scientists have gained many insights by positing that politicians want to be elected and reelected, this starting assumption can be fruitfully modified. A useful way to think about politicians is that they seek to move policy as far toward personal preferences as is possible without crossing the line into sparking public resistance that may lead to defeat at the ballot box. Knowing when rhetorical possibilities allow preferences to be publicly stated and forcefully championed, and when preferences must be compromised for the sake of electoral expediency, is the hallmark of successful political leaders.

If this understanding of rhetoric is accurate, a crucial implication follows: The reasons politicians give for their stands on issues commonly deviate from those that led them to adopt their positions in the first place. The rhetoric expressed in support of a position may bear little connection to the processes by which the preferences lying behind the position were initially formed. Should politicians happen to recall the thinking that led to a certain preference, they would be unlikely to give a complete accounting of it when making public statements. Such a result is indisputable when the true motivation for preferences is self-interest, a notoriously poor defense of one's beliefs in the public arena. Even when public-spirited ideas influence preferences, though, rhetorical advocacy still adapts to the context.

The most common adaptation political leaders make involves simplification. People who make a living in politics have spent far more time thinking and talking about issues than the average citizen. Representing the inevitable complexity of many issues, elected officials often possess many different reasons for their positions. When advocating in public, politicians select from the full set of potential rationales the one or the handful that are most convincing at a given moment for a given audience. That flexibility, which may be deployed instinctively and without conscious intention, allows elected officials to be consistent in their recorded stands even as the rhetoric they offer in support evolves alongside circumstances. Yet when the situation so affords, they may embrace entirely new grounds for their preexisting positions. In attempting to win backing from the mass public, successful politicians seize the rhetorical opportunities available to them.[49]

It often signals weakness, however, when a candidate, party, or other political entity changes positions. The ideal sequence for political actors, one that preserves the desired ends while allowing flexibility on the means, lies in keeping their positions stable while updating their rhetoric as it proves useful or necessary. Such an approach fails when no line of discourse can protect the viability of previously stated positions, and political elites who seek effectiveness in the political realm may be forced not only to change their rhetoric but to change their stances as well. Finding a new position is a second-best alternative, undertaken when simply invoking new forms of rhetoric would be insufficient.

Reprioritizing, Reframing, and Repositioning

When the context changes, I propose, elites generally respond in one or more of three ways: reprioritizing, reframing, and repositioning. Because the interplay of these responses will structure my analysis in the rest of the book, it is worth investigating their characteristics in some detail. Implemented by intellectuals and parties in creative ways, the "3 Rs" of political change will help to explain the course of recent American political history.

Reprioritizing, the first response, resembles the concept of agenda setting widely used in studies of the news media and public policy.[50] Political actors offer and endorse many different policy initiatives, yet they cannot devote the same level of attention to each one. Some proposals are invariably highlighted, attracting a disproportionate share of the available time and energy, while others are deemphasized. A politician, party, or other political entity who reprioritizes takes items it formerly backed at a lower level and raises their prominence, thereby reshuffling the hierarchy of positions presented to the public. Through this approach, the issue stances expressed over time show a strong consistency even as items move up and down the list of priorities.

The second response available after a change in the context is reframing. Whereas reprioritizing relates to the volume of attention *across* issues, reframing refers to the relative hierarchy of arguments developed *within* issues. Issues are inherently multidimensional, meaning that they can be understood through a variety of frames. When one examines a large body of text drawn from different sources, multiple frames usually can be identified, but some will be more commonly featured than others. Often a single dominant frame, or perhaps a small handful, characterizes the issue. Political elites reframe an issue by presenting a different means of interpreting it. Occasionally the frame is entirely new, though more often it rises within the mix of existing frames. Formerly capturing a smaller part of the discourse, such a frame now becomes preeminent.

Reprioritizing and reframing are the preferred options, the ones initially considered when circumstances change. Through such strategies, political elites adapt their rhetoric to the context while retaining the positions they established in the past. When such rhetorical adaptations appear unlikely to be sufficient, a political actor may be forced to adopt the third response: repositioning. Individuals or political organizations who reposition modify their stances, replacing policies they previously stated were meritorious with different ones. Moving beyond merely updating their rhetoric, they revise the policy positions for which the rhetoric is marshaled. In this way they change what they stand for to align themselves with the rhetorical possibilities and constraints of the day.

The repositioning approach is fraught with dangers, which explains why it is usually the least-desirable alternative. For individual politicians, switching positions invites charges of hypocrisy and opportunism. "My opponent used to support one thing," the criticism commonly goes, "and now he [or she] stands for something else." If one's political adversaries can make the charge stick, flip-flopping carries a real price. At the level of parties, too, repositioning is risky. It may increase the party's competitiveness with certain voters, but only at the cost of alienating some core supporters, who then may become less likely to volunteer for the party, extol its virtues to friends and family, or contribute financially. Such people also might vote for a third party—either newly formed or newly invigorated—which can accuse the major party of selling out its venerable principles for crass electoral gain.

In the 2000 election, for example, Ralph Nader crystallized some of the discontent many formerly stalwart Democrats felt toward the party. Nader famously contended that because the Democrats had repositioned so much, they were now interchangeable with the Republicans and it made no difference who was elected. Even though most political observers agreed that the longtime consumer advocate exaggerated greatly in treating the parties as mirror images of each other, it is true that the Democrats repositioned considerably between the 1980s and the present—a phenomenon to which my later chapters will return. Nader drew 2.7% of the popular vote in the 2000 election, a small figure that nevertheless may have affected the outcome of the election. Many of his backers (30%) said in exit polls that they would have stayed home had he not entered the race, with the remainder choosing Al Gore over George W. Bush by a margin of more than two to one. Those votes would have been sufficient to move Florida and New Hampshire into Gore's column, allowing him to earn a solid majority in the Electoral College.[51]

Of special relevance to this book, all three responses to an altered context—reprioritizing, reframing, and repositioning—can instigate policy change by affecting the size of the supporting coalition. When reprioritizing or reframing works, it increases the number of backers for a policy or candidate. An expanded coalition, in turn, becomes more likely to grasp the levers of power necessary to translate policy preferences into policy decisions. That is the desired result: The actors hope that forms of rhetoric congruent with the context will allow wider assent and a larger coalition. By adapting rhetorically to their contexts, political leaders strive to create and expand a space more favorable to their preferences. Not only does the context influence rhetoric, then, but effective rhetoric influences the context and brings policy changes in its wake.

Repositioning, too, can lead to policy change. When many actors shift their positions in the same direction at the same time, the consequence, in effect, is an updated set of preferences that are subsequently reflected in policy.[52] Rhetoric is intertwined with this process because by defining the issue in a manner that successfully taps into the context, the elites taking the offensive have made the desired policy difficult to oppose. Reacting to the judgment criteria made salient through rhetoric, some political figures who otherwise would challenge a certain action now join the coalition. With the base of opposition shrunken through repositioning, it becomes more likely that the coalition's desires will be written into law.

Rhetoric, Strategy, and Manipulation

In explaining how rhetoric is constructed to fit the context, this chapter has emphasized elites' strategic choices—and appropriately so. Strategy development in politics must be investigated to gain a full accounting of who wins and loses and how the game is played. Political strategies contain rhetoric as a key component, perhaps never more so than when politicians and parties hire communication professionals as advisers. Image makers, spin doctors, and media consultants make no apologies for seeking the most attractive rhetorical profile for candidates, parties, and issue positions. This process might be labeled necessary marketing when done by one's own side versus tawdry manipulation when done by opponents. Even without the assistance of these advisers, political leaders sometimes actively consider alternative rhetorical possibilities and choose those deemed most likely to succeed.

When rhetoric adjusts to the context, however, the cause need not be the crafty maneuvering of political elites. Because issues and problems are complex and multifaceted, neither individuals nor institutions simultaneously consider all relevant standards and facts when passing policies.[53] The context affects which elements of a policy attain salience and govern the subsequent decisions. Political actors cannot avoid participating in this winnowing process, for they react to the information they receive and the landscape they observe. The same forces that concentrate public and media attention on certain attributes of issues also operate for elites, thereby providing the primary means of evaluation. When speaking in public, elites reveal their own thinking by constructing their rhetoric based on the prevailing context. Stated another way, elites commonly—maybe even usually—believe their own rhetoric, for they have internalized the decision criteria the context has invited. Even when their preferences are longstanding, elected officials can thoughtfully and genuinely advocate their positions by expressing the reigning principles and sustaining rationales they perceive at a certain moment.

As a practical matter, it is difficult if not impossible to determine whether the rhetoric of political elites, in a particular case, reflects clever scheming, authentic beliefs, or both.[54] Scholars can observe and document behavior but ordinarily can only infer underlying motives. In most studies of politics, however, one need not make those inferences because unobserved drives do not forge coalitions or enact policies; the consequences of interest stem from actions, not motivations. Discerning the internal stimulus is normally unnecessary because the same results—those flowing from actual behavior—occur no matter what happens within the minds of political actors. Whether by explicit intention or unconscious reaction, the rhetoric of political actors capitalizes on public opinion and the social context. The behavior is strategic in its effects regardless of whether it was planned by calculating actors.

Conclusion

The model developed in this chapter covers how rhetoric is formed and then expressed in electoral and policy processes. Different approaches to political communication allow certain insights that are best treated as parts of an integrated whole rather than as separate contributions. Although behavioralists have thoroughly studied the consequences of framing, one important form of rhetoric, comprehending rhetoric's potency requires exploring not only its effects but also the circumstances that influence its construction. Whether intentionally strategic or not, political actors assess their contexts before making claims and appeals. Elites must swim in the river passing through their lands to gain any realistic chance of redirecting the current.[55]

Abiding by the tenet that politicians seek to win the "median voter," scholars of politics commonly examine the positions taken by candidates, officeholders, and parties. A consideration of the role of rhetoric in politics, though, demonstrates the limits of any conception of a static and predetermined median voter. What people want from government depends on the options and arguments presented to them by elites, who in turn react to public opinion and contemporary conditions when crafting their proposals and rhetoric. A position rhetorically defensible under one context becomes untenable under another, ultimately affecting whether preferences can be translated into policy. Without the ability to devise persuasive messages, political actors may downplay their preferences or else fail to influence audiences in ways that achieve policy aims. An analysis of politics therefore gains by examining not just the positions of political elites but also their rhetoric as expressed in speeches, essays, interviews, press releases, campaign advertisements, and formal platforms.

Social scientists commonly strive to push causal chains back as far as possible, the assumption being that explanations should concentrate on root causes rather than the later, intervening variables. Rhetoric can be considered a root cause because it is a means by which political actors, relating to each other in a social enterprise, discover the interests and construct the ideas that allow them to form their preferences. Yet rhetoric later reenters the political process as a downstream variable employed to advocate and justify preferences. The empirical analyses in later chapters address rhetoric mainly in its latter capacity, where it connects preferences and context to coalition building and policy choices. Such an emphasis, however, does not require denying rhetoric's role as a variable operating at the very base of politics. Indeed, I hope that this book is read alongside other works that clarify the ways in which rhetorical dynamics represent foundational forces in politics.

Some readers may wonder whether my model of the origins and consequences of rhetoric inappropriately overlooks other facets of the political domain. The purpose of any model, including the one offered here, is to further our understanding of important phenomena. Models abstract from the real world some small number of elements, whose interactions can then be used to illuminate key relationships. The proper test of a model is the leverage it yields, the amount of explanation relative to the amount of complexity. Parsimony is a virtue in model building, but only when it does not undermine accuracy.

The model I present in this chapter cannot account for everything that steers political struggles and outcomes along particular routes. Formal and informal institutions, for example, are largely excluded from investigation here despite being central subjects of study for social scientists. The evidence and interpretations in the rest of the book attempt to show that my parsimony in studying rhetoric, along with reprioritizing, reframing, and repositioning as three possible responses to a change in the context, leads to new insights into politics. The value of my theoretical framework, then, depends on whether it succeeds in explaining political trends of interest to citizens, scholars, and practitioners. The next chapter puts the principles introduced here into practice, showing how a revised context of pervasive economic insecurity invited rhetorical innovation.

THREE

Economic Insecurity and Its Rhetorical Consequences

On November 2, 2004, eleven states voted to prohibit same-sex marriage, with most of the initiatives and referenda also banning civil unions, reciprocal benefits, and domestic partner laws for homosexuals. These votes capped a year of headline-grabbing moves by interest groups and elected officials that kept the issue in the public eye. Nine months earlier President George W. Bush had announced his support for a constitutional amendment prohibiting gay marriage nationwide. He did not mention the issue in any of his television advertisements during the ensuing campaign, but the controversy continued to stimulate widespread interest when municipalities in several states began wedding gay couples without authorization from judicial rulings or legislative enactments.[1] Same-sex marriage and its civil equivalent clearly struck a raw nerve among Americans on both sides of the issue.

The resounding public response to same-sex marriage led some observers to proclaim that the nation's political life recently had entered a new phase, one marked by tumultuous and unceasing conflict over cultural orientations. The problem with this interpretation of how American politics has developed and changed is that struggles over values, morals, and identities are as old as the republic itself and do not mark a departure from politics as usual.[2] For example, one of the flash points in the modern culture war, debates over adding intelligent design to school curricula, had a direct predecessor in early twentieth-century state laws that forbid the teaching of evolution in the classroom. Similarly, the antiimmigration sentiment expressed in recent years was exceeded in periods such as the 1920s, when hostility to Italian, Mexican, and Chinese entrants brought restrictive immigration laws. More generally, American history is dotted with battles over outlawing slavery, prohibiting consumption of alcohol, passing women's suffrage, and reviving religious commitment and participation. Cultural divisions, in short, are not a new feature of the American political system.

A more specific but equally mistaken inference often drawn from the prominence of same-sex marriage is that social and cultural concerns have displaced economics as the topics that dominate campaigns, public dialogue, and legislative deliberations. Political commentators commonly assume that if issues such as gay rights now attract attention, then it must come at the expense of economics. Conceptions of a nation irreconcilably split between cultural worldviews, with economics pushed to the background, lie behind many of the red-versus-blue maps that are ubiquitous in the first decade of the twenty-first century.[3] As this chapter will show, however, the modern culture war has not distracted Americans from economic worries, for those anxieties have actually intensified rather than diminished. To see how and why this transformation has occurred, one must examine Americans' different economic experiences in the initial decades after World War II compared with the period from the early 1970s to the present.

The Postwar Economic Boom

At the close of World War II, policymakers, business leaders, and union officials sought to prevent the recurrence of economic disaster. Although military preparation and production had effectively ended the Great Depression and the nation's factories, stores, and offices hummed with newfound vigor, concerns remained over whether the gains would be sustainable in the war's aftermath. Using the downturn following World War I as a historical analogy, the most pessimistic observers expected a downward spiral when defense spending invariably would shrink and millions of soldiers would be reabsorbed into the civilian workforce.[4] Some prominent members of the Roosevelt and Truman administrations were more confident, holding that with fine-tuning the economy could maintain high levels of employment and growth.[5] The general public, with memories of mass joblessness and widespread despair still fresh, sided with the fearful forecasters. A poll taken in September 1945 asked Americans, "For the first year or two after the war, which one of these things do you expect: enough jobs for everybody, some unemployment, or a lot of unemployment?" A startling 32% of the respondents chose the most dismal option, with another 43% bracing for at least some unemployment.[6]

Once history could verify or refute the predictions, the record showed that the American economy outperformed even the most optimistic projections of a few years earlier. On the international scene, the nation dominated export markets as the war-shattered economies of Europe and Japan recorded productivity rates only a fraction of those in the United States.[7] Wartime production at home had generated incomes for millions of people who formerly could not find steady work. Under rationing policies that limited the types and amounts of goods available, though, the new paychecks did not translate into higher levels of consumption. When those controls were lifted, the pent-up demand created a huge market that manufacturers and service providers eagerly captured. Sales of homes, cars, appliances, and other consumer goods boomed in the years following the Allies' victory.

The low risk of involuntary job loss represented one of the most noteworthy features of the postwar economy. After the cost-of-living adjustments that unions began winning in the 1940s, the interests of business and labor became closely aligned. Management specialists believed that long-term ties with employees benefited companies through loyalty in the workforce and the job-specific experiences and skills that resulted. Under a norm of employment stability, temporary layoffs during recessions were expected, but a permanent downsizing during economic expansions was not.[8] Stability was further encouraged by shifting control of large corporations from owners to managers, a development that started at the turn of the century.[9] Most executives worked their way up the ranks with the same employer, giving them a personal connection to and understanding of rank-and-file employees. Rewards were normally earmarked for those who built a company by reinvesting profits in expansion rather than returning them to shareholders. These incentives encouraged executives to enlarge payrolls when earnings permitted and to contract only when absolutely necessary. With profits accruing across companies and industries, there was little pressure for major revisions in the employment relationship.

This period did see recessions, mild in most cases and severe in 1958. The trends that people experienced throughout their working lives, though, are more important to this book than the temporary setbacks workers encountered. Judged by these long-term trends, the picture was bright. Buoyed by the availability and security of jobs, wages rose consistently for more than two decades and boosted millions of Americans into the middle class. Strong unions forced management to share productivity gains with workers through increases in wages, establishing a pattern that carried into nonunionized sectors of the economy. Corrected for inflation, the income of the median family more than doubled from 1947 to 1973—a remarkable outcome and one that, by the 1960s, economists and policymakers in the executive branch thought would continue indefinitely with proper applications of macroeconomic policy.[10] Employer-provided benefits spread rapidly as well, allowing a growing share of the population to receive pensions or health insurance through the workplace.[11]

The gains in employment and wages were dispersed across American society, for those without extensive education or skills could readily find jobs in manufacturing or services. Even the nation's most disadvantaged group, southern blacks displaced as agricultural laborers by new methods and machinery of farming, regularly secured employment in urban centers in the South and North.[12] As a result, income became more equally distributed. The Gini Index, a commonly used measure of income inequality, continually fell during the 1950s and 1960s, as did the annual share of income received by the top 5% of families.[13]

Economic Troubles Begin in the 1970s

When examined as a whole, the decades after the early 1970s stand in sharp contrast to the preceding ones. Contemporary eyes naturally turn toward the most recent boom or contraction, making it difficult to situate those events within a longer sweep of history. The economy since the days of bell-bottom trousers has continued to fluctuate, of course, and the business cycle periodically comes out of hibernation. What is most crucial for understanding historical eras, however, is not the variation but rather the averages that Americans encountered over the course of their working lives. Gauged with a variety of indicators, those averages have declined from what the nation saw in the 1950s and 1960s.

On one major dimension, public confidence in the economy's prospects eroded. Perceptions about future economic performance can be measured by the Index of Consumer Sentiment, constructed through regular surveys administered at the University of Michigan. One question on the surveys asks, "Now turning to business conditions in the country as a whole—do you think that during the next 12 months we'll have good times financially, or bad times, or what?" From the inception of the surveys in 1960 through 1972, positive responses outnumbered negative ones every year, and usually by substantial margins—an average of 41%. Beginning in 1973, the pattern reversed itself: Eight of the next ten years registered negative expectations for the performance of the economy. The economic rebound during the mid to late 1980s was insufficient to restore lasting optimism, for not until the close of the century did the numbers approach the levels routinely seen during the 1960s. Those gains proved to be only temporary, however, as the figures turned south again at the beginning of the twenty-first century.[14]

Americans' waning confidence in the nation's future economic prospects was rooted in their workplace experiences. In perhaps the most notable turnabout, employment opportunities slumped when stagflation and declining profits in the 1970s brought cost and competitive pressures to the fore at major corporations. Through restructuring, companies decimated entire communities by eliminating manufacturing jobs, especially in the Midwest and Northeast, and in the 1980s regular downsizing spread to service-sector industries such as banking, insurance, and telecommunications. By the recessions of 1991 and 2001, college-educated men and women in the ranks of middle management and the technology sectors frequently received pink slips that for many symbolized failure, induced despondency, and ended their primary or only source of income.[15]

The transitions in employment corresponded with a changing climate for corporate governance. Increasing numbers of Americans entered the stock market, particularly through retirement accounts, but the proportion of stock held directly by individuals dropped because the new equity owners bought mostly stakes in mutual funds rather than shares of single corporations.[16] Combined with the rising value of assets owned by institutional investors, including pension funds, insurance companies, and private foundations, the center of authority in corporations shifted away from management and back toward owners. Despite their inability to control management on a day-to-day basis, mutual fund directors and institutional investors easily could and did vote with their feet. Shares of stock changed hands much faster than they had when most of the equity market was owned directly by individuals, sending strong signals to executives to deliver short-term profits or else see their companies' stock prices fall.[17] Other innovations, such as incentive-based pay and stock options, also helped reorient executives' focus by aligning their interests more strongly with those of short-term stockholders. The fact that executives were increasingly hired from outside the firm rather than promoted from within further weakened their ties to the company's workforce.

These collective pressures made managers quicker to eliminate employees when doing so seemed to improve the firm's outlook for profits. A comparison of the reasons for layoffs in 1972 and 1994—years reflecting parallel points in the business cycle—showed that in the former year companies usually cited poor results, meaning downturns for the company or industry, as the motivating factor. By the later year, announcements were more likely to note that layoffs reflected a structural change intended to increase the company's competitiveness.[18] No longer confined to recessions, the threat of job turnover had become a regular feature of the labor market during robust times as well. Workers readily sensed the dangers of the new environment: When one compares surveys from years with similar unemployment rates, larger numbers of people in the 1990s than the 1970s believed they might soon face a layoff.[19] With job losses potentially just around the corner, workers understandably felt less secure.

Americans also came to believe that their fates were more tightly linked with the larger economy. Individuals' fortunes have always been connected to the economy as a whole, but people can enjoy greater and lesser degrees of insulation from impersonal economic forces. Industries such as groceries and utilities are less vulnerable to recessions than are luxury goods, for example, and the relationship between individuals and the broader economy can vary over time as well. Those holding stakes in mutual funds —to take one prominent group—cannot help but believe that their portfolios' values change with the nation's economic performance. As the number of stock owners mushroomed through personal retirement accounts, this source of linkage to the economy intensified. Compounding the trend, many of the factors that formerly provided some insulation from the economy weakened. The labor market became more flexible because of a declining rate of unionization, increased outsourcing and international trade, and the ease of eliminating or replacing workers.

The heightened connection between personal livelihoods and the overall economy is documented in a long-running data series. Surveys for the Index of Consumer Sentiment contain two questions that ask respondents to reflect on what has happened to both their own family's financial situation and to broader business conditions over the past twelve months.[20] Answers regarding financial conditions for one's own family and for the nation, the data show, have grown more connected over the last half-century. Quarterly responses to the two questions correlate at .58 in the 1960s, .70 in the 1970s, .88 in the 1980s, and .89 in the 1990s.[21] The distinction between personal and social decision-making, whereby citizens make political judgments according to how well they have done personally versus how well the overall economy has performed, has thereby lessened.[22]

Stagnating wages went hand in hand with uncertainties over employment to make the economy writ large more relevant to individual feelings and fortunes. Average wages closely track productivity, the amount of goods and services produced per hour of work. The crucial dividing year on this measure, as in a variety of economic outcomes, proved to be 1973. Annual productivity growth from 1973 to 2000 averaged 1.7%, slipping to only half the rate of 3.3% per year seen from 1947 to 1973.[23] Wage growth quickly followed suit. After escalating by 38% in the 1950s and 37% in the 1960s, the median family saw its real (inflation-adjusted) income rise by only 10% in the 1970s, 9% in the 1980s, and 12% in the 1990s.[24] Moreover, even the gains in family incomes that did occur in the later decades were primarily the result of a greater number of workers per family rather than pay hikes for individual workers.[25]

Insights into the new environment of wages can be gained from panel studies tracking the same workers over time. A study of the long-term wage trajectories of two cohorts of young men—one entering adulthood in 1966, the other in 1979—found strikingly different outcomes between the groups. Men in the later cohort experienced about 20% lower real wage growth over their first decade and a half in the workforce than did their predecessors.[26] Political scientist Jacob Hacker's investigation based on a lengthy data series revealed a trend of downward mobility alongside the more familiar story from American history of upward mobility. Family incomes since the early 1970s have turned more volatile from year to year, with some people moving down the wage scale as others moved up.[27]

Economic difficulties struck hardest the roughly seven of every ten adults lacking a college degree. The Bureau of Labor Statistics has collected data since 1984 on Americans' experiences of job losses. Unsurprisingly, the results have consistently shown that those with lower levels of education are much more likely to report involuntary unemployment in the previous three years than are college graduates.[28] Whereas workers lacking postsecondary education might have taken reasonably secure and well-paying factory and sales jobs in the 1960s, they more often held positions as cashiers, data entry assistants, and day care workers in the 1990s. The difficulties of paying for food, rent, transportation, and utilities on what can be earned in the low-wage sectors are often perceived intellectually, but sometimes not viscerally, by academics and journalists. To gain an appreciation for the experiences of a growing number of Americans, writer and social critic Barbara Ehrenreich conducted her own experiment by working for several months as a maid, waitress, retail clerk, and nursing home aide. Ehrenreich vividly, and at times wrenchingly, described how difficult it was to pay for rent, food, transportation, and utilities on wages near $7 an hour.[29]

Coupled with gains in real income among Americans with four years of college, the modest wages at the bottom end of the labor market enhanced the already substantial returns of higher education. Calculated as the wage differential between those whose education ran through college versus those who stopped at high school, the "value" of a college degree that stood at 45% in 1973 climbed to 89% by 2000. College graduates now earn nearly twice as much as those holding only a high school diploma.[30] As is well known, the changing structure of the labor market brought more inequality: The average family in the top fifth of the income distribution collected $7.47 for every dollar earned by the average family in the bottom fifth of the distribution in 1973, but the figure steadily rose to $11.02 in 2000.[31]

The Actual and Expected Standard of Living

Analysts of varying ideological stripes agree that workers faced greater threats of employment instability in the post-1973 period than in the first three decades after World War II. For example, few disagreed when Federal Reserve Board chairman Alan Greenspan testified before Congress in 1999 that workers felt less secure in their jobs than in previous times, thereby dampening upward pressures on wages. The question of what has happened to incomes and living standards, however, has created more controversy. Some observers have argued that average Americans, not just the wealthiest group, have witnessed major advances in their material existence. The conflicting interpretations result in part from uncertainties about how to adjust wages for inflation. The widely used Consumer Price Index (CPI), even in its revised versions, does not fully account for improvements in product quality.[32] Measured inflation therefore overstates the actual increase in the cost of living, meaning that real wages have been simultaneously understated.

Another position in this debate rests on evidence that Americans' current levels of consumption far exceed those of a few decades ago.[33] With important exceptions in areas such as health care and education, the costs of goods and services ranging from a gallon of milk to a telephone call to a square foot of a house have fallen in real terms, reducing the amount of work necessary to generate wages sufficient to purchase them. Products like air conditioners, large televisions, and electric coffee makers, considered luxuries in 1970, are now routinely owned by households of modest means. New items such as cell phones, DVD players, and home exercise equipment have penetrated deeply enough into society to now be deemed essential by many American families. One assessment of these trends claims that "by the standards of 1971, many of today's poor families might be considered members of the middle class."[34]

Independent of people's actual standard of living, however, is the intriguing question of whether their lifestyles correspond with how well they think they *should* be doing. As a large body of research has shown, individuals' status, livelihood, and gains relative to their expectations predict social behaviors and psychological attitudes better than do measures of their objective situations alone.[35] This point cannot be overemphasized when considering the political consequences of Americans' perceptions of their economic positions. Although some analysts have claimed that the economy since the early 1970s created opportunities and growing wages across-the-board, no one asserts that these advances were as strong as those achieved in the 1950s and 1960s. Adjusting the CPI to account for product quality strengthens real wage growth in prior decades as well as recent ones, meaning that the years after 1973 still fare worse by comparison. The current era would look better had it not followed a generation-long boom that raised expectations, perhaps unrealistically so, about what workers would see over their lifetimes. Even if a favorable interpretation of the times after baby boomers came of age is the accurate one, many people's material livelihoods still fell short of what they expected. Indeed, some writers who contend that the public and media have grossly overestimated the long-term problems recognize that many Americans' expectations have risen faster than their capacity to meet them.[36]

Public opinion polls offer a statistical view of escalating material demands. One revealing survey asked, "How much income per year would you say you (and your family) need to fulfill all of your dreams?" The median response nearly doubled in just one decade, from $50,000 in 1987 to $90,000 in the last administration of the survey, 1996.[37] Needless to say, family incomes did not double in the intervening years. Another question sought to determine whether or not respondents considered a variety of factors essential for the "good life." Examining the several waves of the survey beginning with its initial application in 1975 and ending with the latest available figures for 1996, answers increasingly centered on the material, as opposed to the spiritual, ethical, or intellectual, aspects of life. The percentage of people identifying a "vacation home," "swimming pool," and a "second color television" rose by more than 20%. The ranks of those citing a "happy marriage" and "children" thinned slightly. Showing that money trumps excitement in modern America, mentions of a "job that pays much more than average" rose by 18% at the same time that answers of an "interesting job" dropped by 8%.[38]

Several explanations could account for Americans' appetites for more and more goods and services. Expanding levels of advertising now include product placements in movies and billboards on the sides of city buses. People's reference points may have shifted as well, from their neighbors—whom they now visit with less often—to the fictional characters and lavish lifestyles they see on television programs.[39] If greater consumption by some encourages emulation by others, the proliferation in income and wealth at the top of the distribution may have raised consumer desires throughout society.[40] The declines in community involvement that Robert Putnam investigates in *Bowling Alone* also may have fueled higher levels of materialism.[41] When citizens were more connected with community institutions and activities, they could draw sustenance and satisfaction from them; with more people retreating to their homes and television sets, they might be more likely to use consumption to meet their emotional needs.

Of course, material aspirations have expanded throughout American history, and it is difficult to determine whether the rate of increase is greater now than it was in earlier ages. Social theorists from Tocqueville to Veblen to Galbraith observed similar facets of American society in the mid-nineteenth century, at the turn of the twentieth century, and in the mid-twentieth century, respectively. Regardless of their origin or their comparison to prior epochs, though, the material demands of the populace have broadened and deepened over the last three decades. The mismatch between what people have versus what they want helps explain why the market for books and articles with a negative outlook on recent decades has often been robust. Even if individuals are not worse off, the redefinition of wants as needs may induce a feeling of losing ground and create a receptiveness to gloomy messages about the nation's standard of living.

At the same time that Americans demanded higher levels of consumption, they confronted stagnating wages in the workplace. Some families initially righted the imbalance by adding a second earner within the household, a strategy that has neared its natural limit now that labor-force participation rates for women approach those of men.[42] For a time, the day of reckoning could be postponed through lower savings rates and higher levels of debt. The debt-to-income ratio of households, calculated as total consumer, mortgage, and other debt divided by after-tax personal income, skyrocketed from 0.67 in 1973 to 1.07 in 2000.[43] A 2004 poll revealed the massive debt burdens by asking why "it is harder to achieve the American dream today" than it was for previous generations. Debt levels ranked as the most common response, easily outpacing the nine other options the survey offered.[44]

As more Americans live from paycheck to paycheck and make burdensome debt payments, they become vulnerable to unforeseen financial shocks. Whereas families with a cushion of savings might absorb the lower income resulting from a job loss or the higher expenses stemming from a medical emergency or divorce, accumulated debt increasingly causes such problems to push people over the financial edge.[45] The number of filings for personal bankruptcy more than doubled in the 1980s and then leaped by another 70% during the 1990s.[46] In a startling indicator of families' financial health, every year more Americans declare bankruptcy than receive bachelor's degrees.[47] Even this drastic and demoralizing step no longer provides an option for some people because Congress has toughened the federal laws governing bankruptcy.

As if the twin pressures of employment instability and debt loads were not enough to unnerve Americans, broad segments of the population have faced threats to their health insurance and retirement income. Owing largely to a decline in employer-provided coverage, the number of Americans without health insurance rose from 23 million in 1976 to 45 million in 2004.[48] Fears of unanticipated and unpayable medical bills have been made more pressing than they were to the uninsured in earlier times owing to massive inflation in health care costs. Meanwhile, in the midst of continual discussion among political elites about the long-term funding of Social Security, the perception that "it won't be there when I retire" has spread, especially among the young. Relatively few people have built up personal savings and paid down debt to offset these concerns.

The sum of these various outcomes can be called "economic insecurity," a concept broader than—though obviously related to—conventional understandings of a "sluggish economy." The economy can be growing steadily, but if people wonder whether layoffs are imminent due to downsizing or globalization, or they hold piles of debt and live a crisis away from bankruptcy, then they do not possess economic security. A strong economy, then, is a necessary though not sufficient condition for economic security, which rests not only on typical measures such as GDP growth and the unemployment rate but also on wages, debt levels, job stability, and the scope of health insurance and retirement coverage. Beyond the objective figures, economic security contains a subjective component because people's fears about such matters as the dangers posed by international competition, the likelihood of layoffs, and the prospects for a collapse in Social Security may exceed the reality. Economic security also hinges on expectations, for a given income can be seen as high or as low depending on the level of material comfort the earner demands. If desires for consumption increase faster than incomes, debt and economic insecurity are the likely results.

An important aspect of this insecurity has been its persistence through upswings and downswings in the post-1970s economy—a point that will have great relevance for my analyses in subsequent chapters. Despite high GDP growth in the last half of the 1980s and again in the few years following the recession of 1991, gains in productivity, job stability, and incomes remained sluggish. Not until 1996 did many indicators improve, led by a productivity growth of 2.7% in 1996–2000 that, while falling short of the averages seen in 1948–1973, nevertheless greatly exceeded the typical figures recorded after 1973.[49] Thus the end of the 1990s saw gains in real wages at all levels of education as a low unemployment rate signaled employer demand even for low-skilled workers.[50] Yet the best economy in thirty years still could not eliminate fears about economic security. A poll taken at the height of the late-1990s boom asked people what would improve their happiness. Greater economic and financial security topped the list of answers, beating alternatives such as better health, more leisure time, greater faith in God or religion, and more opportunities for personal development.[51]

Had the tight labor markets prevailing at the end of the 1990s continued, economic security may eventually have turned a corner. Soon enough, though, the dot-com crash and slowdowns in investment undercut claims that old rules no longer applied. The following years saw a return to strong productivity increases, but job and income growth, especially compared with earlier recoveries, remained weak. Regardless of what happens as the twenty-first century unfolds, the period from 1973 to the present looked very different from the decades immediately following World War II. Although there were fluctuations during each time span in that workers naturally did worse during recessions than in the succeeding recoveries, the differences *between* the periods proved more important for the political effects described later in this book than did the variations within them.

The economic difficulties of individuals and families in recent times, it is important to recognize, were not a postmodern illusion foisted on the public by politicians or the media. Job instability, stagnant wages, high debt levels, and a lack of health insurance affected people's lives directly and forcefully. These problems were too personal, too concrete, to be created by elites through a swirl of words and images unrelated to people's actual experiences. At the same time, the rhetorical and policy responses of politicians, interest groups, and other political actors to the problems were in no way predetermined; later chapters will show how a rightward shift in American politics emerged from the variety of responses made by intellectuals and parties. The underlying stimulus of economic insecurity was real even though the political consequences could easily have taken different forms.

Media and Public Attention to the Economy

Trends in wage growth, employment stability, and consumption desires were intertwined with parallel changes in the content of the news media. Because these complementary shifts in media coverage formed part of the context for political rhetoric, a closer examination of their origins and development is warranted. Several factors affect the volume of attention the news media devote to different phenomena. Owned in most cases by major corporations seeking value for stockholders, news organizations strive to maximize profits by carefully scrutinizing both costs and revenues. When it comes to costs, a news-gathering strategy that can be implemented cheaply holds appeal for all those involved in constructing and producing the news. On the revenues side of the ledger, news organizations can add to their audience shares and advertising income by covering the kinds of stories most likely to attract viewers, listeners, and readers.

Costs became especially pertinent to news organizations in contemporary times. Even as recently as the 1960s, most newspapers and broadcasting stations were locally owned, and television news did not regularly turn a profit.[52] The trend of steady consolidation across media outlets has made reporters and editors increasingly accountable not to traditional journalistic norms and practices but to stockholders and managers.[53] This pressure for making profits led to a relentless search for stories that, while still piquing the interest of the audience, could be developed cheaply. Drawing from figures about production, unemployment, interest rates, and inflation lifted directly from government reports, economic news fit the bill well. Other economic stories in areas involving trade disputes, the stock market, and the actions of the Federal Reserve Board also did not require expensive investigative reporting. Within a news culture of intensive monitoring of costs, coverage of the economy could be predicted to climb relative to other topics.

The realities of the workplace since the early 1970s may have brought a similar result through the demand side by influencing which stories people will devote scarce time to watch, listen, or read. For many of the same reasons that have created economic insecurity—such as international competition, rising debt levels, downsizing during upturns as well as downturns, and the growing ranks of those lacking health insurance—Americans may have become more interested in economic news. With respondents more often reporting that their financial situations are connected with those of everyone else, as described earlier in the data from the Index of Consumer Sentiment, there is greater reason to follow the economy's twists and turns. At the same time, the proliferation of media outlets and competing entertainment programs across radio, broadcast television, cable television, and the Internet intensified the business pressures on news organizations to find and hold an audience.[54] A likely consequence of these factors is profit-seeking news organizations expanding their coverage of the economy over the last three decades in an attempt to capture a greater market share.

The long-term growth in economic coverage can be demonstrated through a content analysis of news stories. Recognizing that no source is fully representative of the entire scope of the news media, empirical studies nevertheless find that the volume of coverage devoted to different issues often correlates highly across news outlets.[55] Similarities in content result from "pack journalism," from various outlets responding to the same occurrences in society, and from the tendency for competing reporters to follow similar criteria and norms when constructing the news. Still, there is some advantage in conducting a content analysis of a prestigious news source that provides leadership to other news organizations. Owing to its long-standing reputation and the availability of data over a lengthy period, the *New York Times* will be used here.

I calculated the proportion per year of front-page stories on economic matters from 1946 to 2004.[56] Paralleling the lead stories in television news that have been shown to exert the greatest impact on the public's issue priorities, front-page stories in newspapers are the ones most often read and discussed.[57] Economic stories here include those on production, employment, and prices within the economy as a whole or within a given sector or company; shortages or surpluses of commodities; the stock and bond markets; monetary policy and interest rates; strikes and labor unrest; and government efforts to affect the economy through means such as wage and price controls, incentives for plant location, community redevelopment, and taxation.

The data show that economic news was relatively uncommon on the front page in the decades immediately after World War II, but the pattern changed greatly thereafter. Although short-term variation can also be identified, for the purposes of this book the differences between periods are most important. The year 1973 represents an appropriate dividing line by marking the beginning of the trends described earlier in the chapter. News coverage changed alongside people's economic experiences: From 1946 to 1972, an average of only 10% of the front-page stories in the *New York Times* addressed the economy, but that level nearly doubled to 18% for the period 1973–2004. During every single presidential administration after Richard Nixon's first term, the average yearly proportion of coverage was higher than the 10% figure from the previous two and a half decades. Among regular consumers of the news, along with those encountering it second-hand through friends, family, or coworkers, the state of the economy moved closer to the forefront of consciousness.

The same pattern appears in measures of public opinion. Whether as cause or effect, news coverage is closely related to the degree to which people attend to different issues. Public attention can be assessed through the Gallup polls that have regularly asked random samples of Americans, "What do you think is the most important problem facing this country today?" These surveys paint a comprehensive portrait of the shifting focus of the American public over a long period. With the rich source of data available, one can determine across different periods the extent to which people prioritized the economy.

The "most important problem" data indicate that for a few years after the Second World War, the economy occasionally topped the list amid a burst of inflation and anxiety about another depression.[58] During the next twenty-five years of employment security and consistent growth in real incomes, references to the economy seldom reached the number-one position. In total, only 17% of the "most important problem" surveys conducted from 1946 to 1972 found the economy in the first spot. By far the most common public concern during that era was foreign affairs, including communism, the threat of war, relations with the Soviet Union, and Vietnam. The issues of civil rights and racial segregation also made multiple appearances in the leading position.

The succeeding decades looked very different. With economic insecurity spreading, Americans regularly cited some aspect of the economy as the foremost problem of the nation. People reacted not only to oil shocks but to an array of enduring difficulties; the energy crises eventually receded even as economic troubles remained regarding international competition, job turnover, downsizing, and wage growth. Expanding desires for consumption put pressure on pocketbooks that led to higher levels of personal debt and bankruptcy. All of these factors would be expected to—and did—make people more closely attuned to the economy. Various components of the economy were the "most important problem" in a remarkable 73% of the surveys from 1973 to 2006.[59] More often than not during this period, the economy stood as the public's leading priority.

For much of the last quarter-century, political commentators assumed that material needs had diminished in importance in American politics.[60] With the economic dimensions of public life fading from the scene, the axis of political conflict supposedly revolved around social and cultural issues such as guns, abortion, crime, gay rights, religious expression, teaching evolution in schools, and moral degradation in movies, music, and television. Thomas Frank, for example, attributes the electoral success of the Republican party to the prominence of those issues.[61] The culture war clearly galvanized many interest groups, who in turn mobilized sizable constituencies on the left and the right. The "most important problem" data, however, contradict any assertion that economic matters moved off the public's radar screen. By comparison with previous decades, the economy attracted much more attention from the early 1970s through the opening years of the twenty-first century.

This finding cannot be easily reconciled with political scientist Ronald Inglehart's oft-cited thesis that postmaterialist values have supplanted materialist orientations in Western societies.[62] Greater physical safety combined with an increased standard of living after World War II, Inglehart argues, caused younger generations raised in affluence to place more emphasis on free speech, environmental protection, women's rights, personal freedoms, and political participation. In fairness, Inglehart sought to identify large-scale, cross-national trends, whereas the focus of this book is on the United States. The topics he defines as postmaterialist certainly occupy space on the public agenda, but in no way have they eliminated basic questions of economic security. One of the ironies of Inglehart's claims about postmaterialist values displacing materialist ones is that he published his initial, pioneering article on the subject in 1971.[63] In a follow-up book he predicted that the patterns he uncovered would disappear if economic troubles returned—and they did, at the very moment he was writing.[64] During a long-term decline in economic security in the United States, worries about jobs, incomes, and growth attracted more attention, not less, from the American people.

When the economy was not the public's foremost concern in recent times, the first spot was usually held by foreign policy. Terrorism and national security overshadowed the economy from September 11, 2001, through most of 2002, but thereafter the economy regained its prominence. Even with the long buildup, execution, and occupation of the second Iraq war and the continuing global war on terror, a majority of Gallup's "most important problem" surveys from 2003 to 2006 found the economy to occupy the number-one position. The intensity of Americans' attention to the economy, then, remained far higher than in the early post–World War II decades.

Economic Context and Rhetoric

The various dimensions of economic insecurity have been extensively documented in books, articles, and reports. The political implications of the growth of economic insecurity, however, have received much less analysis. Major developments in matters critical to everyday lives, of which pocketbook and workplace relationships certainly qualify, should reverberate throughout the political system by creating opportunities for some goals, interests, and players and constraints for others. Changes in people's economic experiences, along with greater media and public attention to them, form a substantial part of the "context" that chapter 2 identifies as a driving force behind the construction of politicians' rhetoric for both mass and elite audiences.

The context affects what kinds of issues and arguments resonate with people. With the rise of economic insecurity, politicians attuned to their constituencies could readily have sensed the benefits of promising that their policies would yield economic gains.[65] The continual prominence of material worries in both the public mind—as seen in the "most important problem" data—and in the mass media meant that politicians could easily surmise that voters would place more weight on economic criteria when judging candidates, officeholders, and policies. Politicians need not even be right in that expectation. For social scientists attempting to explain how and why political rhetoric is constructed, politicians' beliefs about how ordinary citizens make judgments are more important than the actual decision-making processes. Based on the information available to them, politicians would be reasonable in expecting that policies framed in economic terms would become more acceptable to American audiences.

One would predict that both the conduct of campaigns and the substance of governing would be affected by the new context. In a climate of insecurity, elected officials strive both to deliver strong economic performance and to undertake visible policy actions that can be linked rhetorically to the economy. One plausible strategy involves ignoring policies with noneconomic effects and focusing on those closely connected to economic quantities. For instance, whereas formerly governors might have given both time and rhetorical emphasis to public health programs or the organization of government agencies, now they might devote sustained effort to luring new firms and jobs to the state through regulatory exemptions or training programs.

Alternatively, politicians could press with an economic rationale the same proposals made in previous periods, meaning that the change would come not in the policies offered and enacted but rather in the grounds publicly used to support them. With this strategy, political leaders construct their most prominent arguments around the effects a given policy will have on jobs, investment, wages, prices, or business conditions. Policies previously defended through appeals to morality or justice could now be promoted as a means to stimulate economic growth and job creation. Instead of advocating flatter income taxes by asserting the unfairness of taxing individuals at unequal levels—to take one example—a politician could contend that higher rates on the wealthy decrease the incentive to work and invest. Obviously there are limits to this approach because some policy areas, such as criminal justice and civil liberties, do not easily lend themselves to economic arguments. Nevertheless, a wide range of domains, including regulation, education, taxation, agriculture, transportation, energy, labor, and foreign trade, can easily accommodate rhetorical rationales based on the consequences for the economy.

Economic Rhetoric after World War II

By changing the setting within which political debates are conducted, economic insecurity opens the door to processes that can culminate in new policy decisions, while an absence of economic insecurity means that political struggles will be fought on other grounds. These points are illustrated well by the rhetorical themes of the quarter-century following World War II. Because of widespread prosperity, economic arguments were not as powerful as they had been formerly or would later become. Politicians and other political actors usually could gain only a moderate amount of traction by asserting that their preferred policies would bring economic returns. With financial security seemingly assured outside of temporary downturns, as evidenced by the sparse mentions of the economy in the "most important problem" surveys, arguments more contextually potent usually formed the rhetorical basis for programmatic initiatives.

Often the most powerful justification for a given policy was that national defense depended on it. In the opening decades of the Cold War, advocates often could win federal support for a program by attaching it to defense needs, a tendency seen in education, transportation, and trade. Today, even amid a potentially permanent global war on terror, these three issues are most frequently framed around their economic effects. According to the most common arguments advanced in the public realm, stronger schools equip workers to compete for the jobs available in a postindustrial society, robust transportation systems lubricate the economy by moving goods and people, and free trade leads to efficiency gains and lower prices. Although debates surrounding all three issues have always included economic components, for a time policy positions were anchored primarily to national defense.

The rhetorical linkage to defense can be seen in the first major federal legislation on education, the National Defense Education Act of 1958, which authorized financial assistance for programs in science, mathematics, and foreign languages and funded loans for college students. The title of the legislation summarized the prism through which it was presented to the public: Backers framed the statute as an effort to encourage educational achievement in order to beat the Soviets. Yet many people had desired a federal role in education long before the impetus that the *Sputnik* launch provided in 1957. Whereas those efforts formerly were blocked through adherence to the centuries-old norm of exclusive state and local control of education, the USSR's apparent scientific and technological prowess gave advocates an appealing rhetorical opening to allow federal intervention. Even though the framing of education policies around national defense did not last indefinitely, from the perspective of the twenty-first century it is remarkable that such a connection could ever have arisen.

Transportation policies took a parallel track with those in education. The interstate highway system was initially authorized and funded through the 1956 legislation popularly known as the National Interstate and Defense Highways Act. Highways that connected all parts of the continental United States, supporters contended, would allow the rapid movement of troops, weapons, and equipment in the event of war. Of course, those same highways would promote commerce, but the economic frames could not single-handedly justify such a large expenditure of federal dollars. The rhetorical means to win passage emphasized the benefits for defense rather than for the economy. Again, the title of the legislation identifies the central frame through which it was communicated to the American public, a clear contrast to today's situation where transportation policies are normally defined around the economic needs of states, regions, and the naton.

The framing of foreign trade also differed from the modes of discourse common today. Political leaders in this earlier era believed that international exchanges of goods and services facilitated both prosperity and peace, but the latter effect usually received greater rhetorical emphasis. Prominent politicians held that a web of commercial relationships with non-Communist countries would make them less susceptible to leftist revolutions or alliances with the Soviet Union. The 1960 Democratic platform, for example, sandwiched its discussion of trade after sections titled "National Defense," "Arms Control," and "The Instruments of Foreign Policy," and before the sections titled "Immigration," "The Underdeveloped World," and "The United Nations"—an indication that trade was grouped with foreign and defense policy. The platform writers framed international trade as one part of a multifaceted approach to ensure lasting peace and protect national security.

Important statutes and platform planks on education, transportation, and trade show that in the immediate postwar decades, politicians commonly responded to the context by invoking noneconomic arguments, especially those relating to national defense. That does not mean that economic frames were ignored; indeed, they did provide the main rhetorical justifications for policies in the domains of energy and agriculture.[66] While stating that a certain policy should be adopted because it will aid the economy is never a poor rhetorical choice, such a claim will be more successful at certain moments than others. For most of the quarter-century after World War II, economic frames were less potent than they had been during the Depression or would become from the early 1970s to the present, and political actors responded in predictable ways when constructing their rhetoric.

In the latter half of the period of liberal ascendancy in American politics running through the Great Society, then, policy developments did not revolve predominantly around economic implications. Of the most important liberal statutes from the 1940s, 1950s, and 1960s, very few mimicked President Kennedy's Keynesian-inspired tax cut in being sold to the public predominantly with claims about the consequences for the economy. Instead, the rhetoric of liberal officials and their allies within interest groups, social movements, and the intellectual community normally stressed other goals. The rhetoric surrounding the 1964 Civil Rights Act and the 1965 Voting Rights Act emphasized social justice and fair treatment, not the effects on the economy, as did similar efforts for combating gender discrimination and revising immigration policies to hinge on family reunification rather than national origins. Needless to say, the wave of environmental legislation that swept the nation was framed around nonmaterial objectives, and the expanded reach of the federal government into consumer protection—for which new legislation covered food additives, drug safety, truth in lending, and greater inspection of meat and poultry—sought not to promote economic growth but rather to guard against its undesirable side effects.

Because Keynesian doctrines were generally accepted in the economics profession, liberals of that era could compete effectively with conservatives in answering the question of how to encourage job creation and boost people's incomes. When the national dialogue turned to achieving broadly based prosperity, liberals possessed an intellectually coherent answer. Most of the time, though, policy deliberations invoked other criteria. With wages growing much faster than inflation, jobs usually plentiful, and pension and health plans covering more workers, economic security was not as prominent a concern as it would soon become. Therefore, politicians and other political actors pushing for any given policy usually had relatively little to gain by contending that it would produce favorable effects on the economy. The 1960s are commonly remembered as a decade filled with idealistic fervor, sentiments that became possible because anxiety over economic security had been largely removed from national discussion.

This chapter concludes with an important point explored more fully in the rest of the book: The decline in economic security beginning in 1973 encouraged major revisions in rhetoric and policy, whose interactions reverberated throughout American politics. Conservatives would soon gain the upper hand in winning political power and making public policy, but the right's rhetorical effectiveness, and the corresponding shift in elite and mass politics, was not inevitable. The success of conservatives in changing the course of policy depended on a network of allied intellectuals who could offer to both political leaders and the general public clear reasoning and convincing appeals for broad approaches to taxation, regulation, government spending, and the welfare state. The next chapter describes how conservatives built their intellectual and rhetorical capacity by first examining a period when it was lacking, the Depression.

FOUR

The Building of Conservatives'
Intellectual Capacity

Throughout the New Deal and shortly thereafter, the vast majority of the nation's public intellectuals—those who offer, normally through the written word, learned commentary, opinions, or insights for an educated public—held left-of-center views. Despite attracting support from most of the business community and on many editorial pages, conservative viewpoints found little voice among intellectuals. One could not identify self-sustaining groups of conservative thinkers who were offering first principles, tracing chains of logic, and exploring policy implications. The sorry state of conservatism's intellectual wing was observed long ago by George Nash, whose comprehensive account of intellectual activity in a later period—the first three decades after World War II—received a warm reception from the very people he described. Nash writes that in the 1930s and continuing through the end of the war, "no articulate, coordinated, self-consciously conservative intellectual force existed in the United States. There were, at most, scattered voices of protest, profoundly pessimistic about the future of their country."[1]

The Depression obviously encouraged political actors to base policy proposals and the arguments for them on an economic language geared toward promoting a recovery. The onset of a new context, though, does not automatically induce corresponding modes of rhetoric. The context is best regarded as providing possibilities and invitations, but taking advantage of them requires an intellectual capacity within which appropriate ideas can be developed and disseminated. Ideas do not gain influence simply by being internally coherent, thoroughly elaborated, or effectively presented. They also must circulate broadly, a process that usually depends on more than just the creative scholar working in isolation. Even when one pioneering figure towers over the others, the providing of details, resolving of contradictions, and connecting to contemporary issues typically are performed by subsequent thinkers who connect with an audience outside of narrow intellectual circles.

Without this kind of robust intellectual capacity, an ideological movement is constrained in how it can react to major changes in the social, political, and economic context. When formulating their own preferences and devising rhetoric for mass and elite audiences, political leaders commonly borrow from, and are influenced by, intellectual discourse. The need for a network of individuals and institutions that can discover, refine, and publicize ideas can be seen by analyzing conservatives' ineffective opposition to the New Deal. From the standpoint of research design, one cannot accurately assess the effects of a phenomenon without also considering a case marked by its absence. My analysis of a period when the right's intellectual capacity was missing (the New Deal) therefore complements the chapters to follow that examine an era (the post-1970s) when it was present.

Conservative Opposition to the New Deal

Without interconnected research institutes, freelance intellectuals, and journals of opinion, conservatives failed to advance a well-argued explanation of the causes of and solutions to the Depression. President Hoover initially pointed to rising waves of turmoil within European economies, which then spread internationally and surged onto American shores. Among other political and business leaders, the view was common that economic downturns formed a natural and self-correcting part of capitalism, making periodic slumps inevitable and in some ways desirable. Hoover's secretary of the treasury, Andrew Mellon, and some members of the Federal Reserve Board believed that the 1920s had seen an outbreak of speculative excess that only "liquidation," including mass bankruptcies, could purge from the system.[2] This analysis was more conventional wisdom than intellectual perspective, however, and it was not defended in detail anywhere with the reasoning and evidence that could serve as guideposts to political leaders.

Within the discipline of economics, Say's Law (which stipulates that supply creates its own demand) maintained some adherents. Advocates of classical economics claimed that production and consumption spontaneously coordinate through the price mechanism, making downturns the product of government mismanagement of the money supply. Moreover, prolonged unemployment cannot exist, since prices and wages will eventually fall such that employment will be restored. If government would avoid interfering with the natural workings of the market, the argument continued, the economy would right itself.[3] Again, though, conservatives lacked an intellectual infrastructure that could borrow and apply these principles and bring the case to larger audiences. After all, Jean-Baptiste Say had been dead for a century and Adam Smith for even longer. The usefulness of classical economics and its modern counterparts was inherently limited without skillful writers who could gain inspiration from existing works, incorporate new sources of information and data, and extend the ideas to the current situation.

The social sciences in general, and economics in particular, were not as fully developed in methodological and theoretical sophistication as they would become in later decades. The inchoate state of the social sciences, however, cannot explain the failure of conservatives to advance a persuasive and widely publicized diagnosis of the Depression. After all, the same limitation applied at the other end of the political spectrum, yet liberals and leftists suffered no shortage of articles and books that helped explain the crisis. Proto-Keynesian ideas, for example, had been expressed by many observers who directed attention to policies designed to counter weak consumer demand. William Foster and Waddill Catchings, among others, advocated government spending on public works to lift consumer demand and thereby boost employment.[4] Perhaps the most vigorous government intervention of all—national planning—received laudatory reviews from many intellectuals. Surveying periodicals from 1923 to 1933, two sociologists counted 1,598 articles on planning as a means to restore balance in the economy.[5] The Roosevelt administration, in short, could draw from several distinct lines of thought holding that industrial capitalism was imperfect but amenable to improvement through government action.

The scarcity of talented writers and thinkers on the right meant that FDR's responses to the Depression encountered no sustained and effective intellectual challenge. It certainly was not the case, though, that a detailed, constructive alternative was impossible to formulate. In 1963 economists Milton Friedman and Anna Schwartz published a book attributing the Depression's length and severity to a contraction of the money supply, defined to include a wide array of bank deposits and financial instruments. Friedman and Schwartz condemn the Federal Reserve Board for failing to react with a loose monetary policy.[6] Related accounts of why a recession became the Depression blame other government policies, especially the Smoot-Hawley Tariff passed in 1930 and the whole panoply of New Deal programs. It has now become a staple of conservative writing about the period to argue that the federal relief, recovery, labor, taxation, and social insurance programs made the Depression deeper and more painful than it otherwise would have been.[7]

Some authors have even attempted to quantify the adverse impact of Roosevelt's efforts, finding a greater gap with each passing year between the economy's actual performance and that which would have occurred in the absence of those policies.[8] Although similar assertions that Roosevelt made a bad problem much worse were occasionally offered at the time, none was constructed in a systematic way with intellectual rigor. If works like those published later had been available at the time, along with the necessary means of publicity and distribution, conservatives might have been more successful in resisting the policies and rationales of the New Deal. The crucial need was for an intellectual infrastructure that could convincingly attribute the causes of the Depression to foolish actions by government officials rather than shortsighted corporations or flaws in capitalism.

The absence of an articulate, widely known intellectual case equating unregulated capitalism with prosperity, and big government with stagnation, helps solve a rhetorical puzzle regarding the grounds for opposition to the New Deal. When times are tough and economic security is low, one would expect policy discussions to reflect this context and thus to revolve around economic dimensions. Competing advocates will champion their set of policies as necessary to increase production and create jobs. When times are prosperous, by contrast, deliberation about policy alternatives—even when the same issues are considered—will focus less on their economic consequences. Arguments that are economic in character will not vanish but will recede in the amount of time and emphasis devoted to them within the overall debate. Different kinds of arguments, such as promoting justice, strengthening values, maintaining communities, or protecting freedom, will rise in stature and form the basis for decisions.

Extensive criticism of the New Deal based on economic consequences could have emerged, at least after Roosevelt had been president long enough to be the country's focal point. During his first two years in office, the opposition was disorganized, and the initial burst of national optimism following his inauguration would have been difficult to counter. At that point, it would have been futile to press the case that Roosevelt's policies would worsen the Depression; in a sense, there was nowhere lower to go, and while in office the previous administration had not successfully addressed the despair or halted the downturn. The second half of FDR's initial term, however, presented new opportunities. He became the nation's recognized leader whose policies had taken effect, and yet national conditions in 1935 were only slightly better than in 1933. The unemployment rate, while down a few points since Inauguration Day, remained remarkably high at about 20%. This would have been a propitious time for rivals to attack the president's policies for failing to spark a sustained recovery, with a follow-up claim that more of the same would prolong the Depression and cause additional misery.

Roosevelt's political competitors did not accept the compelling invitation to employ that line of reasoning and make it the centerpiece of their rhetoric. Their surprising omission is evident in the congressional debates surrounding one of the most salient pieces of legislation involving taxing and spending, the 1935 Social Security Act. The omnibus package contained not only the old-age pensions that came to be known as Social Security but also unemployment insurance, welfare, and aid to the blind. Ultimately, old-age pensions proved to be the most contentious part of the legislation. The political alignments were closer than one might suspect judging from the overwhelming 372–33 vote in the House of Representatives. A motion to recommit the legislation to committee with instructions to delete the controversial section failed by just 149–253. Had a few dozen of the supporters been converted into opponents, Social Security as it existed for the next several decades might never have been enacted.

It would seem that an economic argument would have been an effective way to kill Social Security. Because no benefits would be paid until several years after revenues were first collected, the bill in the short run amounted to a payroll tax split equally between employers and employees in the affected sectors of the economy. Adversaries could have argued that passing such a tax in the middle of the Depression, without even the stimulation provided by connected spending, was foolish. Employers subject to the tax would either have to cut payroll, thus increasing unemployment, or pass along higher prices to consumers and cause production declines when fewer goods were purchased. Employees, meanwhile, would find their wallets thinner because of the tax, forcing consumption to fall and the Depression to continue.

Opponents occasionally made such a case, though not nearly as strongly or widely as one would predict. The economic argument had to compete with others that absorbed most of the time and energy on the floor of the House of Representatives, such as claims that the bill granted vast authority to an administrative agency, that it was unconstitutional, that the revenues would eventually be insufficient to pay the benefits, and that federal control would overtake state responsibility.[9] All of those arguments enjoyed some currency and under certain circumstances could carry the day; in the midst of the Depression, however, none carried an explicitly economic appeal. Explaining to citizens, fellow legislators, or opinion leaders that you opposed Social Security because it strengthened the federal government was unlikely to resonate as firmly as stating that it would deepen and prolong the unprecedented industrial and agricultural collapse.

A similar pattern characterized arguably the most important piece of regulatory legislation passed in the same year, the Public Utility Holding Company Act. This act required the breakup, unless specific efficiency criteria were met, of holding companies that controlled large numbers of other enterprises producing electricity. The key vote this time came in the Senate, where an amendment to strike the central component of the bill failed by just a single vote, 44–45. The legislation established government restrictions on how private businesses conducted their affairs. Decades later, as chapter 5 will show, such regulations were criticized most often through arguments about their expected effects on the economy. During the Depression, when such a case would have delivered a powerful punch, the dissenters mainly invoked other reasons. Senators from both parties attacked the vagueness of the delegation of power, the potential for federal control over all utilities, and the inability of the bill to solve the stated problem.[10] Although all of those reasons potentially could justify opposition to the bill, none tapped into intense economic fears by asserting that the bill would worsen and deepen the Depression.

Continuing this pattern of rhetoric into the next election, the 1936 Republican platform did not place the economy front and center. The opening section instead alleged betrayal, abuse, and dishonesty by the incumbent administration. According to the GOP's platform, "The powers of Congress have been usurped by the President," the administration "has been guilty of frightful waste and extravagance, using public funds for partisan political purposes," and Democratic policies have "destroyed the morale of our people and made them dependent upon government."[11] Even though production remained low and many jobholders wondered if they would soon join the breadlines, only one of the fifteen specific charges in the lead section referenced the Depression. Later the document did propose policies to reverse the crushing stagnation and decline, but taken as a whole it is surprising that jobs, growth, and incomes were not the dominant subjects. The New Deal had clearly not solved the Depression, so the staggering economy would be expected to form the focal point of an effective opposition. Instead, the country's stagnation was merely one of several problems and critiques the Republican party linked to the New Deal.

Outside of electoral politics, perhaps the largest organized resistance to FDR's policies came from the American Liberty League. Established by wealthy industrialists in 1934, the group became a veritable communication empire, using radio appearances and formal statements to supplement its primary activity of sending its large series of pamphlets to legislators, newspapers, public libraries, and executive branch officials. Like the opposition within Congress, the American Liberty League contended that federal programs were hurting production and delaying recovery, but again that argument was subordinate to others. Various pamphlets contended that recently enacted policies pitted class against class, violated the Constitution, relied on coercion and impinged on freedom, and replaced private decisions with political controls. The organization went so far as to label the New Deal an unadulterated power grab by Roosevelt, representing a push toward a Fascist or Marxist dictatorship.[12]

During and shortly after the second downturn of 1937–1938, the opposition finally elevated economic arguments to the number-one position in its arsenal of rhetorical weapons. Senator Robert Taft (R-Ohio), for example, gave a forceful speech describing how the New Deal had imperiled the nation's prosperity.[13] By then, however, the criticism was too late, for the labor and social insurance programs had already passed and were beginning to be institutionalized. The question is naturally raised, why did those who resisted the New Deal not use economic arguments more frequently and thoroughly in the previous years, when there was still some possibility of preventing the passage of policies they found odious? One key reason was the lack of a well-developed and solidly grounded alternative, namely that free and unfettered markets, with low taxes, minimal regulation, and strong protections for private property, could revive the nation's standard of living. Opponents could not identify a group of books or articles, whether in the popular domain or scholarly circles, that centered on that theme. Some works did state the case, of course, but only alongside the development of other points. Nowhere did it receive the kind of exclusive and comprehensive treatment necessary to establish its usefulness for policy debates.

The scale and scope of the Depression had undermined the belief that government should stay out of the economy. Recognizing this fact, however, only begs the question of why the discrediting was so thorough and widespread, for crises and catastrophes do not interpret themselves.[14] Caught without the intellectual infrastructure required to create and communicate persuasive explanations, conservatives could not convincingly present the merits of the minimalist state. Had conservative politicians claimed that government programs jeopardize economic progress, they would have done so without corroborating support from intellectuals who, through prior study, reflection, and writing, would have prepared the arguments for acceptance. Without such allies and a climate of favorable economic ideas, critics of the New Deal acted, perhaps without explicitly recognizing it, as if they could not win a debate couched in economic terms.

At first glance one might assume that heightened attention to questions of economic performance would invariably benefit the right rather than the left. Through analyses of intellectuals, parties, and public opinion, later chapters will demonstrate that the period from the early 1970s to the present has followed such a pattern. Who wins and loses when the economic context gains importance, however, cannot be predicted with a simple rule of thumb. There is nothing intrinsic to the economy that dictates who will prevail if it becomes the central reference point for political decisions. During the Depression conservatives attempted to steer the national conversation toward other, noneconomic criteria for judging policies. Lacking economic ideas that others would find persuasive, conservatives chose other grounds on which to fight, grounds that might produce some damaging blows and maybe even victory.

As it turned out, that strategy failed miserably. The opposition would have faced an uphill battle in any event, but had there been substantial intellectual support for an alternative to the New Deal's attempt to restore prosperity, perhaps conservatives could have blocked or modified its core policies, and a different course may have become possible. An ideology without a critical mass of intellectuals invariably faces difficulties in the political arena, especially when times of rapid change open windows of opportunity for redirecting the ideological thrust of government.[15] During moments of a new context it becomes crucial to have ideas available that can both explain why prevailing problems exist and identify effective responses. It always has been and always will be difficult to beat something with nothing.

The Establishment of Intellectual Outlets on the Right

The ability of the right to combat one set of ideas with another, and to move from negative resistance to seizing control of the debate with a positive agenda, greatly increased over the next half-century. Dispirited and disorganized during the 1930s, the greatly outnumbered conservative intellectuals soon multiplied their ranks and founded publications to formulate and communicate their ideas.[16] In 1944 *Human Events* became the first conservative weekly, initially covering mostly foreign affairs and communism and later addressing domestic issues. The Foundation for Economic Education, which debuted in 1946, published works extolling free markets, antistatism, and private property. In 1950 a revamped version of *The Freeman* appeared, quickly becoming a valuable forum for journalists and scholars alike. Five years later William F. Buckley, Jr., inaugurated *National Review*, the first conservative journal to attain the visibility and respect of established periodicals on the left. Over the succeeding decades, Buckley's magazine played an important coordinating role in bringing together the often fractious elements of the right.

Conservative intellectuals shared the conviction that the scholar Richard Weaver summarized in the title of his landmark book *Ideas Have Consequences*.[17] But these ideas, visionary leaders were beginning to realize, must reach and resonate with wider audiences to wield the desired influence. Politics and society would shift rightward only when conservative ideas were articulated more clearly, defended more forcefully, and applied more directly to the practical issues of the day. Despite following the long-since abandoned practice of equating the New Deal with socialism, libertarian theorist Frank Chodorov neatly summarized what could be learned from earlier defeats: "If socialism has come to America because it was implanted in the minds of past generations, there is no reason for assuming that the contrary idea cannot be taught to a new generation. What the socialists have done can be undone, if there is a will for it."[18] Thus through persuasion and proselytizing, conservatives could remake the nation.

Shortly thereafter conservative publisher Henry Regnery remarked that he started Regnery Press, which would later grow into a successful and profitable business, because "men don't live by bread alone, it is ideas that shape history," and in the war of ideas liberals and leftists dominated. "So long as they control the means of communication," he continued, "they don't have to worry too much about a slight set-back in Washington. If we want to do anything, we must work on the level of ideas."[19] The pioneering work of Buckley, Regnery, and others was followed by new publications in the 1970s and 1980s such as *American Specta-*

tor, *New Criterion*, and *Reason*, which provided space for various strands of thinking on the right. Meanwhile, *Commentary*'s formerly liberal orientation moved with that of its editor, Norman Podhoretz, into neoconservative territory.

The results of these cumulative efforts can be seen by examining figure 4.1, which plots over time the circulation of political magazines on the right as a share of the total circulation of all political magazines.[20] The figure shows the multiplying of conservative magazines and journals over a seventy-year period and their increased ability to find an audience, relative to what was happening on the left.[21] In the 1920s and 1930s, as the graph indicates, there were few major outlets for conservative thought, with *The Freeman* (1920–1924) and *American Mercury* (founded in 1924) the sole exceptions. Indeed, figure 4.1 probably overestimates that era's conservative presence on the nation's bookshelves and coffee tables; the calculations do not include the largely liberal literary reviews that published articles with political content even though politics was not their main focus.[22] The dearth of conservative magazines and journals changed gradually during the postwar years, and by 1980 the right had reached rough parity with the left in its capacity to get commentary, analysis, and advocacy into the hands of interested readers.[23]

While the emergence of conservative magazines clearly reflects the passion, energy, and talent of their founding editors and publishers, their funding was also critical to their success. Except under unusual circumstances, political magazines are assuredly not profitable; the vast majority, whether on the left or right, regularly lose money.[24] Abandoning even the pretense of earning a profit, such periodicals are commonly produced by nonprofit organizations created solely for that purpose. With large subsidies required for their establishment and year-to-year operations, conservative publications turned to individual philanthropists to finance their cause. In some cases, the funding instigated a virtuous cycle by paying for better writers and editors, which then attracted higher circulations, in turn providing more revenues and more donors who saw their money making a difference.

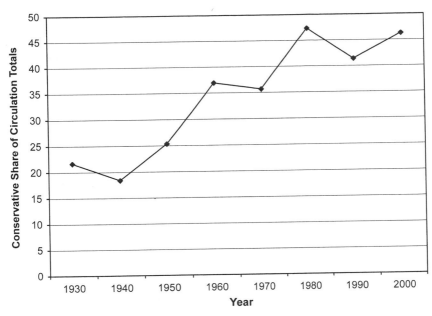

Figure 4.1. The Emergence of Conservative Magazines

The right's ability to establish and maintain a group of magazines and journals also hinged on the contributions of several conservative foundations. One study of a sample of periodicals discovered that those on the right received several times more revenues in foundation grants than those on the left.[25] To build a pipeline of future writers, foundations on the right subsequently broadened their portfolios to include conservative newspapers on college campuses.[26] Given the pessimism of conservative intellectuals in the 1930s and 1940s, it is remarkable how quickly the right assembled a group of vibrant, high-quality publishing outlets. Over time, then, conservative ideas became more thoroughly known, methodically reasoned, and politically effective.

Writers, at least the best ones, can affect public policy in subtle and indirect ways. An ideology unsupported by new articles, pamphlets, reports, and books to show its power and relevance will turn stale, whereas one blessed with talented writers and thinkers will articulate its core principles, propose solutions to the nation's problems, and frame its discourse to appeal to both elites and the mass public. Sometimes this influence comes through shaping the views of future policymakers. People who run for office are drawn from the most politically active and aware segment of the population, those most likely to pay attention to contemporary writing about politics and public affairs. Such writing can help them clarify their values, envision policy directions, and apply their beliefs to issues currently under discussion. For policymakers already in power, intellectual tracts can help strengthen the resolve of partisans who need personal reassurance as well as effective arguments that satisfy and in some cases inspire and convert constituents.

Think Tanks: Modern Incubators of Ideas

Working symbiotically with the conservative magazines and journals, a growing number of think tanks has emerged whose residents, fellows, and affiliates often appear on the byline as contributors to periodicals such as *National Review*, *The Weekly Standard*, and *Public Interest*. Think tanks have long dotted the American political landscape, with the initial handful founded at the beginning of the twentieth century. These early institutes sought dispassionate, expert knowledge that could be developed through scientific methods and used for societal improvement.[27] They were nonideological in the sense that the conclusions of their studies ranged across the political spectrum. An emphasis on maintaining balance and objectivity can be found in some think tanks today, such as the Brookings Institution, Council on Foreign Relations, Institute for International Economics, and Resources for the Future. Some individuals working for these institutes surely hold predispositions that affect the objectives, inferences, and interpretations of the research they perform, but the organizations' leaders do not view their mission as furthering a particular point of view.

During the 1970s a new kind of think tank emerged that sought not to discover knowledge but to promote an already established ideology, devoting as much or more effort to spreading the implications of their research than to completing or acquiring it. Research became a weapon of political struggle, a means of championing a vision for society and public policy. One of the pioneers in this regard was the Heritage Foundation, known for its vigorous efforts to market its studies to policymakers and journalists. A quote from the then in-house magazine *Policy Review*, directed at prospective state-level think tanks though seemingly self-referential, summarizes the modern approach and mentality:

> Everything you do, every day, must involve marketing in as many as six dimensions. Market your policy recommendations, market the principles and values behind them, market the tangible publications and events your organization is producing. Market the think tank concept itself. Then market your specific organization. And never stop marketing yourself and the other key individuals who personify the organization.[28]

Such all-directional marketing takes a variety of forms. Perhaps the cheapest and easiest is sending copies of studies, along with executive summaries more likely to be read, to legislators, staffers, administrators, and journalists. Requiring more time, researchers are expected to cultivate reputations with policymakers and reporters as reliable sources of information and willing contributors of analysis, opinions, or quotes. Think tanks often host conferences and forums to facilitate their personnel's contact with reporters and policymakers. Their own staff, and sometimes their ghostwriters, pen op-ed pieces to distribute to newspapers and syndicates, and their researchers stand ready to accept invitations for appearances on television or radio shows. Institutes with sufficient funding can package radio commentary or television footage for distribution to broadcast stations always on the lookout for ways to cut their own production costs.

The hope of influencing politics or society lies behind the activities of think tanks on matters such as Social Security or environmental regulation, or even on less applied topics such as the structure of families or the role of religion in people's lives. That goal may be short-term, such as improving the prospects of passing a piece of legislation, or it may be long-term in slowly building support for an idea. Either way, the link to policy is always present. The Hudson Institute is representative of its sister organizations in that it contains a clause within its mission statement explaining that it "produces independent, high-quality research and competes boldly in the debate of policy ideas. Hudson works to counsel and guide policy change, applying our ideas whenever possible alongside other leaders in communities, businesses, non-profit organizations and governments alike."[29] To meet this goal of providing counsel and guidance, researchers at think tanks are expected to establish relationships and legitimacy with policymakers and reporters. A researcher who participates in a congressional hearing or is quoted widely in the news media is sure to be recognized and rewarded for doing valuable work.

Deeply concerned with the visibility and impact of their ideas, think tanks diligently track their citations in the mass media. One of the first appeals they take to prospective contributors when seeking grants or donations is some version of, "Look how many times our researchers were quoted in news stories or called on for commentary." For example, the Cato Institute's annual report for 2002 highlighted 448 major television appearances, 483 radio appearances, and 474 citations along with 118 op-eds in high-circulation newspapers.[30] Although policy institutes do distribute a substantial amount of dry, technical analysis, their drive for political influence leads them to produce a steady stream of easily readable publications that contribute to public dialogues about politics. Consistent with the purpose of informing, reinforcing, and persuading audiences that include nonspecialists, prose written with complicated syntax and particularized jargon either is not constructed in the first place or else is reworded by copy editors. Given the goal of winning hearts and minds, the easy understanding following from accessible prose trumps any benefit from precision of thought and expression that complex writing might allow.

The Financing and Impact of Think Tanks

The 1970s were remarkable years for the formation and growth of conservative and libertarian think tanks. Many prominent policy institutes were founded, including the Heritage Foundation (1973), the Manhattan Institute, originally the International Center for Economic Policy Studies (1978), and the Cato Institute (1977). Also in the 1970s, the American Enterprise Institute and the Hoover Institution, older organizations without a national reputation, enlarged their budgets and enhanced their visibility. Whereas the conservative movement had already created and nurtured publishing outlets for books, articles, and opinion pieces, think tanks offered an institutional innovation that could seamlessly merge research, publicity, and advocacy.

Notwithstanding the eminence of their new competitors on the right, centrist and nonideological think tanks continued to occupy a prominent niche in media and policy circles. One of the most venerable of all think tanks, the Brookings Institution, perennially appeared at or near the top of citation lists. In its early years Brookings's scholars struck conservative notes as prominent critics of New Deal and Fair Deal policies such as national and regional planning, deficit spending, and executive reorganization.[31] The ideological tendencies of the organization subsequently evolved with the times, aligning with the liberal mainstream in the 1960s and early 1970s. Since the early 1980s, Brookings can be justifiably called centrist or nonideological because it has employed a diverse array of scholars.[32] Two of its recent presidents, Bruce MacLaury and Michael Armacost, were Republicans. Conservatives such as Richard Haass in foreign policy, Ron Haskins and Lawrence Mead in welfare policy, and Diane Ravitch in education policy have published works under Brookings's imprint. In fact, the reputation for balance, expert analysis, and scientific standards achieved by Brookings and other think tanks operating as "universities without students" appears to enhance their credibility as sources for news stories.[33] To the extent that calculating an average is possible, the ideological tenor of Brookings' research output falls somewhat left of center. The organization is certainly not liberal, however, in the way that the Heritage Foundation, Manhattan Institute, or Hudson Institute is conservative.

Reflecting a marriage of dollars and dogma, financing from a variety of sources contributed mightily to the formation of think tanks on the right. Neoconservative intellectual Irving Kristol asked corporations, in a piece originally published in the *Wall Street Journal*, to make philanthropic contributions to scholars and institutions who could publicly articulate the virtues of free enterprise.[34] William Simon, who had served as secretary of the treasury in the Nixon and Ford administrations, observed firsthand the constraints on policymakers when conservative initiatives did not rest on sufficient intellectual grounding. He wrote that business, to protect itself from government intervention, must "funnel desperately needed funds to scholars, social scientists, writers, and journalists who understand the relationship between political and economic liberty. . . . I know of nothing more crucial than to come to the aid of the intellectuals and writers who are fighting on my side."[35]

These and other appeals reinforced a greater willingness on the part of the business community to fund the development of ideas. Recent regulations in worker health and safety and in environmental and consumer protection, combined with a persistent slump in profits, had left major corporations feeling beleaguered. Many business leaders believed that the climate of ideas, as established within academia and the media, set the stage for the enactment of policies that undermined the system of free enterprise.[36] Calls for contributions to conservative think tanks whose proposals would benefit business thus found a favorable reception. Corporate money made a crucial difference in the inception or expansion of many conservative think tanks, especially the American Enterprise Institute.[37]

Much larger in total dollars was the funding from individuals—especially those who gave in large chunks—and foundations.[38] A handful of foundations, including the Bradley, Smith Richardson, Olin, Carthage, Allegheny, and Sarah Scaife Foundations, were particularly generous in financing conservative institutes. The leaders of these foundations, like those who started and edited conservative periodicals, believed in the power of ideas. William Simon, for one, seized the chance to implement his plan for aiding the intellectuals and writers on his side when he became president of the Olin Foundation in 1977. Assisted by individuals, foundations, and corporations, conservative think tanks became established players in national and state policymaking arenas.

Although liberals formed their own think tanks, among which the most prominent in the 1980s and 1990s were the Center on Budget and Policy Priorities, Economic Policy Institute, and Institute for Policy Studies, as a group they receive far less financing than their counterparts on the right. A compilation of a large sample of think tanks found that the conservative institutes oversaw budgets *four times* as large as the liberal ones.[39] Bigger budgets allow a think tank to pursue its core activities, such as calling attention to studies, reports, and proposals, more thoroughly and effectively. Within a group of six national newspapers, budgets strongly predicted how many citations each think tank received. Placed in that context, the high number of citations to the conservative ones, collectively referenced across the newspapers at five times the rate of those with liberal dispositions, is understandable.[40] Budgets probably bear some relationship, however imperfect, to the policy influence of think tanks.

This influence should not be considered independent and autonomous but rather interactive, for think tanks work cooperatively with ideological allies. Even think tanks for which one need not read their studies to know what conclusions will be reached, and who therefore find their research dismissed by opponents as being biased and flawed, can leave a mark on public policy. Using their ability to marshal and package information, they supply policymakers with ideas, appeals, imagery, and statistics to use in building coalitions with colleagues or constituents. Scholars from research institutes can also do the policymaking themselves when they accept posts in the executive branch. The presidential administrations of Ronald Reagan and

George W. Bush, for example, drew heavily from think tanks in filling advisory and executive positions.[41] When researchers leave think tanks for formal government service, current and former givers among foundations, corporations, and individuals see the concrete results of their financing.

Other channels of influence are more indirect. All of the available means of communication, from op-ed pieces to quotes given to journalists to commentary on broadcast media, feed into public opinion. Research institutes can provide the reasoning, evidence, and symbols adopted by shapers of public opinion such as columnists, clergy, editorial writers, interest groups, and talk radio hosts. Over the long term, the ideas of think tanks produce seeds that can germinate years later. Future policymakers often form their preferences by drawing from the ideas circulating as they become politically active. Ideas sometimes merely provide rhetorical cover for a preference formed through other means, but their influence can extend more widely. Even political actors with strong predispositions need to elaborate the intervening steps between guiding principles and concrete programs, a task for which ideas are well suited.[42] Once understood and internalized, ideas can lead to preferences that are sincerely held and honestly expressed.

The dominance of conservatives within the population of ideological think tanks brings advantages in the many pathways of influence, a point that observers on the left have repeatedly lamented.[43] Ironically, the conservative institutes draw much of their funding from foundations that are not especially large within the world of philanthropy. Far more foundation money is available for liberal than conservative causes, but foundations whose giving patterns indicate a liberal orientation award most of their grants to service providers and advocacy groups rather than think tanks.[44] The liberal foundations that do make grants to research institutes tend to give in ways that do not build the capacity for future influence. They most often contribute for specific projects rather than general operating support and give for one year rather than for the long term.[45] Even as liberal fortunes improved with the multimillion-dollar launch in 2003 of the Center for American Progress, the conservative think tanks continued to expand, and it probably would take years of patient institution-building for liberals to compensate for lost time.

Conservative Intellectualism and Its Consequences

Several decades ago, no one would have predicted that conservatives would soon fervently embrace the power of ideas. Conservatives were known as practical and down-to-earth men of affairs who focused on doing rather than theorizing. It was liberals and leftists, entrenched in the literary world and academia, who controlled the intellectual arena. The literary critic Lionel Trilling could scoff, with only a little exaggeration, that "In the United States at this time liberalism is not only the dominant but even the sole intellectual tradition . . . the conservative impulse and the reactionary impulse do not, with some isolated and some ecclesiastical exceptions, express themselves in ideas but only in action or in irritable mental gestures which seem to resemble ideas."[46]

Recognizing the need for a space to hone conservative ideas and introduce them to more people, imaginative organizers and thinkers on the right set out to reverse this course. There was a self-conscious strategy to form outlets for their writing, with the hope of educating both political leaders and the active part of the general citizenry. With *National Review* paving the way, conservative writers would soon be able to choose from a variety of publishing venues. Later, with the aid of funding from business, individuals, and foundations, conservatives built an extensive set of think tanks to provide a research capacity and apply their principles to the major issues of the day. The reward structures at think tanks, especially the ideological, marketing-oriented ones, quickly developed to direct researchers toward seeking influence with policymakers and the public. Funding for book publishers, training programs, and student newspapers on college campuses rounded out the interconnected network of writers, researchers, and publicists.

How is this intellectual capacity related to the central themes of this book, the political responses to economic insecurity that shifted American politics to the right? Intellectuals, it should be remembered, form only one part of a much larger story. When considering their role within more encompassing developments, the relevant factor is not the population of intellectuals at any given point in time but rather how the outlets and institutions of intellectual life have evolved. What can be said with certainty is that farsighted leaders on the right constructed an alternative universe to academia that has allowed conservative ideas to find expression and gain resonance. Whereas in the middle of the twentieth century one could realistically assert that conservatives lacked an organized and effective intellectual movement, soon thereafter such a statement was no longer accurate.

By using their writings to interpret the worlds around them, intellectuals—whether from the left, the right, or elsewhere— give other political actors conceptual tools to envision and implement creative approaches to public policy. The need for a ready cache of intellectual perspectives becomes especially important during times of flux, when possibilities present themselves for large-scale transformations in the scope, functions, and purposes of government.[47] To identify prevailing problems and point the way toward solutions, ideological movements require both available ideas and the capacity to distribute them to receptive audiences. By the 1970s the right's recently formed intellectual outlets and institutions positioned it well to take advantage of any major changes in political, economic, or social conditions that would allow new policy initiatives and the rhetoric to support them. The rise of economic insecurity offered just such an opportunity, and the next chapter examines how conservative intellectuals responded.

FIVE

The Move to Economic Arguments
by Conservative Intellectuals

Stephen Moore's article "How Big Government Makes America Poorer" appeared in the March 2004 issue of *The Insider*, a then-monthly magazine published by the Heritage Foundation.[1] Making full use of his limited space, Moore argued that government's foolish and counterproductive policies worsen the nation's economic health. The problems begin with excessive taxes that "inhibit growth by reducing the private sector's capacity and willingness to expand."[2] When combined, according to Moore's data, federal, state, and local taxes absorb more than 40% of workers' paychecks. Having grown throughout the twentieth century, this tax burden severely weakens "workers' incentive to work and employers' incentive to hire."[3]

Moore sees government's wealth-destroying effects continuing into the regulatory domain, where businesses must comply with environmental, health, safety, and consumer protection requirements. "Draconian regulations promulgated without any regard to costs and benefits," Moore asserts, "slow down the engine of economic progress in America."[4] He also contends that government expenditures should be excluded from the statistical calculation of the nation's gross domestic product (GDP). The standard measure of GDP "includes public sector expansion as a good not a bad" and, accordingly, encourages further government spending.[5] Subtracting the public sector from GDP would

formally acknowledge that "government growth doesn't enhance our private sector markets—it displaces them."[6]

Any close observer of American political life will immediately recognize Moore's arguments, for conservatives have repeatedly expressed them in recent decades. In fact, the arguments
are so familiar that if Moore's byline were replaced by some other
conservative's name, no one would know the difference. Because
conservatives so often invoke economic consequences when justifying their policy stances, one can easily slip into making the
ahistorical assumption that similar rhetoric has always accompa-
nied their advocacy of low taxes, minimal regulation, and as few
social programs as possible. As this chapter will show, however,
such an assumption is erroneous. Despite the stability of the positions conservative intellectuals have embraced, the rhetoric offered in defense of those positions has evolved to incorporate a
much larger economic component.

My goal in this chapter is to explain how and why the supporting rhetoric changed. Before beginning my analysis, I take account of the various forms of conservatism. Like any prominent
ideology, conservatism has often been marked by competing
strains, with the most durable cleavage separating the traditionalist and religious right from the libertarians. Differing markedly
on topics such as drugs, abortion, pornography, police powers,
school prayer, and public promotion of morality, the two camps
nevertheless have forged greater unity on matters of government
intervention in the economy. Because my analysis in this chapter
focuses on policy areas with economic aspects, I have largely
avoided the internecine battles among conservatives regularly
occuring in other domains.

Still, an advantage to comparing intellectuals operating
within only one strain is that one avoids inappropriately mixing
together change over time with change from one kind of conservatism to another. It would not be surprising, for example, to discover different forms of reasoning between the traditionalist
Russell Kirk and the libertarian Charles Murray even when they
consider issues such as taxation, government regulation, and the
welfare state. To ensure that apples are compared with apples, I

begin by tracing the argumentation within three landmark books that fall squarely within the libertarian branch of the broader conservative tradition: Albert Jay Nock's *Our Enemy, the State* (1935), Friedrich Hayek's *The Road to Serfdom* (1944), and Milton Friedman's *Capitalism and Freedom* (1962). Standing as milestones of libertarian thought, the books' publication dates bracket the middle decades of the twentieth century.

Prior to World War II, few conservative intellectuals attracted a nationwide audience. Given the significance of the 1930s to the future course of American politics, though, it is important to include writings from that decade when charting the development of conservative rhetoric. Albert Jay Nock was arguably the best known of his small cohort of like-minded intellectuals who were active during the Depression. Although his *Our Enemy, the State* achieved only limited acclaim at the time of its initial release, its lasting influence was confirmed by its being republished on two occasions. Postwar intellectuals such as William F. Buckley, Jr., and John Chamberlain paid homage to Nock for informing their views.[7] Through *The Road to Serfdom* and *Capitalism and Freedom*, respectively, Friedrich Hayek and Milton Friedman sparked more discussion and controversy at the time of publication, and both books remained prominent on conservative reading lists in the decades thereafter. Reflecting their broad influence, Hayek and Friedman each drew a passionate following inside and outside academia. Most importantly for this chapter's purpose, the books by Nock, Hayek, and Friedman each illustrate how conservatives expressed themselves within particular historical eras.

Albert Jay Nock and the Tyranny of State Power

In *Our Enemy, the State*, Nock distinguishes between a government, which must restrict itself solely to protecting freedom and promoting security, and a state, which possesses all-encompassing powers and responsibilities. Some people invariably exploit others through the state, which Nock believes has replaced the government in America. Borrowing from the analysis of Charles Beard, Nock depicts the drafting and ratification of the Constitution as an attempt by merchants, financiers, and speculators to bolster the central government at the expense of state and local governments, where small farmers and ordinary citizens had enjoyed strong representation.[8] Even more so in recent times, the country has seen "a great redistribution of power between society and state."[9]

Nock deems this redistribution dangerous because of the vast control it gives the state over people's lives. After centuries of state expansion, citizens owe allegiance to distant, arbitrary, and self-aggrandizing rulers. Within the federal government, Nock sees a further consolidation whereby the executive asserts itself over the other branches, leading to a system that looks, feels, and acts like a monarchy.[10] Such centralization inevitably brings a proliferation of agencies, boards, and commissions that force officials at lower levels of government, who help in administering programs, to act as de facto agents of the federal government.[11] Nock forecasts a continuation of this process because "Every intervention by the State enables another, and this in turn another, and so on indefinitely."[12]

Nock devotes extensive attention to policies regulating business. He does not identify specific legislation by name, but he almost certainly warns against recently enacted federal laws. The National Industrial Recovery Act of 1933, for example, used federal authority to promote cooperation among private enterprises in setting prices and standards. Nock writes: "When the State intervenes to fix wages or prices" that ought to be determined by an individual businessman, "it proposes to confiscate his power and exercise it according to the State's own judgment of what is best."[13] Nock does not claim that these programs should be curtailed because they imperil job creation, cause lower wages, or undercut the standard of living. Instead, he grounds his opposition on the argument that freedom is best assured under decentralized government institutions and unregulated private enterprise.

Friedrich Hayek and the Dangers of Socialism

With *The Road to Serfdom*, Friedrich Hayek hoped to reach intellectuals and political leaders in Britain and, to a lesser extent, the United States. Published near the end of World War II, the book warned that Fascist Germany and Communist Soviet Union shared the same fundamental belief system despite the wartime alignment of one country as enemy and the other as ally. Hayek saw fascism's roots not in modern propaganda, capitalist competition, or excessive individualism, as thinkers of his day held, but in the growth of state power over the individual. He contended that intellectual currents in Britain and the United States —the embrace of national planning, the acceptance of state authority—paralleled those in Germany during and after World War I that culminated in the Nazi's seizure of power. The obvious implication was that the two countries where he would spend most of his adult life were heading in the same dreadful direction.[14]

Hayek's chief concern is socialism, by which he "means the abolition of private enterprise, of private ownership of the means of production, and the creation of a system of 'planned economy' in which the entrepreneur working for profit is replaced by a central planning body."[15] Hayek prefers private competition as a means of organizing the social life of a nation, since it does not rest on the "coercive or arbitrary intervention of authority."[16] Rejecting the notion that socialism could ever arise through democratic means, Hayek holds that central planning suffers from a lack of information from the polity on how to proceed. People could agree in advance on the desirability of planning, but they could not possibly decide, or even anticipate, how that planning can and should be carried out in practice.[17] Even the pretense of democracy will be compromised: "The conviction grows that if efficient planning is to be done, the direction must be 'taken out of politics' and placed in the hands of experts—permanent officials or independent autonomous bodies" exempt from popular or parliamentary control.[18]

When *The Road to Serfdom* is read in its entirety, it becomes obvious that the economic consequences of planning represent only a minor theme. It is to the concept of freedom, and how planning destroys it, that the future nobel laureate returns time and again. Though the particulars of their assessments differ, Hayek therefore echoes Nock's deep-seated resistance to state authority. Hayek closes the book on his main theme: "The guiding principle that a policy of freedom for the individual is the only truly progressive policy remains as true today as it was in the nineteenth century."[19] This unrelenting defense of freedom helps explain why he became, and remains, a towering figure in the libertarian tradition, which celebrates freedom as a goal in its own right rather than a utilitarian method to achieve better economic outcomes.

Milton Friedman and the Relationship between Economic and Political Liberty

Written more than a decade after the end of World War II, *Capitalism and Freedom* did not mirror *The Road to Serfdom* by raising the specter of fascism. Yet the normative ideal of freedom remained a foundation upon which to build a political philosophy, and in some respects Friedman followed in Hayek's footsteps. Friedman stated at the outset that he will demonstrate how capitalism, defined as a system through which individuals and enterprises interact voluntarily in the marketplace, promotes both economic and political freedom.[20] In contrast to his purely academic writings, with this book Friedman sought a wide audience, eventually selling more than a half-million copies.[21] *Capitalism and Freedom* is commonly considered Friedman's most significant contribution to public discourse about politics, though his stature within his home discipline of economics resulted primarily from other works.

In Friedman's view, economic liberty exists when individuals rely on their talents and abilities to produce as they see fit. The use of the market for as many activities as possible avoids the conformity costs associated with political decisions and their inevitable forcing of a minority to submit to a majority.[22] Whereas a market system allows a diversity of views and permits all to be satisfied, since each person can choose which goods and services to purchase, state action necessarily involves coercion by preventing individuals from freely exercising choices.[23] Economic liberty also serves an instrumental purpose as a necessary precondition for political liberty.[24] Friedman believes that the proper role of government covers only specific functions with definite boundaries. Government responsibilities should be limited to defining and protecting property rights, enforcing contracts, upholding law and order, and correcting for monopoly power and other market imperfections.[25]

In a new preface written for a reissue edition, Friedman remarks that two decades earlier he and a handful of fellow travelers "were deeply concerned about the danger to freedom and prosperity from the growth of government."[26] This warning about the danger government poses to both freedom *and* prosperity is revealing, for much had changed in American society during the twenty years between the book's initial appearance and his 1982 preface. Most important, achieving and maintaining economic security rose from one of many concerns to rank as a dominant interest of both politicians and the public. Had Friedman written *Capitalism and Freedom* in the 1980s rather than the 1960s, he almost certainly would have given considerable attention to the government's threat to prosperity. It was clearly an exaggeration, though, for him to claim in retrospect that the book included prosperity as one of the two pillars on which he rested his case. Friedman certainly stresses freedom, as the book's title indicates; his musings on prosperity, though present, are distinctly secondary in the amount of space and emphasis he allocates to them.

Intellectuals, Rhetoric, and Context

This chapter's interpretation of conservative rhetoric within its context parallels a leading approach within intellectual history, the subfield of history focusing on influential thinkers and how they interpret and alter their worlds. Scholars in this area study not only the internal dynamics of important texts but also the relationship between texts and their external environments.[27] Even the most profound and original intellectuals absorb and reflect the values, controversies, and unstated assumptions and mentalities of their societies and communities. Knowing this, subsequent scholars who interpret an earlier writing and assess what the author meant commonly situate the work within the historical, cultural, and intellectual currents of its day.[28] Social and political forces are shown to feed into the elaboration of ideas that then return to affect beliefs and practices within the very societies from which they came. Intellectuals thus draw from their contexts while contributing new modes of thought and inspiring new forms of action in areas such as labor, religion, gender, warfare, and human rights.

Using these interpretive principles, the books by Nock, Hayek, and Friedman are best understood within the political and economic milieu in which the authors lived and wrote. The establishment of powerful states in Hitler's Germany and Stalin's Soviet Union made the dangers of centralization salient to American political elites from the 1930s to the 1960s. With those examples and their violations of personal liberties as the backdrop, conservative intellectuals gravitated toward policy arguments based on freedom. The role of government in society also had changed closer to home, adding relevance to long-standing beliefs about the wellsprings of freedom. Although this period of liberal ascendancy put conservatives on the defensive, Hayek and Friedman presented arguments that tapped into the prevailing political and intellectual context.

For Nock's book and other conservative rhetoric during the Depression, the reliance on freedom as a framing device also reflected the absence, described in chapter 4, of a convincing and broadly publicized case for promoting prosperity through limited government and unregulated capitalism. A rational political movement responding to the Depression would prefer to present its policies as a solution to the widespread misery, unemployment, poverty, and despair. Attacking laws and executive actions with arguments that they violate freedom, as Nock did, was at best a distant second in rhetorical potency. Yet conservatives faced a daunting dilemma: The merits of their economic program seemingly had died with the onset and persistence of the Depression, and few writers and thinkers were available to perform a resurrection. Later on, the right reinterpreted the length and severity of the Depression as the product of government failures rather than problems inherent in the variety of capitalism existing at that time. Relying on economic consequences to uphold conservative principles and to refute liberal ones could have been effective during the Depression, if only conservatives had possessed an intellectual infrastructure to construct and disseminate the reasoning and evidence.

During the postwar decades, conservatives founded intellectual institutions and gained additional adherents. Hayek and Friedman, central figures in this story, served with great ability and vigor as public intellectuals. These two men, one should remember, were first-rate economists who easily could have, and actually did in their scholarly publications, evaluate policies by assessing the implications for prices, productivity, wages, employment, and growth. At first it seems puzzling that they grounded the appeals in their best-known popular works in the concept of freedom rather than prosperity, thereby passing up the chance to play on their home turf.

The theoretical framework I advance in this book points to a ready explanation for why they chose that path: As public persuaders they composed their messages to conform to the context, though without necessarily doing so through planning and forethought. In an era of prosperity, arguments about freedom potentially could trump—at least in the public arena—those based on economic criteria. The bypassing of their own academic expertise in economics in favor of public arguments about freedom happened during the writing process, *before* readers had the chance to respond positively to the books. In Friedman's case, by the 1960s political leaders and the mass public had come to assume that economic progress was likely, if not quite taken for granted. Less leverage could be gained than had been possible earlier or would be obtainable later from elevating economic outcomes as the leading justification for touting unregulated markets over government action. A thoughtful advocate would certainly mention policies' economic consequences, as Friedman did in *Capitalism and Freedom*, but a more compelling case could be marshaled by placing the emphases elsewhere.

Operating in the exalted realm of ideas, intellectuals sometimes view their writing as immune from the rhetorical dynamics that drive politicians' discourse. If the goal is seeking truth, as most intellectuals assume, then one should forthrightly follow premises to their logical conclusions rather than worry about currying favor with the intended audiences. In reality, choices regarding what language to offer, how to frame an argument, and how to capitalize on audiences' predispositions pervade even technical disciplines such as economics.[29] However, this adaptation by intellectuals to the context and audience commonly, maybe even usually, occurs unconsciously. In the case at hand, Hayek and Friedman surely accepted their own arguments about freedom; they were not simply searching for the best hook for their preexisting preferences. By all accounts the two men sincerely believed that a commitment to freedom required adhering to their desired policies, and they wrote their books to bring that case to a wider public. Hayek and Friedman failed to see major policy changes in the 1950s and 1960s, but a new context would soon allow their intellectual successors to introduce a different, and ultimately more successful, line of argument.

Conservative Criticism of Government Regulation

From the early 1970s onward, the onset and persistence of economic insecurity revolutionized the opportunities for the public defense of conservative policies. With American workers feeling the pressures of economic insecurity, positions justified in economic terms became more persuasive. In contrast to the Depression, conservatives now possessed a sufficiently robust intellectual infrastructure to construct and communicate the case for why government regulation—an important policy area experiencing many new laws and executive actions—imperiled the nation's economy. Some of these efforts drew on academic articles and books that critiqued the regulation of airlines, telecommunications, and trucking. The push for policy revisions crossed the ideological spectrum as liberals and conservatives alike worked to dismantle much of the traditional regulation of prices and entry conditions across a range of industries. Ralph Nader's network of consumer groups, for example, believed that industry-specific regulation led to corruption, bureaucratic mistakes, and overly cozy business-government relations. Centrist writers at the Brookings Institution also advocated the repeal of price-and-entry regulation. With Presidents Ford and Carter backing reform and Senator Edward Kennedy (D-MA) providing leadership within Congress, the mid-1970s started a period of opening regulated industries to competition.[30]

The deregulation movement provoked much more controversy when it moved beyond industry-specific regulation and into what is commonly called "social regulation," which applies across many sectors of the economy. Building on predecessors from earlier in the twentieth century, social regulation appeared with full force in the 1960s and 1970s. The new policies restricted the internal decision-making of companies regarding their production processes, how they treated their workers, and how their products affected consumers and the environment. The sweeping scope of social regulation covered such matters as pollution control and waste disposal, the health and safety of work sites, the harm that products caused to consumers, and discrimination against current and prospective employees. In a time of optimism about addressing long-dormant problems, rising budgets and growing staffs characterized regulatory bodies such as the Environmental Protection Agency, Occupational Safety and Health Administration, Consumer Product Safety Commission, Equal Employment Opportunity Commission, and National Highway Traffic Safety Administration.

Under the guidance of conservative think tanks, especially

the American Enterprise Institute (AEI), intellectual criticisms of social regulation flowered in the mid to late 1970s. Chafing under the recent wave of regulatory initiatives, many corporations and trade associations channeled funds into think tanks in order to craft and disseminate these messages. The responses of business to a then-unfavorable political climate included financing an intellectual culture—represented most clearly by the think tanks—that would undermine the regulatory and welfare states. Assisted by these contributions, AEI scholars such as James Miller attempted to show how regulation stifled innovation, weakened production, and reduced employment. The organization started a public policy journal devoted to the issue, titled *Regulation* (now published by the Cato Institute).

The new journal quickly left its mark on public and legislative deliberations. Working with coauthor Robert DeFina, Murray Weidenbaum—then the director of the Center for the Study of American Business at Washington University in St. Louis—devised a means of estimating business's costs of complying with regulations. In 1978 Weidenbaum published a summary of his data in *Regulation*, and he projected that the regulatory drain on the economy would soon exceed $100 billion per year.[31] Despite their criticisms of his methodology and assumptions, even his foremost opponents were forced to acknowledge his influence in Congress and the media.[32] In a book released the following year, Weidenbaum blamed proliferating regulation for precipitating the decade's slowdown in productivity growth.[33]

When consumer and environmental laws began passing in the 1960s, conservative intellectuals had only occasionally stepped forward to assert that regulations would jeopardize the economy. The intellectual opposition that did challenge the laws typically offered arguments about the proper responsibilities of government, the unwarranted intrusion into private enterprise, or the lack of a compelling problem to be remedied.[34] These critics probably believed that social regulation also threatened the economy, but the times were not propitious for spotlighting that concern in the political sphere. From the early 1970s to the present, however, opponents reframed their arguments to stress the economic harm posed by consumer and environmental protection.[35] Working collaboratively with sympathetic minds from the intellectual world, the regulated industries themselves contended that existing and proposed policies were job killers. The wrangling in the Pacific Northwest over "timber workers versus spotted owls" symbolized this rhetorical cleavage on the proper range, techniques, and stringency of government regulation.

Many conservatives had long been skeptical of using government action to protect consumers and the environment and to oversee workplaces. The resistance to social regulation flowed from the same philosophical orientation that rejected the welfare state and progressive taxation. The reframing of regulation around economic consequences, though, signaled a major change in rhetorical emphasis. The decline in Americans' economic security after the early 1970s invited particular kinds of arguments, those relating to jobs, incomes, and the economy more generally. Adroitly reacting to the newfound opportunity, though again with motivations that could be unplanned or unintentional, conservative intellectuals penned their writings accordingly. By introducing economic criteria for evaluating policies, these intellectuals-as-rhetors increased their prospects of winning political debates.

Changes in the Rhetoric on Government Regulation in *National Review*

The reframing of social regulation can be seen more systematically through careful study of the pages of a conservative intellectual journal. Provided that standardized procedures are employed and the findings are replicable, a content analysis can pinpoint the magnitude, timing, and scope of the rhetorical changes. *National Review* is a natural choice for the periodical to investigate because of its perennial standing as a forum for conservatives of all stripes. Since its founding by William F. Buckley, Jr., the magazine has welcomed contributions from journalists, scholars, and polemicists that cut across the usual divisions among conservatives. Unlike other magazines on the right that were founded later or ceased publication after a short run, *National Review* allows comparisons over time. Because its first issue hit the newsstands nearly two decades before the long-term decline in economic insecurity, a content analysis can incorporate articles published both before and after economic matters advanced markedly in the priorities of the public, political leaders, and news media.

To investigate the development of conservative economic rhetoric, I conducted a content analysis of all *National Review* articles addressing social regulation from the magazine's inception in 1955 through 2004.[36] The central classification for each article is a binary decision of whether or not the primary (or only) arguments about the desirability of regulatory policies were economic.[37] For an article's dominant arguments to be mainly economic, they must receive more emphasis and space than all others combined. Recognizing the many different connotations of "economic," I use the term here only in its most conventional sense: "Economic" matters are those commonly understood to define and create people's material well-being, such as jobs, incomes, prices, growth, inflation, investment, productivity, savings, competitiveness, and the health of industries. Thus an article stating that requiring companies to install pollution-control equipment would cause factories to close and inflation to increase would count as offering an economic frame. Noneconomic arguments include everything else, such as the intrusiveness of government controls, flaws in the underlying science, a concern that regulatory agencies become bloated bureaucracies, the lack of a need for regulation because problems are not severe or are improving on their own, and the inability of regulatory efforts to alleviate the problems they are supposed to address.

The results of this classification show an important development in conservative rhetoric. Before the troubles over economic security began in 1973, opposition to social regulation did not rest mainly on economic grounds. For example, a 1963 article criticized President Kennedy's calls for consumer protection, holding that such measures embodied an inaccurate assumption that consumers could not protect themselves and, in any event, would create vague standards and empower government agencies.[38] In resisting prospective regulation to improve automobile safety, one author argued that the policies would deny people free choices and would improperly permit government control of managerial decisions.[39] During a wave of environmental legislation, *National Review* printed an article describing how the harm to the environment from industrial pollution had been grossly exaggerated.[40]

Some articles published before 1973 did base their opposition to regulatory efforts mostly on economic consequences, of course, but the number that did so rose markedly thereafter. In 1980 an editorial pinned the drop in productivity growth on government regulation in areas such as pollution and safety.[41] As Congress was debating revisions to the Clean Air Act in 1990, the pending bill was assailed for its high costs and negative effects on unemployment.[42] A few years later an article maintained that safety and other regulations imposed on automobile manufacturers in the 1970s had crippled their ability to produce cheap vehicles, ultimately forcing Volkswagen to pull the original Beetle from the U.S. market.[43]

For purposes of comparison over time, a transition can be identified beginning in 1973. As documented in chapter 3, that year saw the beginning of a lasting decline in productivity growth. Differing from what prevailed from the 1940s through the 1960s, Americans' economic experiences from 1973 to the present included greater difficulties with wages, employment stability, personal debt and bankruptcy, and health and pension coverage, all within a setting of rising expectations for material lifestyles. Although the oil shocks of the 1970s contributed to these problems, the forces of change outlasted the temporary energy shortages. Conservative rhetoric, represented by *National Review* articles on social regulation, responded forcefully to the altered context. In total, 50% of the articles published from 1973 to 2004 used primarily economic arguments to demonstrate the merits or, much more commonly, the flaws of government regulation. Showing statistically the reframing of the issue, the figure for articles before 1973 had been much lower at 29%.[44]

The importance of conservative intellectuals, then, went well beyond the simple fact that the right commanded a larger, more encompassing, and better-funded set of outlets for honing and conveying ideas than existed a few decades earlier. To affect the terms by which politics is contested, an intellectual capacity must be deployed effectively; resources do not directly translate into influence. Conservative intellectuals made the most of their capacity by updating their communication strategies. Writers and publicists in think tanks, *National Review*, and other institutions did not repeat the same arguments in service of continuing policy goals. As the reframing of social regulation indicates, thinkers discovered and adopted the most persuasive rhetoric to advocate the policy initiatives they held dear. Although the right's goals on regulation had remained fixed for decades, the rhetorical means by which they could be accomplished changed drastically. Conservative intellectuals made their messages compatible with the surrounding environment, understanding, whether consciously or unconsciously, that such a move greatly enhanced their likelihood of success.

The Emergence of Supply-Side Economics

The right's intellectual wing not only used its analytic abilities to impugn government regulation but also unveiled the broader theory of supply-side economics. Coming to full fruition near the end of the 1970s, this theory centered on the incentives for producers to provide capital and for workers to provide labor. In studying what causes economies to grow and the standard of living to rise, supply-siders covered a wide range of policies: trade barriers, monetary policy, exchange rates, property rights, and government regulation. The perspective aroused the greatest controversy for its views on taxation, the policy domain on which supporters focused most often. A key concept in supply-side economics is the "wedge," the difference between what employers pay for labor and the after-tax income of employees. The higher the wedge, the lower the incentive for businesses to offer jobs and for workers to accept the jobs available.

Such thinking led to claims that reducing the level of taxation would bring substantial economic benefits. Cutting taxes, especially on the upper brackets, would unleash an entrepreneurial spirit, resulting in greater savings, wages, and economic growth. In the strongest version of the doctrine, reducing marginal rates would so stimulate the economy as to increase, rather than decrease, tax revenues relative to what would have been collected otherwise. The underlying reasoning came to be called the Laffer curve, named after the economist Arthur Laffer. The famous curve, which plots tax revenues against tax rates, shows no government revenue at a rate of either 0%—no surprise there—or, more interestingly, at 100%. The amount of revenue grows as tax rates climb above 0% but at some point flattens and heads south, leading to the place where zero revenue is collected at a tax rate of 100%. With no take-home pay under a requirement that the government collects their entire income, people either refuse to work or evade the tax.

From the Laffer curve, supply-siders inferred that tax cuts would pay for themselves, thus helping balance the budget and even raising additional money for other programs. In the words of George Gilder, who wrote a best-selling book championing supply-side theory, "The fact is that tax cuts provide the only desirable way of either balancing the budget or supporting new spending for defense."[45] To those unversed in this theoretical framework, such a statement would seem preposterous; most people would reject out of hand a belief that cutting taxes would generate additional revenues for government. Within the confines of supply-side economics, however, the claim simply captured the predictable effects of taxation on private behavior.

Elements of supply-side economics borrowed from the books and articles of earlier times, as the advocates themselves were quick to note.[46] Supporters cited particular passages from the writings of classical English and French economists such as John Stuart Mill, Adam Smith, Jean-Baptiste Say, and the Physiocrats. Among American thinkers, supply-side economics revived the reputation of Andrew Mellon, a Pittsburgh industrialist and banker who served as secretary of the treasury from 1921 to 1932. In congressional testimony and in his 1924 book *Taxation: The People's Business*, Mellon reasoned that excessive taxation decreases the government's revenues; when taxation becomes too high, people either do not work—and thus do not earn taxable income in the first place—or else shelter their income in illegal or nontaxable sources.[47]

Supply-side rhetoric did not vanish with Mellon but in fact appeared throughout the post–World War II period. Frank Chodorov attacked the graduated income tax, for example, through references to productive investment and personal initiative: "Why expand my business, why work overtime when my increased income will leave little for myself?"[48] He continued by relating the supply-side metaphor that government revenues decline under progressive taxation because it kills the goose that lays the golden eggs.[49] Using similar logic, Charles Gavin's entry into the postwar debate vilified graduated income taxes for undercutting the efficiency of the economy. Because individuals and businesses shift income into other activities or years solely to avoid taxes, "Progressivity thwarts the maximum productivity of goods and services of which our society is capable."[50] Even though neither Chodorov nor Gavin made those arguments the focal point of his tract, both mentioned the economic effects nonetheless.

What changed in the 1970s, then, was not the presence of supply-side rhetoric but rather the frequency and centrality of its use. When economic security was strong from World War II through the early 1970s, the doctrine held only limited potency. Judging taxation according to its economic implications was not the best way to promote one's policy preferences, and conservatives consequently stressed other standards and goals when taking positions on taxation. In the more recent period beginning in 1973, conservative intellectuals backed largely the same policies as before but with different reasoning: In rhetorical defenses the economic consequences took center stage rather than appearing as mere props. With the decline in Americans' economic security, old arguments suddenly acquired new resonance that encouraged intellectuals to reinvigorate them.

Several parts of the conservative intellectual infrastructure fueled this revival of supply-side economics. Although a handful of academic economists participated, the movement did not rely on the professional economics literature for sustenance. Instead, outlets and institutions outside of academia carried the ideas to journalists, politicians, and the general public. The Smith-Richardson Foundation, for example, helped underwrite the most influential popular exposition, Jude Wanniski's 1978 book *The Way the World Works*.[51] One of his articles on taxation, as well as others of a similar vein, appeared in a neoconservative journal, *The Public Interest*. Under the leadership of Robert Bartley and with Jude Wanniski as an editorial writer, the editorial page of the *Wall Street Journal* distributed supply-side viewpoints through the mass media.[52] The growth of supply-side economics consummated a marriage of opportunity and capacity—the opportunity provided by the economic context wedded to the intellectual capacity that conservatives had worked for decades to build.

By the mid-1980s, relatively few intellectuals willingly embraced the supply-side label. The budget deficits accruing shortly after the implementation of President Reagan's 1981 tax cuts discredited the grandest claim of supply-side economics, the assertion that tax cuts would stimulate the economy so much as to create more rather than less revenue for government. That turnabout did not bury the broader theory, however; on the contrary, the softer, less extreme version of supply-side economics became absorbed into the mainstream conservative view on taxation and thus no longer needed a separate label. Almost every conservative from the late 1970s to the present who talked about taxes in general, and progressive income taxes in particular, proclaimed their large and negative effects on the economy. The converse held as well: Tax cuts, especially on the upper brackets, offered the surest route to a permanent increase in growth, investment, and productivity.

Popular and scholarly recollection of supply-side economics usually views its origins and consequences as temporally bounded. That was the theory created in the mid to late 1970s, the story typically goes, which died after deficits accumulated in the Reagan years. The conventional account is wrong at both ends of this time interval. Not a new theory at all, supply-side economics was an old one repackaged with modern examples, analogies, and data. Long present but buried in conservative writings, it rose to the surface in articles, books, and reports circulated by the right's newly robust intellectual infrastructure. The strongest version maintained few adherents in later decades, and yet the theory never faded away. Conservatives continued to press the need for proper incentives for producers and workers; although the supply-side label receded from the political scene, intellectuals and politicians on the right repeatedly highlighted the connection they perceived between taxation and economic vitality.

Changes in *National Review*'s Rhetoric on Taxation

The pages of *National Review* preserve for posterity the transformation of conservative rhetoric on taxation. As was the case for social regulation, a content analysis can provide numerical estimates for the proportion of articles framed in economic terms, thereby adding precision to the inferences that can be drawn. In the following analysis, I examine all editorials, columns, and ordinary articles about taxation from the inaugural issue in 1955 through 2004. To be included, each article must contain at least one paragraph explaining the reasons why a certain position should be embraced or rejected. The classification applied not to the main thesis of the article but rather only to that part making explicit arguments for the merits (or lack thereof) of tax policies. By gauging the amount of space and degree of emphasis given to different arguments, I determine whether the author's advocacy was or was not based primarily on economic reasons.[53]

Table 5.1 lists examples of economic and noneconomic ar-

TABLE 5.1
Examples of Economic and Noneconomic Arguments about Taxes

Economic Arguments

Cutting marginal rates leads to growth, job creation, and higher tax
revenues
High taxes fuel inflation
Reagan tax cuts stimulated the economy
Tax-advantaged enterprise zones would attract businesses
Progressive taxes discourage work, investment, and productivity
Budgetary models should account for effects of taxes on the economy
Europe's economies suffer from overtaxation
Tax bill will increase efficiency and competitiveness of industry
Taxes are lowering people's standard of living
Clinton's tax proposal will sink the economy
Talk of raising taxes caused stock market to fall
Corporation and capital gains taxes impede investment
Taxes on business pass through to consumers via prices

Noneconomic Arguments

Progressive taxes violate equal treatment before the law
Taxing relies on coercion, impinges on freedom
The American people want lower taxes
Opponents are using faulty numbers on taxes
A tax hike would feed big government and the welfare state
The IRS is unfairly implementing tax laws
A large surplus means we should give the people their money back
The proposal to raise taxes will simply lead to more spending
It is socialist to tax some at higher rates than others
Spending should be cut before we consider tax increases
A flat tax is fair and easy to understand, eliminates loopholes
The bill to cut taxes will not hurt charitable giving
The rich pay their fair share of taxes
Hidden taxes like a VAT cause the total tax burden to rise
Tuition tax credits would foster diversity and quality in education
Voters are penalizing politicians who raise taxes
Sin taxes restrict liberty by trying to change behavior
Taxing higher incomes to achieve equality is simply class envy
The tax-exempt status of a certain organization should be upheld
It is unfair for inflation alone to raise someone's taxes via bracket creep
Corporate taxation is unjust because it is double taxation of capital
The tax code is too complex
Taxes lead to government waste

guments about taxation that have appeared, most of them multiple times, in the pages of *National Review*. For instance, if an author declared that a bill to cut marginal tax rates would accelerate growth and lead to higher tax revenues, the article would be counted as economic, as did those containing assertions that taxes on capital gains or corporate incomes lead to lower levels of savings and investment. Articles categorized as noneconomic include those claiming that progressive taxes are unjust because they reflect class envy, because they violate the principle of equal treatment before the law, or because the underlying attempt to promote equality is socialist. In popular discourse the term "economic" sometimes takes an expansive meaning, but it is used here in a more precise way. Arguments about the proper distribution or redistribution of society's resources, for instance, involve criteria of fairness or justice and hence count as noneconomic.[54]

Using the classifications for each article, it is possible to chart the incidence over time of economically based frames. Conservatives have long been animated more by taxation than regulation, a disposition reflected in the far greater number of articles published on taxes. This deeper source of data, a total of 758 articles spread across five decades, permits an investigation of short-term as well as long-term trends. Figure 5.1 provides a graph of the data, averaged across all the articles appearing during each presidential administration. Higher scores indicate a greater reliance on framing arguments about taxation in economic terms. During the first and second Eisenhower administrations, respectively, only 25% and 47% of the articles used mostly economic arguments. A representative article published in 1958 stated that taxation is based on coercion and violates freedom, for which the only proper response was to allow individuals to decide when, whether, and how much they would pay in taxes.[55] The next issue included four responses that extended the references to compulsion, liberty, and confiscation.

The figures on economic frames for the Kennedy-Johnson, Johnson, and first Nixon administrations were 57%, 20%, and 32%, respectively. The economy became a prominent touchstone in the early 1960s when President Kennedy justified his Keynesian-inspired tax bill through its presumed relationship with economic

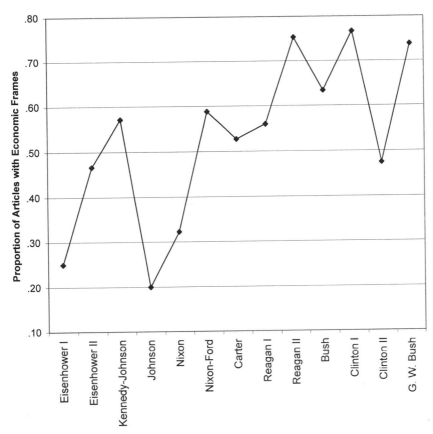

Figure 5.1. Economic Frames in National Review Articles on Taxes

growth. Unlike the Republican minority in Congress, most authors in *National Review* endorsed the bill and echoed the president's framing of it. Shortly thereafter, though, noneconomic themes reemerged. Progressive taxes were criticized as a Marxist attempt to impose equality, and the IRS was condemned for improperly investigating the tax-exempt status of organizations on the right but not the left.[56]

When considering the period before 1973 as a whole, one observes that economic frames predominated only a minority of the time. Just 37% of the articles advocated their positions primarily through references to economic effects. For the succeeding years a contrasting picture comes into view, with consequences for the economy continually visible as the stated reason for positions on taxes. The data from *National Review* articles reach peaks of 75% during Reagan's second term, 77% during the first Clinton administration, and 74% during George W. Bush's first term. A typical editorial in 1978 held that a bill to reduce taxes on capital gains would cause employment, incomes, and tax revenues to soar.[57] Another piece published in 1987 maintained that President Reagan's cuts in marginal rates had instigated a period of mass prosperity, a contention that appeared dozens of times in the 1980s and 1990s.[58] When taken in its entirety, the period from 1973 to 2004 saw a substantial reframing: Economic arguments were dominant in 64% of the articles, a figure nearly double the level of 37% registered for the period from 1955 (the first year of *National Review*) through 1972. Thus from being frequently used but still remaining in the minority, economic frames subsequently grew to define two-thirds of the relevant articles.

The only period that deviated from the post-1972 pattern was President Clinton's second term. At only 49%, the level of economic frames in *National Review* articles had fallen by more than fifteen points below the average after 1972 and had sunk to depths not seen since the 1960s. This decline can be interpreted as a reaction to the robust economic growth, low unemployment, and strong wage gains of the late 1990s. Because Americans were faring better in material terms than at any time in the recent past, a message of changing federal policies to create a more prosperous economy—whether coming from the left, the right, or the center—lacked the potency that argument held in the two previous decades. With tax policies needing other rationales, conservatives began to argue that the forecasted surpluses belonged to the people rather than the government and that without tax cuts government bureaucrats would ratchet up spending.

Beyond the frames employed, *National Review* published relatively few articles on tax policies during Clinton's second term, averaging ten per year, or less than half the rate of the twenty-four articles per year seen over the previous five administrations. If this book's analysis is accurate, the turn away from the issue occurred because the most persuasive argument about taxation since the early 1970s had been cut down to size and reduced in effectiveness. With its best player relegated to the bench, *National Review* frequently chose not to play the rhetorical game on taxes at all. As soon as the economy stalled at the beginning of 2001, however, taxation moved up the list of conservative topics, and the leading rhetorical edge was a connection to the economy. The long-term projected surplus did not change until George W. Bush signed his tax cut into law on June 7, 2001, so the argument that the surplus was the people's money could well have continued. That argument was now less potent than one relating taxation to the economy, however, and so the proportion of articles framed with economic arguments jumped to 76% in 2001.

The Strength of Alternative Frames

As seen in the books by Albert Jay Nock, Friedrich Hayek, and Milton Friedman and the articles in *National Review*, conservative intellectuals placed their greatest emphasis on arguments about freedom, not the economy, in the immediate post–World War II decades. Frequently applied to the issues of regulation and taxation, the call for freedom retained considerable appeal all the way up to the present. Indeed, in the opening decades of the twenty-first century, freedom made an unexpected resurgence as a means of justifying policies. After the failure to find weapons of mass destruction or evidence of Saddam Hussein's involvement in the terrorist attacks of September 11, 2001, President George W. Bush shifted his rhetoric on the reasons for the American invasion of Iraq. The president did not reposition—he continued to maintain that the Iraq war was well worth the cost in lives, money, and intangibles—but he reframed his rhetoric so that it moved away from national security and toward freedom and democracy for the Iraqi people.

In most cases, though, the rhetorical potency of freedom as a means of framing issues—especially domestic ones—declined during and after the 1970s. Under conditions of greater economic insecurity, the material dimension of politics assumed an exalted status. Intellectuals and politicians could consult the "most important problem" surveys described in chapter 3, or simply talk to their friends and family, to understand the fears people held about achieving and maintaining a decent standard of living. The rise and perisistence of economic insecurity posed an obstacle needing to be overcome with serious thinking, sustained planning, and robust action. Recasting old ideas in an explicitly economic language could reshuffle the deck of national politics, making possible shifts in policy otherwise unthinkable.

Because ineffective arguments eventually exit mainstream political discourse, all enduring categories of arguments—including those involving personal freedom and economic consequences—are strong and potentially decisive in building coalitions for policy alternatives. Of course, these two alternatives are not the only ways of framing issues that have persisted across American history. Other kinds of arguments through which political elites have routinely framed issues include equality, morality, community, and racial exclusion and inclusion.[59] Still, political actors have regularly applied freedom-oriented and economic arguments to a range of issues in recent times as well as in earlier eras. Accordingly, my analysis here explores these arguments in some detail while recognizing the need for and value of complementary studies that concentrate on other arguments.

Both freedom-based and economic appeals hold deep roots in American culture and history. Demands for freedom have been embedded in the nation's political traditions from the Revolutionary War through the opening years of the twenty-first century. Whether the discussion covers property rights, civil rights, or some unspecified kind of rights, freedom and liberty have continually been upheld as essential to the American identity. Similarly, materialist values were evident in colonial America from the very beginning—most notably in the Chesapeake region—and the desire for upward mobility and wealth accumulation continued in later centuries. The goal of delivering "a chicken in every pot" has been incorporated into the rhetoric of every astute politician.[60] Advocating a policy or program because of its purported connection to freedom or effects on the economy, then, has always brought political rewards. For this reason, neither means of framing issues will ever disappear from political rhetoric. Anyone who studies a large sample of rhetoric from any point in American history will encounter policies framed in these two ways.

To say that something always occurs, however, does not mean that it persists with the same intensity. The amount of attention each argument receives varies considerably over time, as one would expect given changes in the historical context that affect the needs and wants of audiences. The lower the level of economic security, the more successful are arguments holding that a policy will boost employment, wages, and living standards. Because concerns about economic security never completely vanish, and because people desire more goods and services even when they already live in abundance, one can predict that economic arguments will always be present—as indeed they were in the two decades after World War II. The crucial distinction is one of degree, and conservatives' economic arguments became much more prevalent when the context changed beginning in 1973.

Arguments based on freedom and the economy differ in their persuasiveness not only relative to each other but also compared with other arguments. From the end of World War II through the 1960s, conservatives faced an intertwined rhetorical and political conundrum: By using the concept of freedom when explaining the merits of their domestic positions, they convinced and motivated part of the American population, yet they could not secure a lasting majority. Arguments about freedom competed with those from other perspectives, for political conflicts at the aggregate, national level incorporate multiple voices. Liberals linked contemporary circumstances and durable American values by advocating policies that invoked fairness, social justice, and the opportunity for all citizens to lead a better life. With worries about economic security receding, these alternative means of framing issues won favor with the American public. Conservatives needed a shake-up of the context before they could successfully highlight an interpretive dimension based on economic criteria, a move that would soon expand their supporting coalition.

From Intellectuals to Politicians

Intellectuals like Nock, Hayek, and Friedman and the contributors to publications such as *National Review* form one crucial part of a larger story about politics. By developing and elaborating ideas, the thinking class helps motivate actual or prospective candidates and lead them in directions they might not otherwise go. In an important channel of influence, the very preferences of political leaders draw from ideas discussed in intellectual circles. The intelligentsia also can provide the rhetoric, including forms of reasoning and the supporting evidence, for elected officials who wanted similar policies anyway but would have defended them on other, less persuasive grounds. Politicians who might have downplayed a certain position, recognizing that it could not be adequately presented to the public or political elites, possess new rhetorical tools if intellectuals have created effective frames on the issue.

Mass audiences' encounters with ideas usually come secondhand through exposure to the rhetoric of these political leaders. Although relatively few citizens read intellectual writings, some of the ways of thinking contained therein nevertheless penetrate public consciousness. When sufficiently simplified for popular consumption, ideas can help politicians mobilize public support for policy proposals. Candidates and officeholders, that is, creatively adopt and adapt ideas in the process of devising rhetoric for public constituencies. I pursue these points further in the next chapter, which shows how conservatives' rhetorical renewal moved beyond intellectuals and into the realm of politicians. By opening up space for the rhetoric of key figures in the Republican party, most notably Ronald Reagan, conservative intellectuals contributed to a long-term process of policy change.

SIX

The Rhetorical Adaptations of
the Republican Party

On the opening day of the Oklahoma legislature in 1965, Governor Henry Bellmon delivered his state-of-the-state address to a packed legislative chamber. A Republican elected in 1962 to a four-year term, Bellmon moved from topic to topic while making policy recommendations to his legislative colleagues. Placing his central themes elsewhere, he nevertheless mentioned the economic condition of the state and pointed to positive movement on several fronts. To promote further economic progress, he proposed building highways, boosting tourism, developing the state's water resources, and funding an agricultural experiment station and extension service. When Bellmon discussed other areas such as education, the budget, health and welfare, public safety, civil rights, and government operations, he usually defended his proposals on noneconomic grounds.

While serving a second tour of duty as Oklahoma's governor in 1989, Bellmon delivered an address vastly different in content and tone from the one a quarter-century earlier. Most noticeably, this time he gave far more space and emphasis to economic matters. Like many other governors of the 1980s, he explained the steps he deemed necessary to improve the state's "business climate." Throughout the speech Bellmon backed his policies with arguments that they would create additional jobs, stimulate new investments, and produce higher incomes. Besides repeating his earlier framing of transportation, tourism, and agriculture around economic needs, the Oklahoma governor now stressed the economic benefits of proposals involving tax cuts, education standards, training programs, business incentives, and workers' compensation. In the speech's conclusion, Bellmon challenged the legislature to work together on jobs, industrial development, and economic prosperity.

A comparison of the 1965 and 1989 speeches by Governor Henry Bellmon yields two lessons. First, the volume and depth of coverage given to the economy differed in degree rather than kind. Economic matters featured much more prominently in the later one even though they attracted some attention in the earlier one. Second, that change occurred despite the fact that both speeches took place during long economic expansions. Real GDP growth for the four quarters up to and including the ones marked by the speeches was strong in both 1965 (5.2%) and 1989 (4.1%). As had been the case for well over a decade, however, in the later year financial anxieties were pronounced among the American population in ways not captured by some commonly used macroeconomic indicators.

The emergence of economic insecurity can be traced to 1973, for that year saw the beginning of a long-term drop in productivity growth that soon manifested itself in job instability and slack wages. Americans' average levels of consumption steadily rose in the succeeding decades, but economic security entails much more than just the number of goods and services people can purchase. As earlier chapters have shown, recent times have brought uncertainties in employment, higher levels of personal debt and bankruptcy, and perceptions of financial vulnerability. This widespread insecurity encouraged elected officials to focus more attention on the economy and to present economic justifications for a greater number of policies. Given by the same person with the same upbringing and values, Henry Bellmon's 1965 and 1989 speeches illustrate how politicians adapted to the changed economic context.

The rhetorical responses of Republicans were not unique to Bellmon, as can be seen through a content analysis of state-of-the-state speeches by the party's governors. Typically given on the first day the legislature formally meets, these messages afford governors their best opportunities to influence the upcoming legislative session and are usually reported extensively in the mass media. Indeed, ordinarily the state-of-the-state address is the most important speech in a given year, and governors use their time in the spotlight to cover many different policy areas. Because Republicans hold fifteen to twenty governorships even in the worst electoral years for the party, we have many examples available to measure and compare over time the incidence of economic arguments.

Although it is not feasible to analyze every speech from a lengthy period, a paired comparison of years can yield ample information. I identified two years each of strong and weak economic performance both before and after the decline in economic security that began in 1973 and persisted into later decades.[1] My intent in gathering eight years of data was to make a series of apples-to-apples comparisons, for it would be misleading to place the best years after 1973 against the worst years before, or vice versa.[2] Appropriate pre-1973 choices for strong years were 1955 and 1965, both taking place during upswings in national economic performance.[3] I compared them with the post-1973 years of 1989 and 1999, which also recorded high growth rates. From the pool of weak years, when the economy struggled to rebound from temporary downturns, I included 1949 and 1961 from the pre-1973 period and 1983 and 2001 from post-1973.[4]

Reprioritizing in Republican Governors' Speeches

One potential response to an altered context involves reprioritizing, in which parties and politicians take goals or policies they formerly endorsed and push them up their list of concerns. With the rise of economic insecurity, political actors could reprioritize by moving objectives and initiatives related to the economy to a higher place within the group of all those supported. For parties, the economy and issues linked to it would shift to earlier spots in formal platforms and would receive more emphasis and elaboration; for politicians, those matters would now appear more often and more prominently in speeches, press releases, and campaign advertisements. Like other elected officials, governors can reprioritize by changing the amount of attention they allocate to different subjects.

As a rhetorical genre, governors' state-of-the-state addresses follow certain conventions based on the expectations that the speaker and audience bring to the situation.[5] Governors typically identify their priorities by describing a series of goals to achieve in the near future. Usually appearing at the end of the speech, the goals—as defined here—reflect broad themes rather than specific legislative proposals. For the analysis that follows, I coded each sentence in the goals section according to its content. The crucial determination was whether or not the subject of each sentence was economic in nature, with the economic category encompassing references to concepts such as employment, prices, industry, payrolls, production, growth, and prosperity.[6] Noneconomic goals included cooperating across party lines to pass legislation, showing accountability to the public, providing leadership on difficult questions, and leaving a legacy that future generations will respect. Issues such as taxes, education, welfare, and health care count as economic only if the speaker explicitly connects them to the economy. With the information from this classification, it is possible to calculate, for each governor and year, the proportion of sentences in the goals section whose content was economic.

The data created by tabulating Republican governors' goals are summarized in table 6.1, where it is immediately apparent that the economy gained status as a priority.[7] GOP governors offered many kinds of goals over the last half-century, with economic ones becoming more numerous in the most recent times.[8] The comparisons show more than a doubling of attention to the economy not only in the weak years (from 11% to 24%) but also the strong ones (from 8% to 20%). This finding is exactly what one would expect from knowing, as described in chapter 3, that financial security has become a challenge for many Americans

TABLE 6.1
Reprioritizing in Republican Governors' Speeches

	Pre-1973	Post-1973
Strong years	8%	20%
Weak years	11%	24%

Note: Cell entries are the percentage of sentences focusing on the economy in the goals section of Republican governors' state-of-the-state addresses.

even when the economy performs well. Responding to those worries, the governors did not turn away from the economy in the late 1980s and late 1990s when standard indicators such as growth, unemployment, and inflation recorded favorable numbers. The governors seemingly recognized that a "good" economy was not "good enough" to alleviate the problems of economic insecurity pervasive among the population.

Reframing in Republican Governors' Speeches

A second rhetorical response to the emergence of economic insecurity involves reframing, which occurs when political actors such as governors embrace the same position as before but revise their stated rationales. Many policies formerly defended with noneconomic reasons would now see economic consequences receive the top rhetorical billing. Whereas reprioritizing involves shifting attention across issues, reframing refers to changing the arguments offered within issues. Previously advocated differently, a reframed position now rests on alternative rhetorical grounds. Reprioritizing and reframing are connected, though, in that an issue might rise on the priority list precisely because an appealing frame, one suited to the context, has become available. Political actors are more likely to accentuate an issue when they possess a persuasive means of framing it.

To assess the degree of reframing, the same issue must be studied over time. Although most topics do not consistently recur among the governors and over the years, two areas of policy attract interest in almost all of the state-of-the-state speeches: education, whether at the elementary, secondary, college, or adult levels, and taxation, whether on sales, incomes, properties, or estates, or as tax credits and exemptions for particular activities. Accordingly, my analysis of governors' framing and reframing concentrates on the rich body of data available on education and taxes. For both domains, the focus here is on the arguments given rather than the underlying proposals.[9] The key classification indicates whether each sentence included economic or noneconomic reasons for accepting the proposals in question.[10]

I summarize the resulting data for education and taxes, respectively, in tables 6.2 and 6.3. In every instance governors framed these two issues more often in economic terms in the years after 1973 than before, with the reframing usually large in magnitude. The reframing appeared when comparing both good and bad years, making the trend pervasive and robust. The frequency of an economic means of framing education, for example, rose from 29% in the strong years before 1973 to 48% in comparable years thereafter. While Republican governors stressed the desirability of promoting and strengthening education throughout the periods under study, over time they became more likely to give economic justifications for their policy proposals. The words of John Rowland (Connecticut, 2001) are typical among those holding office in recent decades: "Providing a world class education to every student is the best way to ensure we have a world class workforce for the new economy of tomorrow."[11]

The rhetorical reframing of taxation follows a pattern similar to education. Republican governors have long sought to hold the line on taxes—this was a central plank of the party since the New Deal—but they now present different arguments than in earlier decades. Typical of the post-1973 governors who asserted

TABLE 6.2
Reframing on Education in Republican Governors'
Speeches

	Pre-1973	Post-1973
Strong years	29%	48%
Weak years	16%	61%

Note: Cell entries are the percentage of sentences focusing on economic arguments within the pool of all sentences containing explicit arguments about policy proposals regarding education.

a sizable and negative relationship between taxes and the economy, John H. Sununu (New Hampshire, 1983) praised his state's avoidance of general sales and income taxes: "This tradition has served and will continue to serve as an attractant and a stimulus to quality economic growth. This growth creates jobs and opportunities for our citizens."[12] The party's governors in the early post–World War II decades, by contrast, less often made claims about the economic consequences of taxes.

Besides education and taxes, which are discussed in almost every speech and thus allow for systematic comparisons, Republican governors in recent times commonly framed other topics around economic needs. Many of the prescriptions for jobs and growth were nonpartisan, consensual ideas such as establishing public-private partnerships, building highways and airports,

TABLE 6.3
Reframing on Taxes in Republican Governors' Speeches

	Pre-1973	Post-1973
Strong years	25%	34%
Weak years	22%	38%

Note: Cell entries are the percentage of sentences focusing on economic arguments within the pool of all sentences containing explicit arguments about policy proposals regarding taxes.

investing in emerging technologies, and promoting the state through tourism, exports, and internal development. Other policies framed in economic terms took a more partisan cast, including restricting unions, curtailing environmental regulation, passing tort reform, limiting workers' compensation and unemployment compensation, and loosening policies on zoning and land management. For example, Frank Keating (Oklahoma, 2001) called for a statewide vote on right-to-work legislation, stating emphatically: "Eight states are gaining one or more Congressional seats, six of them are right-to-work states. Right-to-work means growth, higher income, and higher jobs."[13] Illinois governor George Ryan asked in 1999 for an array of regulatory reforms because small businesses "need our help. And one of the best ways we can help is to get out of the way. That means regulatory relief, now."[14] Republican governors' penchant for advocating policies with economic arguments, then, went well beyond the issues of education and taxes.

A Comparison of Barry Goldwater and Ronald Reagan

The rhetorical adaptations of the GOP characterized the federal as well as the state level, as revealed by a comparison of two of the party's luminaries of the twentieth century: Barry Goldwater and Ronald Reagan. With the exception of George McGovern, Barry Goldwater suffered the worst electoral drubbing among major-party presidential candidates since World War II. In 1964 Goldwater corralled just 38% of the popular vote, a tally far short of triumphant Lyndon Johnson's 61%. Ronald Reagan, by contrast, outshone all other presidential candidates from the post–World War II era. Dwight Eisenhower, Richard Nixon, Bill Clinton, and George W. Bush won election and reelection, but only Reagan achieved two landslide victories in besting Jimmy Carter by ten points in 1980 and Walter Mondale by eighteen points in 1984.

The contrasting fates of Goldwater and Reagan become

more remarkable in light of their nearly indistinguishable policy positions. Despite scattered differences, the broad outlines of their views fit together snugly. The two ardent anti-Communists believed in confronting the Soviet Union through a posture of military strength; both vehemently opposed an expansive welfare state; and both sought to shrink or eliminate many government programs. In his twilight years in the 1980s and 1990s, Goldwater became known for iconoclastic views outside the mainstream of the Republican party, such as support for abortion rights and allowing gays to serve openly in the military. The earlier Goldwater, though, showed clear commonalities with Reagan, leading political observers to link the men together in American history. Upon Goldwater's death in 1998, a wide array of activists and commentators remarked that his most important legacy came when his ideas resurfaced more successfully in the beliefs and commitments of Reagan.[15]

Schooled to regard elections as Downsian battles over the median voter and legislative politics as dominated by the distribution of "ideal points," many political scientists downplay the importance of studying rhetoric. In examining candidates' and officeholders' stands while overlooking their rhetoric, political scientists have missed an important difference between Goldwater and Reagan. Notwithstanding the similarity of their positions, the two towering figures in conservative politics persuaded in different ways. Reagan is commonly remembered as a sunny optimist whose folksy examples, self-deprecating humor, and ingratiating personality played well with the electorate; Goldwater occasionally came across as dour, negative, and solemn. The rhetorical contrasts go much deeper than personal styles, however, and into the very substance of the particular arguments they offered. These differences, heretofore largely unnoticed by scholars and journalists alike, show how rhetoric flows from and conforms to its context.

The analysis that follows focuses on the periods when the two Republican standard-bearers built support for their respective nominations and campaigned for office: 1960–1964 for Goldwater and 1976–1980 for Reagan. Both men boasted distinguished political careers either before seeking the White House (in Reagan's case) or both before and after (in Goldwater's case), but the purpose here is to contrast them as presidential nominees of the Republican party; hence the appropriate scope can be narrowed to the periods when they emerged as actual or potential presidential candidates. During those years each aspiring candidate used many forums to reach prospective voters; and as is true for everyone running for office, most of their statements along the campaign trail quickly faded from the scene as public and media attention turned elsewhere. The analysis here of prioritizing and framing examines only their most prominent writings and speeches, those that exerted the most influence on each candidate's prospects for electoral victory.

Prioritizing by Goldwater and Reprioritizing by Reagan

Prioritizing through rhetoric can occur simply when a candidate expends more words, paragraphs, and pages on one issue than another, but it also includes elements such as placement or highlights in a speech. The earliest parts of a speech often direct the flow for later sections, and sometimes speakers make their prioritizing explicit through statements such as "The most critical issue facing us in this election is . . ." Barry Goldwater's prioritizing is remembered above all else for his vigorous anticommunism, a topic that dominated his address at the 1964 Republican national convention. Immediately after the obligatory paragraph beginning with the words "I accept your nomination with a deep sense of humility," Goldwater emphatically clarified the stakes of the Cold War: "The good Lord raised this mighty Republic to be a home for the brave and to flourish as the land of the free—not to stagnate in the swampland of collectivism, not to cringe before the bully of communism."[16] Time and again the Arizona senator returned to the threat of Communist aggression and the conduct of foreign affairs more generally, stressing that only strength and vigilance in the face of Soviet expansionism would allow the

United States to achieve a lasting peace. The economy, by contrast, was barely mentioned in the speech.

Goldwater's best-known rhetoric prior to his convention address was contained in *The Conscience of a Conservative*.[17] With few legislative accomplishments in his Senate years, little political clout in Washington, DC, and a small constituency in his then-sparsely populated state, the Arizona senator first received broad national exposure after the book appeared in March 1960. Eventually selling more than 3.5 million copies, his magnum opus defined for its era what a conservative stood for and against. *The Conscience of a Conservative* differs somewhat from the convention address in allocating fifty-three pages to domestic matters and, along with a chapter on principles equally applicable to all areas of policy, only forty pages to what Goldwater calls "The Soviet Menace." Although foreign policy does not capture more pages than domestic issues, neither does it rank much behind. Forcefully articulating his views on the Cold War, Goldwater writes: "If an enemy power is bent on conquering you, and proposes to turn all of his resources to that end, he is at war with you: and you—unless you contemplate surrender—are at war with him."[18] Notably, the domestic agenda that Goldwater advanced places the economy as only one of several concerns.

In his infamous "daisy girl" television advertisement during the election of 1964, Lyndon Johnson sought to reinforce this reputation of Goldwater as a strident and, to some, a reckless cold warrior. The visual images, building from an idyllic setting toward a dark conclusion, showed a young child plucking the petals off a flower during the countdown to an atomic bomb's explosion. The commercial was Johnson's means of asking voters whether they wanted Goldwater's finger on the nuclear button. The advertisement's importance to Goldwater's prioritizing across issues lay in confirming what his speeches and writings already indicated: No one doubted that he placed the struggle against communism at the top of his priorities.

Sixteen years later Goldwater's ideological companion, Ronald Reagan, shifted the rhetorical emphases. In the speech announcing his candidacy on November 13, 1979, Reagan set the tone for the campaign to come: "No problem that we face today can compare with the need to restore the health of the American economy and the strength of the American dollar."[19] By calling the economy the number-one concern for the election, Reagan clearly stated his priorities. Toward the end of the speech Reagan turned to international politics and the global conflict with communism, but those matters received much less space than did the economy. This structuring of the speech is especially noteworthy when considering the Soviet Union's invasion of Afghanistan only a few months earlier and the Carter administration's defense buildup in response. Given Reagan's own anti-Communist orientation and the recently renewed Cold War, it would have been entirely plausible for him to make foreign affairs the highest rhetorical priority for his impending candidacy—and yet the economy received the most attention.

These rhetorical patterns continued throughout his quest for the nomination, culminating in an acceptance speech of which more than half addressed economic matters and described his proposals for reform. Reagan stirred the convention delegates with criticisms of "an economic stew that has turned the national stomach."[20] Again, while foreign policy was not ignored, it received much less elaboration and stayed entirely offstage until his economic program had been described to listeners and viewers. Reagan's most prominent speech after the convention, the only one printed in full in the *New York Times*, was devoted completely to the economy and to his proposals to improve the prospects for higher employment, faster growth, and lower inflation.[21] Reacting to his campaign's promise of bold action, extensive coverage of the speech followed in the mass media.

During September, October, and November of the general election campaign, Reagan purchased airtime to broadcast seventeen television advertisements.[22] Two that were not directly relevant to Reagan's prioritizing across issues dealt exclusively with his background, experience, and leadership capabilities. Of the remaining fifteen commercials, only two covered foreign affairs compared with thirteen that focused on the economy and

Reagan's programmatic initiatives to improve the nation's economic performance. Reagan's television spots, in fact, discussed domestic issues *only* in the context of the economy. Gauged by the time allotted to issues, the former head of the Screen Actors Guild prioritized the economy over foreign affairs by more than a six-to-one ratio.

Framing by Goldwater and Reframing by Reagan

The differences in the two candidates' framing of issues closely parallel their prioritizing. The most prominent frame in Goldwater's rhetoric, characterizing both his writings and speeches, is freedom. He throws down the gauntlet early in *The Conscience of a Conservative*, constructing a persona for his followers and italicizing the key points to ensure a lasting imprint on the reader:

> for the American conservative, there is no difficulty in identifying the day's overriding political challenge: it is *to preserve and extend freedom.* As he surveys the various attitudes and institutions and laws that currently prevail in America, many questions will occur to him, but the Conservative's first concern will be: *Are we maximizing freedom?* I suggest we examine some of the critical issues facing us today with this question in mind.[23]

Goldwater applies the yardstick of freedom throughout his subsequent chapters. Current policies routinely undermine freedom, Goldwater declares, whereas his preferred policies will advance it. The "closed shop" intrudes on the right of association of prospective union members, for example, and federal interventions in education, agriculture, and race relations violate the constitutional freedoms of individuals and states. In defending his program for winning the Cold War, Goldwater asserts: "For Americans who cherish their lives, but their freedom more, the choice cannot be difficult."[24] For a broad range of issues, then, the concept of freedom provides the criteria for choosing one course of action over another.

Consistent with his driving motivation, Goldwater expounds on the dangers to freedom in an illuminating chapter titled "Taxes and Spending." In contemporary discussions, he explains, "We have been led to discount, and often to forget altogether, the bearing of taxation on the problem of individual freedom."[25] Goldwater laments that government has usurped the rights of a man to the fruits of his labor, for "a third of what he produces is not available for his own use but is confiscated and used by others who have not earned it." *The Conscience of a Conservative* demands a lower tax rate in general and the repeal in particular of progressive income taxes by arguing that they impinge on people's freedom to use their earnings however they choose. Holding that progressive taxes violate the principle of equal treatment before the law, Goldwater calls them "repugnant to my notions of justice."[26]

Goldwater's acceptance speech, as the best rhetorical analyses have indicated, reflects his trademark style in featuring freedom as its driving frame.[27] From the very outset, he holds that "this party, with its every action, every word, every breath, and every heartbeat, has but a single resolve, and that is freedom."[28] Freedom, and the related concept of liberty, is paramount in his famous line, "I would remind you that extremism in the defense of liberty is no vice."[29] The words *freedom* and *liberty*, along with their cognates, are used forty-two times over the course of the speech. That basic means of framing Goldwater's positions is repeated so often that a viewer or listener who sleeps through most of the oration, awakening periodically when the roar of the crowd reaches a crescendo, still will have heard the call for freedom.

Like Goldwater, Reagan opposed the progressive income tax and pressed for cutting federal spending and devolving many programs to states, localities, and individuals. The nature of the dominant frame, however, was thoroughly transformed. Advocating certain policies based on their economic impact replaced Goldwater's concern with their connection to freedom. Nowhere was this transformation clearer than on the issue of taxation, where Reagan in his convention address held: "We are taxing ourselves into economic exhaustion and stagnation, crushing our ability and incentive to save, invest and produce."[30] Later in the campaign, Reagan added that high rates of taxation "cripple productivity, lead to deficit financing and inflation, and create unemployment. We can go a long way toward restoring the economic health of this country by establishing reasonable, fair levels of taxation."[31]

Even as tax cuts formed the preeminent component of Reagan's economic program, his proposals extended to the spending side of the ledger and to government regulation. In his 1979 speech announcing his candidacy, he explained that "the key to restoring the health of the economy lies in cutting taxes. At the same time, we need to get the waste out of federal spending. . . . We must force the entire federal bureaucracy to live in the real world of reduced spending, streamlined function and accountability to the people it serves."[32] Reagan also adopted economic frames in advocating deregulation, the third pillar of what came to be labeled Reaganomics. The problem, Reagan stated during the general election campaign, was this:

> Government regulation, like fire, makes a good servant but a bad master. No one can argue with the intent of this regulation—to improve health and safety and to give us cleaner air and water—but too often regulations work against rather than for the interests of the people. When the real take-home pay of the average American worker is declining steadily, and eight million Americans are out of work, we must carefully reexamine our regulatory structure to assess to what degree regulations have contributed to this situation. In my administration there should and will be a thorough and systematic review of the thousands of Federal regulations that affect the economy.[33]

Reagan cast the issues of taxation, spending, and government regulation in quite different terms than did Goldwater even though their underlying stands were similar; stated more simply, the rhetoric changed even as the positions did not. Goldwater's framing closely matched that of Friedrich Hayek's *Road to Serfdom* and Milton Friedman's *Capitalism and Freedom*, whereas Reagan drew from the intellectual currents appearing two decades later. It certainly was not the case, however, that the 1964 and 1980 nominees of the Republican party would have rejected each other's reasoning. In fact, occasional echoes of each man's rhetoric were evident in the speeches and writings of the other. For example, in his closing paragraph in the chapter titled "Taxes and Spending," Goldwater wrote:

> And let us, by all means, remember the *nation's* interest in reducing taxes and spending. The need for "economic growth" that we hear so much about these days will be achieved, not by the government harnessing the nation's economic forces, but by emancipating them. By reducing taxes and spending we will not only return to the individual the means with which he can assert his freedom and dignity, but also guarantee to the nation the economic strength that will always be its ultimate defense against foreign foes.[34]

Remarkably, Goldwater's words do not appear until the final paragraph of the chapter. The sentences quoted here are the only ones in the *entire chapter* that discuss the benefits for the economy of implementing his philosophy on taxes and spending. Because they stand out against the standard of freedom that infuses the chapter as well as the book, the statements sound superfluous and perfunctory. In a rhetorical approach that contrasts with how the right has discussed taxes and spending in the last three decades, Goldwater does not bother mentioning their economic effects until the closing sentences of the chapter. It is almost as if he is saying, "In case I haven't convinced you with my primary arguments, let me add a subordinate one to the mix."

In Reagan's speeches, the effect of taxes and spending on the economy was never the secondary claim; instead, that effect continually stood at the forefront of his rhetoric. Again, Reagan did not reject Goldwater's argument that taxes and spending impinged on personal freedom. Framing involves the amount of time and emphasis devoted to a particular theme rather than whether it is referenced in passing. Political actors must make choices when constructing their rhetoric; they cannot expound on all the plausible reasons for their stands on issues, especially given the severe limits on the amount of time they can hold an audience's attention. They therefore must present their best arguments and deemphasize or even omit the weaker ones. Every major argument of Goldwater was offered by Reagan at some point and vice versa, but the balance shifted between those that were dominant and those merely mentioned. Despite the similarity of their menu of arguments, the two candidates ordered vastly different portion sizes when preparing their campaign rhetoric.

Supply-Side Economics and Reagan's Coalition Building

Intellectual movements commonly precede innovations in the political realm, a tendency illustrated well by the linkage between supply-side economics and Reagan's rhetoric. The renewed intellectual case for supply-side economics emerged mostly between Reagan's 1976 and 1980 presidential campaigns, thereby providing rhetorical opportunities to sustain his long-standing advocacy of tax cuts. Throughout his political career he fought high taxes and especially progressive income taxes. Reagan made supply-side arguments as early as 1958, though prior to 1980 he did not frame the issue predominantly in those terms.[35] During the 1976 campaign challenging Gerald Ford for the Republican nomination, Reagan could have proposed supply-side tax cuts as a solution for the nation's economic problems; the decline in economic security that began in 1973, after all, was in full swing. The former California governor asked for reductions in government spending but not for large tax cuts. The intellectual movement for supply-side economics had just begun to gel, and so Reagan did not have full access to what would soon offer a fund of powerful rhetorical resources for cutting taxes and reducing progressivity.

By 1980 the case for supply-side economics had been widely disseminated through op-eds, reports, books, and articles in opinion journals, allowing Reagan to claim that he could simultaneously reduce taxes, increase defense spending, and balance the budget because of the greater revenues the tax cuts would generate. To be sure, the doctrines Reagan embraced were regularly challenged, and George H. W. Bush famously called them "voodoo economics." But if in 1980 the claims were controversial, only four years earlier they would have been inconceivable. During the 1976 election, let alone the 1964 contest that pitted Goldwater against Johnson, a candidate could not have made the promises Reagan would later utter without being dismissed as ignorant about economics. The intellectual movement for supply-side economics helped transform an idea previously seen as foolish into one often deemed plausible or even probable. Intellectual developments, then, opened up possibilities for political change, and Reagan soon capitalized on them.

After Reagan's victory in the 1980 election, supply-side economics added rhetorical leverage that proved valuable in constructing a coalition sufficiently large to enact the tax cut into law. Reagan won nearly unanimous support in both the House of Representatives and the Senate among Republicans, an achievement underwhelming in retrospect but noteworthy at the time because of the party's historical commitment to balanced budgets. Skeptics of the revenue-raising potential of lower tax rates, such as Howard Baker, the majority leader of the Republican-controlled Senate, and Pete Domenici, chair of the Senate Budget Committee, accepted revenue forecasts that they previously might have deemed unrealistic. Reagan also won the consent of many Democrats, a vital step to victory given that Republicans did not hold the majority in the House of Representatives. On July 29, 1981, in the key vote to adopt the Reagan-backed tax bill as a substitute for the version passed by the Ways and Means Committee, forty-eight Democrats joined a winning coalition with all the Republicans save one to bring Reagan's tax plan closer to enactment.

Throughout the early months of 1981, Reagan continued to frame the tax-cut bill primarily in economic terms. In a nationally televised address on February 5, 1981, that sought to build public support, the president summarized his main argument: "Excessive taxation has robbed us of incentive."[36] His state-of-the-union address two weeks later followed up: "It's time to create new jobs, to build and rebuild industry, and to give the American people room to do what they do best."[37] In a spring speech to a joint session of Congress, the president asked, "Let us not overlook the fact that the small, independent business man or woman creates more than eighty percent of all the new jobs and employs more than half of our total work force. Our across-the-board cut in tax rates for a three-year period will give them much of the incentive and promise of stability they need to go forward with expansion plans calling for additional employees."[38]

Shortly after the tax program's passage into law, a political scientist surveyed members of the House of Representatives about the reasons for their votes. Among supporters, the most common option chosen was "to stimulate the economy."[39] Reagan's framing of the bill, in other words, was accepted by the legislative coalition that passed it. During the debate on the floor of both chambers of Congress, backers again and again contended that passage would bring economic benefits. Given that 77% of the correspondence House members received from constituents endorsed the president's program, this framing seemed to appeal to a broader audience as well.[40] Polls found lower levels of support among the mass public than among citizens who contacted their legislators, but Reagan nonetheless articulated the best case for his proposal and gave it the greatest chance to win wide assent.

Complementing the tax cuts in 1981 was a package of spending cuts that curtailed such programs as Medicaid, housing, job training, food stamps, assistance to states, and Aid to Families with Dependent Children. Reagan continually tied the economic benefits of his agenda to the spending side of the ledger, and the taxation and spending proposals received joint billing in the president's rhetoric. Reagan cited current policies in both domains—"high taxes and excess spending growth"—as the driving forces that "created our present economic mess."[41] Through reforms involving government spending in addition to tax rates, policy changes could "increase our national wealth so all will have more."[42]

Because the spending bill faced heavy opposition, which the tax bill largely avoided, enactment hinged on the rules established for congressional debate and voting. Congressional politics in this instance, as well as within legislatures more generally, cannot be understood without considering institutional rules on such matters as whether amendments are permitted. Backers of the president in Congress quickly perceived that holding the spending cuts together as one omnibus package would be essential for its passage. With the spending cuts collected under one umbrella, Reagan and his allies could argue for their necessity as an economic measure to bolster savings, growth, and job creation. A persuasive economic frame would have been harder to attach to each and every component; instead, specific arguments about the merits of individual measures would have made the spending reductions more difficult to achieve.[43]

After eluding Barry Goldwater's best efforts at reform and revision, public policy changed when subjected to the rhetorical pressure and substantive direction of Ronald Reagan. Not merely a historical footnote, the contrasting rhetoric of the two men contributed to the divergence in their political fortunes. By framing issues in ways congruent with the surrounding economic context, Reagan turned the positions on which his ideological predecessor had failed miserably into winning messages for both electoral campaigns and legislative actions. He ultimately attained most of his goals on taxation but enjoyed considerably less success on government spending. The 1981 spending cuts recouped nowhere near the amount of revenue lost through the tax cuts, an outcome whose consequences I will examine more fully in the next chapter. Still, when the issues of taxes, spending, and government regulation are considered together, rhetorical innovation helped shape Reagan's victories on the same issues where Goldwater fell miles short.

Changing Priorities in Republican Platforms

Some of the rhetorical distinctions between Barry Goldwater and Ronald Reagan were personal or temporary, reflecting their different backgrounds and styles and the unique events during the years when each man received the Republican nomination. For example, the blunt Goldwater pulled no punches when discussing the major issues of the day; Reagan, while no less forceful, was more circumspect in his choice of words. In 1964 Goldwater attempted to build momentum by alleging corruption in the incumbent Johnson administration, whereas Reagan's momentary opportunities in 1980 included the presence of American hostages in Iran. Most of the rhetoric characteristic of the two men, however, transcended personal qualities or temporary occurrences and reflected a response to enduring contexts.

These changes in historical periods extending beyond particular candidates can be seen by examining the full set of Republican platforms spanning the half-century that concluded in 2000. Party platforms fit into a basic template of placing their most pressing issues, programs, and arguments early in the text, relegating less important matters to later sections. To find the themes that the party is highlighting, one can determine for each election the subject of the first substantive section following any preamble, introduction, or declaration of principles. In particular for this book, it is useful to assess whether the lead section deals primarily with the economy or with another topic such as war, foreign policy, rights, freedom, race, or corruption. Economic subjects are defined here to include references to and programs asserted to affect prosperity, employment, prices, growth, inflation, the standard of living, and the health of industries.

From 1948 to 1972 only one of seven Republican platforms began by addressing the economy.[44] Four of the opening sections focused initially on foreign affairs. Of the remaining two, 1948 commenced with praise for the legislative record of the Republican Congress, and the 1968 platform began with a cluster of domestic concerns. During this period the economy usually received attention only after the party made its defining statements on foreign policy, defense, peace, freedom, and the Cold War. In 1960, for example, the lead section concentrated on foreign policy and asserted that the Eisenhower-Nixon administration "has demonstrated that firmness in the face of threatened aggression is the most dependable safeguard of peace." The party promised to check "the global offensive of Communism, increasingly aggressive and violent in its enterprises," and to promote independence for the peoples of Latin America, Asia, Africa, and the Middle East. In 1964 Barry Goldwater likewise focused on foreign affairs and anticommunism, issues representative of rather than exceptions to the priorities during surrounding elections.

This does not imply that Republican candidates from 1948 to 1972 deemed the economy unimportant. Richard Nixon, for instance, believed that economic performance was crucial to recent election outcomes, including his own defeat in 1960.[45] After finally prevailing in 1968, Nixon told aides that decisions on economic matters had to be guided by political considerations, presumably because of the consequences for his public support.[46] Although Nixon perceived his own political fortunes to be intertwined with the economy, my analysis concentrates not on how important the economy was to political leaders' thinking in a general sense but on how central it was to their rhetoric. The question of what is "really" most important to candidates and parties is difficult to determine and, for present purposes, irrelevant. What matters is the prioritizing in publicly expressed advocacy, for inner beliefs cannot exert any impact on an audience unless they are communicated through words, sounds, or images. The economy usually did not receive top billing in Republican platforms during the quarter-century following World War II, nor was it connected rhetorically to a large number of issues. When discussed, the economy tended to play a subordinate and limited role as support for positions on fiscal and monetary policy rather a framing device for a wide range of domestic issues.

Beginning with Gerald Ford's campaign in 1976, the Republican party elevated the economy to the most prominent place in the platform. This change came more than a decade before the end of the Cold War and thus cannot be understood as a response to the dissolution of the Soviet Union. Even after the Cold War heated up in the late 1970s and early 1980s, economic matters remained central within the party's platforms. That level of prioritization reflected the productivity slowdown, wage stagnation, and other financial troubles that began in the early 1970s and continued into succeeding decades. The rhetorical evolution that followed can be seen in six of the seven platforms from 1976 to 2000 that made the economy the centerpiece of the first substantive section.[47] The single exception occurred in 1992, when the Republicans began with an ill-fated pitch for families and family values. The overall trend in platforms is clear: From its status as one of several priorities in the immediate postwar decades, the economy vaulted to the top of the list after the Nixon years.

In other words, the increased prominence of the economy in the 1980 platform was not a unique and temporary aspect of Reagan's efforts to defeat Carter during a time of high inflation, for the decline of economic security was a long-term rather than short-term phenomenon. Problems with slow wage growth, job instability, downsizing, globalization, debt and bankruptcy, and a lack of health insurance have persisted over time. In three-fourths of the polls taken since 1973, the American public cited the economy as the "most important problem" facing the nation. As the data in chapter 3 indicate, the news media devoted far more attention to economic matters from the early 1970s to the present than in the decades immediately following World War II. With economic insecurity at the forefront of people's minds, Republicans adapted messages to audiences by reprioritizing issues and reframing the expressed reasons for their positions.

The Rhetoric of George W. Bush

At the end of the 1990s the economy was performing at its strongest level in thirty years, temporarily dampening many of the fears, frustrations, and anxieties regarding the economy. Any attempt by Republicans to draw further attention to the relatively prosperous times would risk reminding the electorate that the gains had occurred during a Democratic administration. With economic arguments suddenly less effective, especially for Republicans, George W. Bush found other arguments for proposals such as the plan for tax cuts he unveiled at the end of 1999. Bush's most important speech in the campaign of 2000, his convention address accepting his party's nomination, naturally covered this crucial plank of his domestic program. Bush introduced it by saying, "Another test of leadership is tax relief. . . . Today our high taxes fund a surplus. Some say that growing federal surplus means Washington has more money to spend. But they've got it backwards. The surplus is not the government's money; the surplus is the people's money."[48] Bush went on to pledge that he "will act on principle" in promoting tax cuts, with three such principles getting anaphorically spotlighted in the speech: "On principle, every family, every farmer and small-business person should be free to pass on their life's work to those they love. . . . On principle, no one in America should have to pay more than a third of their income to the federal government. . . . On principle, those with the greatest need should receive the greatest help." Bush's convention speech did not make a single claim about the positive consequences of his tax cuts for the economy. Of course, he occasionally made such statements during the lengthy campaign, but in 2000 they were not the featured selling points of his proposal. In 2000, then, economic arguments were less common than Bush's primary themes on taxation and were omitted entirely from his most prominent speech.

With an economic slowdown developing in the fourth quarter of 2000 and first quarter of 2001, strengthening and protecting the economy regained their rhetorical potency and returned to their usual post-1973 position as overarching rationales for many domestic positions. Bush adjusted his rhetoric to take full advantage of the new context. This verbal evolution had reached its conclusion by the time of his weekly radio address on February 3, 2001, in which he announced that he would soon formally submit tax legislation to Congress. Unlike the convention speech, the radio address did not make its case by establishing a set of principles. Instead, Bush opened with a more practical appeal: "Good morning. This coming week I will send to Congress my tax relief plan. It is broad and responsible. It will help our economy, and it is the right thing to do."[49] Within the short body of the message, Bush elaborated:

> There's a lot of talk in Washington about paying down the national debt, and that's good, and that's important. And my budget will do that. But American families have debts to pay, as well. A tax cut now will stimulate our economy and create jobs. The economic news these days is troubling—rising energy prices, layoffs, falling consumer confidence. This is not a time for government to be taking more money than it needs away from the people who buy goods and create jobs.

Note how Bush's focal point during the campaign, where he called the surplus "the people's money," had shifted. Instead, Bush now contrasted the surplus with the debt of American families and, in turn, argued that turning the surplus into tax cuts would stimulate the economy and create jobs.

The reframing carried into the very title of the legislation, "The Economic Growth and Tax Relief Act of 2001." Prior to passage in the House of Representatives, the legislation received one hour of debate on March 8, 2001. In either all or part of their remarks, 71% of the supporters who spoke that day portrayed the legislation as a response to the economic situation facing the country.[50] Under time constraints that typically allowed only one or two paragraphs per speaker, most of those voting yea closely followed the framing reflected in the legislation's title. The most effective way to advocate the legislation involved promising favorable effects on jobs, growth, and prosperity, and House members mirrored the president in stressing the favorable economic consequences they anticipated.

Despite the revised messages American citizens received in 2001 about Bush's tax cuts, the purposes of the proposal had remained constant over the preceding two years. In fact, those purposes could not have changed, for the legislation Bush submitted in 2001 was nearly identical to the plan he offered at the beginning of his campaign back in 1999.[51] The changes came not in the ends he intended to further but in the means of persuasion. Notably, for the rest of his tenure in office, the president's speeches and statements on taxes sounded more like the Bush of 2001 than the Bush of 2000. He pushed for additional tax cuts in the middle years of his first term, contending that they were needed to ensure a healthy economy. Again, Bush's framing of the issue found expression in the title of his legislative initiatives. The "Jobs and Growth Act of 2003" reduced taxes on capital gains, dividends, and small businesses and accelerated the 2001 enactments.

Bush used similar forms of economic rhetoric to marshal support for his proposals in other areas, including education, energy, and trade. The president's state-of-the-union address of 2002, for example, outlined an ambitious domestic agenda for the remainder of his first term:

> When America works, America prospers, so my economic security plan can be summed up in one word: jobs.
>
> Good jobs begin with good schools, and here we've made a fine start. Republicans and Democrats worked together to achieve historic education reform so that no child is left behind. . . .
>
> Good jobs also depend on reliable and affordable energy. This Congress must act to encourage conservation, promote technology, build infrastructure, and it must act to increase energy production at home so America is less dependent on foreign oil.
>
> Good jobs depend on expanded trade. Selling into new markets creates new jobs, so I ask Congress to finally approve trade promotion authority.

Over the course of his administration, Bush presented similar economic arguments when recommending a new program for job training, the curtailment of federal spending, the reauthorization of welfare reform, and the passage of legal reform. On other occasions Bush insisted that the nation's economic vitality required rejecting the Kyoto global warming treaty, establishing a guest worker program, loosening regulations of power plants, and opposing regulations to address repetitive stress injuries in workplaces.

The 2004 Republican platform supporting Bush's reelection, it should be noted, differed from those of the previous quarter-century in that terrorism and national security eclipsed the economy in the setting of priorities. The opening section of the platform, titled "Winning the War on Terror," praised the Bush administration's previous efforts to defeat terrorism and charted future directions for a second term. Economic concerns, captured in the second major section of the platform, were still emphasized but fell a rung on the ladder of priorities. Yet even as the party's prioritizing changed, its framing on domestic issues usually did not. Thus the GOP platform outlined a plan to make America competitive in the global marketplace, pointing to the prospective economic benefits of such policies as the right to work, lower taxes, tax reform, trade agreements, fewer regulations, educational achievement, research and development, an independent energy supply, and limiting government spending. On tort reform, for example, the platform declared: "Junk and frivolous lawsuits are driving up the cost of doing business in America. . . . That is money that could be used to invest and hire new employees." Even the wide wake of an open-ended global war on terror could not alter the party's reliance on economic justifications for its positions on taxation, regulation, the welfare state, and other issues.

Simply stated, then, President Bush's reaction to the terrorist attacks of September 11, 2001, was to change his prioritizing of domestic issues but not his framing; he continued to construct his rhetoric on many domestic policies around the expected economic effects. This response differed from political rhetoric during the first decade of the Cold War, when—as described in chapter 3—political leaders at the federal level framed issues such as education, transportation, and trade around the needs of national defense. In the opening years of the twenty-first century, these issues were discussed largely in economic terms despite the heightened prioritizing of terrorism and national security. With aspects of economic security continuing to bedevil the American population, Republican politicians in federal and state offices connected their domestic proposals to the prospects of additional jobs, higher incomes, and faster growth.

Republicans and the Economy

According to many scholars and journalists, American politics tilted to the right in recent decades because Republicans routinely downplayed the economy and instead focused their attention, particularly during elections, on social and cultural issues. On the contrary, as this chapter has shown, economic issues were continually accentuated in campaign platforms, the state-of-the-state speeches of governors, and the rhetoric of the GOP's presidential candidates. Republican politicians did not hide their economic agenda behind closed doors for fear that the mass public would recoil. Consistently framing policies in economic terms, the party's candidates and officeholders believed their approach would broaden, not narrow, the size of their electoral coalition. Rather than running away from the economy, the GOP made it a higher priority and linked more issues to it.

The conclusions of this chapter, which focus on the construction of political rhetoric, thus complement those in recent works by several other scholars. Larry Bartels carefully examines the common claim, made famous by Thomas Frank's *What's the Matter with Kansas*, that Republicans have been winning elections by using cultural appeals to attract the white working class.[52] Bartels demonstrates that whether class is defined by income or education, the GOP's long-term gains among white working-class voters are almost entirely confined to the South, where the repeal of Jim Crow laws ended the Democratic party's grip on the region. Moreover, economic issues more strongly predict the voting choices of the white working class than do social and cultural issues.[53] Related research by prominent and respected political scientists rejects the assertion that class-based cleavages have diminished or vanished in the American electorate.[54] Given the substantial amount of time and emphasis Republican campaigns have devoted to issues associated with the economy, it should not be surprising that the relationships among income, education, and voting remain robust. The Republicans' rhetorical strategies documented in this chapter raise the question of what the Democrats did in response, the subject I investigate next.

SEVEN

Democrats and the Long Shadow
of Deficit Politics

The writers of the Democratic party's platform in 2000 felt no need to motivate their programmatic initiatives by first invoking a set of abstract principles. Instead, the document moved immediately to practical matters in asserting that the most important purpose of government was to promote a strong economy. The opening paragraph declared emphatically, "This election will be about the big choices we have to make to secure prosperity that is broadly shared and progress that reaches all families in the new American century."[1] The first substantive section then methodically described the policies designed to achieve the sought-after prosperity. By leading off with the economy, the Democrats made their priorities explicit.

In clear contrast, the party's platform a half-century earlier devoted much less attention to the economy and connected relatively few initiatives to it. In 1948 the Democrats opened with a noneconomic appeal, stating that their presidents led the nation to victory against Germany and Japan and joined with other world leaders to establish the United Nations. The text advocated a foreign policy backed by a strong military, international controls against the spread of atomic weapons, humanitarian aid through the Marshall Plan, and the diplomatic recognition of Israel. Later sections addressed the economy by offering measures to combat inflation, reach full employment, achieve higher incomes, and stabilize agricultural production. Overall, though, the economy received only intermittent coverage from the party compared with its central role five decades later.

This difference in the level of attention paid to the economy in the Democratic platforms of 1948 and 2000 was not anomalous but in fact characterized the surrounding elections as well. In only three of the seven post–World War II elections from 1948 to 1972 (43%) did the Democrats focus the first substantive section of their platform on the economy. Instead, issues related to foreign policy and national defense usually occupied the most prominent spot. From 1976 until 2004, by comparison, Democrats began with appeals on jobs, growth, and prosperity in seven of the eight elections (88%). The only exception was in 2004, when economic matters fell to the second slot, behind national security.

The context that precipitated the changing emphases in platforms was a marked increase in economic insecurity. Despite the fact that levels of consumption easily exceeded those of earlier generations, financial anxieties became a daily reality for many Americans. Encapsulated in factors much broader than simply the quantity of goods and services people consumed, or even the size of their incomes, economic insecurity included more job instability, widespread international competition, volatility of income downward as well as upward, and greater problems with the costs of and access to health care. When combined with the expanding perceptions of what constitutes a decent material lifestyle, those problems caused Americans to experience higher levels of debt and personal bankruptcy. Although the oil shocks of the 1970s came and went, these broader trends lasted into succeeding decades.

Earlier chapters identified three possible reactions by political elites to major changes in the context: reprioritizing, reframing, and repositioning. Reprioritizing and reframing are rhetorical responses through which the advocated positions remain constant but the rhetoric publicly offered in support adjusts to the context. Political actors who reprioritize choose to redirect attention toward certain issues and away from others, and those who reframe creatively update the public arguments they advance for any given issue. When political elites undertake the third strategy, repositioning, they move beyond merely revising their rhetoric and instead actually modify their stances.

Elevating the economy to the first section of the Democrats' platform is a clear example of reprioritizing, for it means giving greater emphasis to issues related to the economy. The Republicans undertook the same approach in their platforms and, in fact, reprioritized at both the state and federal levels. Following the increase in economic insecurity, Republican governors spent more time on economic goals in their state-of-the-state speeches. Did Democratic governors follow a similar course of action? To answer that question, I analyzed their speeches using the same procedures and coding the same years as the ones I presented in chapter 6 for Republicans. The results closely conform to the patterns we have already seen: When comparing the years of weak economic growth before 1973 with comparable ones thereafter, the share of sentences describing economic goals in Democrats' state-of-the-state speeches tripled from 7% to 24%. Likewise, in the years of strong growth pre- and post-1973, economic goals doubled from 8% to 17% of the relevant sentences. Paralleling the Republicans, Democratic governors continued to make the economy a high priority even in the boom years of the late 1980s and late 1990s, a wise rhetorical choice given that economic insecurity remained widespread even when GDP grew at a brisk rate.

The Issue Emphases of Presidential Campaign Advertisements

Additional insights into the parties' similar levels of reprioritizing can be gleaned from examining their presidential campaigns, an investigation of which will also illuminate Republicans' long-term gains in electoral strength. As Republicans regularly won elections from the 1980s to the 2000s, political analysts pointed to several potential causes. According to many scholars and popular writers, Republicans triumphed because presidential campaigns concentrated on social and cultural concerns—God, guns, and gays, for short—instead of economic issues. Thus the strategic decision of Republicans to underscore the former themes, combined with the failure of Democrats to refocus attention on bread-and-butter questions that dealt with people's standard of living, created a campaign environment favorable to the GOP. In the words of one political scientist, "politics is now fought largely in terms of social and cultural issues" because that is how the Republicans "chose to contest elections."[2]

Despite its widespread currency, this understanding of campaign dynamics rests upon a shaky foundation. To find out if the parties have pushed economic subjects to the sidelines of their campaigns, I conducted a content analysis of each presidential nominee's advertisements from the beginning of the television era, 1952, through 2004. Paid television ads reveal the issue priorities of a campaign, for those ads, along with speeches, are a means of communication over which candidates and their advisers maintain complete control.[3] Given the need for any successful campaign to "stay on message," a candidate prioritizes certain issues by running more ads on them. When an issue fails to receive any mentions in ads, the candidate has deemphasized it either intentionally or as an inevitable byproduct of focusing his or her attention elsewhere.

The analysis that follows includes all television ads broadcast during the general election campaign, defined to begin on September 1 and conclude the day voters cast their ballots.[4] I coded each ad according to the issues it addressed, using fractions for those covering more than one issue.[5] The issues appearing in the ads are grouped here into five broad categories—foreign affairs, the economy, social welfare issues, social and cultural issues, and a residual category for other topics—along with thirty-nine subcategories.[6] After calculating the distribution of ads for each nominee, I averaged the data for each party for the elections before and after 1973. Table 7.1 shows the results of the classifications, with the figures representing the averages across six and eight nominees, respectively, for each party in the two periods.

Several pertinent observations emerge from the data reported in table 7.1. When comparing the periods 1952–1972 and 1976–2004 on social welfare issues such as Social Security, health care, and education, the figures increased noticeably among Republican candidates (from 10% to 19%) and slightly among Democrats (from 26% to 28%). Meanwhile, the volume of attention given to foreign affairs dropped by half among both Republicans (from 42% to 20%) and Democrats (from 29% to 15%). That result could be predicted from the platforms of the two parties, where foreign affairs typically dominated the opening section during the earlier period but not the later one. In 2004, however, attention to foreign affairs strongly rebounded in the ads of both George W. Bush (39%) and John Kerry (40%).

For the purposes of this book, the most important difference between the two periods is that the share of advertisements about the economy soared among nominees of both parties, from 29% to 49% for Republicans and 30% to 43% for Democrats. During presidential campaigns from 1976 to 2004, television viewers saw innumerable claims and counterclaims about taxes, jobs, growth, inflation, energy, government spending, and the standard of living. The 2004 election registered levels below those of the recent past (20% for Republicans and 30% for Democrats), but the economy still attracted a considerable number of ads. With the rise and persistence of economic insecurity, the parties opted to increase—not decrease—the proportion of ads addressing the economy. From the standpoint of this book, that finding is entirely expected; yet when placed against common beliefs that economic matters faded from the campaign scene, the data are striking.

A related piece of the conventional wisdom, that the parties have increasingly waged their campaigns by emphasizing social and cultural issues, also fails to withstand the evidence. Over the last half-century, that category declined slightly among Republicans (from 14% to 8%) and was stable among Democrats (8% and 9%). George W. Bush's bid for reelection in 2004 did not represent

TABLE 7.1
Issue Priorities in Presidential Campaign Advertisements

	Democratic Percentages 1952–1972	Democratic Percentages 1976–2004	Republican Percentages 1952–1972	Republican Percentages 1976–2004
Foreign affairs	**29**	**15**	**42**	**20**
Military strength/spending	6.7	1.8	6.9	8.3
Arms race/nuclear war	7.7	4.0	1.2	1.5
Korea/Vietnam/Iraq	4.9	2.6	7.6	0.9
Terrorism	0.0	2.1	0.0	3.0
Peace	5.6	0.7	11.1	3.8
Cold War/communism	1.5	0.1	7.3	1.1
Other foreign affairs	2.9	3.3	8.1	1.7
Economy	**30**	**43**	**29**	**49**
General	2.5	4.7	1.1	5.4
Deficit/balanced budgets	0.0	4.3	0.6	3.7
Taxes	4.4	10.4	7.0	10.9
Trade/international competition	0.2	2.9	0.7	0.6
Agriculture	3.2	0.3	0.8	0.9
Inflation/prices/interest rates	3.7	2.3	5.8	9.7
Jobs/unemployment/job training	4.9	10.0	2.2	7.8
Standard of living/incomes/ min. wage	4.2	2.9	5.4	2.3
Government spending/waste	0.3	2.7	4.2	5.8
Other economy	6.9	2.9	0.9	2.1
Social welfare issues	**26**	**28**	**10**	**19**
Social Security/pensions	4.6	5.2	4.6	3.6
Medicare	8.1	3.3	0.1	2.9
Education	5.4	6.4	2.3	6.4
Welfare/poverty	4.4	4.3	0.9	0.9
Health care	0.6	6.1	0.5	4.1
Housing	1.4	0.0	0.3	0.0
Cities	1.2	0.7	0.8	0.0
Other social welfare issues	0.0	2.1	0.0	0.7
Social and cultural issues	**8**	**9**	**14**	**8**
Crime	1.8	2.8	11.1	2.3
Drugs	0.8	2.8	0.0	3.6
Moral breakdown	0.0	0.0	0.0	0.4
Church and state	0.2	0.8	0.0	0.2
Abortion	0.0	0.2	0.0	0.3
Gay rights	0.0	0.0	0.0	0.0
First Amendment	0.0	0.0	0.0	0.5
Gun control	0.0	1.0	0.0	0.4
Judicial appointments	0.0	0.1	0.0	0.1
Civil rights/desegregation	4.9	0.8	2.9	0.2
Other social and cultural issues	0.2	0.0	0.0	0.3
Other	**7**	**4**	**6**	**4**
Environment	0.5	2.3	0.4	1.0
Corruption	4.1	0.2	4.7	0.6
Miscellaneous	2.4	1.5	0.4	1.3

a reversal on this score, for his campaign's attention to social and cultural issues fell below the Republican average in the post-1972 elections. Across the two periods under study, most mentions of social and cultural issues centered on crime, drugs, and civil rights. The issues arousing the strongest passions on the Christian right—church and state, abortion, gay rights, and judicial appointments—rarely appear in campaign ads.

Of course, this does not imply that campaigns bypassed entirely the cluster of issues important to Christian conservatives. Candidates' stances on those issues are typically communicated to targeted groups, under the radar screen of a broader public, through churches, direct mail, and word of mouth. Still, judged by the messages constructed for a broad cross section of voters, those on which electoral majorities are built, the choices of presidential candidates came through loud and clear: The economy stood out as the highest rhetorical priority from 1976 to 2004. Some conceptions of what it means to be part of the "economic issues" cluster would subsume not only those classified here under "the economy" but also those labeled "social welfare issues." Policy areas such as Social Security, Medicare, and housing certainly contain economic dimensions and are commonly labeled as such by scholars. Whether one prefers a restricted definition, as I used earlier, or an encompassing one that includes social welfare issues, economic matters greatly increased their share of the references among both Republicans and Democrats.

The results of my analysis of campaign advertisements thus reinforce the conclusions drawn from governors' state-of-the-state speeches and party platforms. During campaigns and while governing, the parties reacted to greater economic insecurity by reprioritizing the economy, thereby pursuing the same approach in one key respect. Yet on the other two responses to an altered context—reframing and repositioning—the parties sharply diverged. As chapter 6 documented, politicians from the GOP paired their reprioritizing with a strong dose of reframing. The current chapter will show that leaders from the Democratic party, by contrast, turned more often to repositioning as a second response to the new context. The course of policy and elections in recent times can thus be stated succinctly: Republicans—with an important exception described in the following section—largely changed their *arguments*, whereas Democrats changed their *positions*.

The origins and consequences of these strategies are complicated stories. For this reason, the rest of the chapter will cover a substantial amount of ground, spanning such areas as Republican positions, Democratic positions, and public opinion on deficits. By the end of the chapter, the relationships of these matters to each other, as well as to the policy and electoral changes I seek to explain in this book, will be apparent. To understand why the Democrats did not follow the Republicans by reframing and instead adopted a posture of repositioning, I first examine the cascade of political effects instigated by arguably the most influential politician of the last half-century, Ronald Reagan.

Republicans and Balanced Budgets

As chapter 6 revealed, Ronald Reagan embraced largely the same policy positions as Barry Goldwater but separated himself from his fellow westerner by advocating those positions through different forms of rhetoric. In one area, however, Reagan did alter a trademark stance of his ideological predecessor. Faithfully staking a hard-earned reputation and career on championing balanced budgets, Goldwater during the 1950s assailed the relatively small deficits incurred in some years by the Eisenhower administration.[7] When President Kennedy later stated that deficits could boost aggregate demand and thereby expand the nation's payrolls, the Arizona senator countered that "deficit spending is not now and never has been the answer to unemployment."[8] The conservative icon loudly and repeatedly called for lower and flatter taxes, but the principle of balanced budgets took precedence: To preserve fiscal responsibility, Goldwater declared forcefully, "spending cuts must come before tax cuts."[9]

Although Reagan in the 1980 presidential campaign also proposed balancing the budget, he thoroughly transformed the means of achieving it. Reagan's supply-side philosophy allowed him to reconcile his promises that "We must balance the budget, reduce tax rates and restore our defenses."[10] Cutting taxes and simultaneously opening a new line of expenditure would seem to make balancing the budget impossible—unless the tax reductions would increase, not decrease, federal revenues. Like Goldwater, Reagan desired spending cuts that would contribute to balancing the budget, holding that "Waste, extravagance, abuse and outright fraud in Federal agencies and programs must be stopped."[11] His main difference with Goldwater lay in the supply-side philosophy, which, as a practical matter, meant that progress on the spending side of the ledger need not be achieved before moving on taxation.

After triumphing in the 1980 election, Reagan quickly sought to enact his tax program into law and used the opening months of his administration to mobilize public and congressional support. With the assistance of many Democrats, Congress expanded the president's bill and added to its costs. Reagan won some decreases in domestic spending in 1981, especially on programs benefiting low-income citizens, but the savings were considerably smaller than those lost through tax cuts. On other federal spending, once in office Reagan had to specify the waste, fraud, and abuse he wanted to eliminate, an undertaking that brought little relief to the federal treasury. His 1981 budget lowered the forecasted deficit for future years through what came to be known as the "magic asterisk," which stood for "future savings to be identified."[12] As history would soon show, the requisite savings never materialized. Meanwhile, entitlement programs grew markedly during the 1980s, making the deficits a product of social spending as well as tax cuts and defense increases. Goldwater never forgave Reagan for abandoning the traditional prescription of ensuring spending cuts before proceeding to implement tax cuts. "Had I been in Reagan's place," the retired senator remarked in 1993, "this country never would have gone $3 trillion in debt."[13]

Reagan's expectations and tactics on the deficit have long sparked controversy. Senator Daniel Patrick Moynihan once accused him of intentionally creating a large deficit to bludgeon Congress into curtailing domestic programs, an approach later dubbed "starve-the-beast." Reagan certainly recognized the usefulness of deficits as a political tool; in his 1980 campaign and later as president, he often metaphorically and mirthfully warned that Congress would not restrain spending until its allowance shrank. The available evidence suggests, however, that Reagan desired not actual deficits but rather the prospect of potential deficits.[14] For example, he signed into law tax increases during his first term, especially a large one in 1982 that offset part of the revenue losses from the tax cuts of 1981. Although it is difficult to ascertain politicians' deepest beliefs, there is good reason to believe he was genuine in espousing supply-side reasoning and expected his tax cuts to contribute to, rather than detract from, a balanced budget. Such faith was not new to Reagan: As early as 1958, nearly a decade before his entry into politics, he articulated the central supply-side claim that cutting tax rates would increase tax revenues.[15] A perennial optimist who spoke in anecdotes and aphorisms, Reagan easily could have believed that tax cuts would pay for themselves.

Whereas Reagan seemed to be a true believer, some of his intellectual allies in the 1980 campaign pointed instead to the electoral advantages of tax cuts, even those that might push budget deficits to new heights. An editorial in *National Review* lamented that the previous insistence on balanced budgets had devastated the GOP's public standing:

> During the past thirty years of inflation the Republicans championed The Balanced Budget while the Democrats denied there was a problem. The budget could of course be balanced either by reducing expenditures or by increasing taxes. The Republicans sturdily but blindly advocated both, became famous as The Enemy of the Little Guy, and dwindled to a permanent minority in Washington.[16]

The political case for tax cuts could be put in even stronger terms. Skeptical of supply-side economics, Irving Kristol nevertheless summarized its electoral appeal for Republicans in an opinion piece published on May 16, 1980, shortly after Reagan offered a revised version of the Kemp-Roth tax cuts then circulating in Congress. The allure of Kemp-Roth was overwhelming despite, or even because of, its potential for causing gaping deficits:

> when in office the liberals (or social-democrats, as they should more properly be called) will always spend generously, regardless of budgetary considerations, until the public permits the conservatives an interregnum in which to clean up the mess—but with the liberals retaining their status as the activist party, the party of the "natural majority." The neo-conservatives have decided that two can play at this game—and must, since it is the only game in town. . . . And what if the traditionalist-conservatives are right and a Kemp-Roth tax cut, without corresponding cuts in expenditures, also leaves us with a fiscal problem? The neo-conservative is willing to leave those problems to be coped with by liberal interregnums. He wants to shape the future, and will leave it up to his opponents to tidy up afterwards.[17]

Within the strategic stance that Kristol endorsed, balanced budgets are for chumps. Why not let the other party take the tough stands and suffer the voters' wrath at election time? In the quotation here, Kristol did not outline a starve-the-beast approach to shrinking the federal government. Instead he described, albeit with wording not quite so bald, a starve-the-Democrats plan for winning elections. He assumed that whoever takes the initiative in distributing largesse, whether in the form of reducing taxes or increasing expenditures, holds an inherent advantage in earning the loyalties of voters. If the Republicans could become more assertive in delivering benefits to the electorate, they could reverse a long period in the political wilderness. Meanwhile, with the Democrats having lost their "natural majority" and ruling only during infrequent "liberal interregnums," they would become the janitors reduced to cleaning up budget messes left by Republicans.

In the next presidential contest and over the following two decades, the advice of Irving Kristol proved prescient. When Reagan ran for reelection in 1984, the opposition seized on the deficits just as Kristol had predicted. The Democrats soon became stern advocates of fiscal responsibility who curtailed the scale and scope of their domestic proposals. While confronting the deficit appeared to benefit one of the party's presidential candidates, Bill Clinton, a closer examination will reveal the mixed legacy he left for policy and for subsequent Democratic nominees. The budgetary repositioning of the parties thus created two effects: it shifted policy to the right and undermined the Democrats' electoral fortunes. My investigation of the causes and consequences of the Democrats' move toward fiscal restraint begins with Walter Mondale's ill-fated 1984 campaign, and then I turn to Clinton's emergence as candidate and president.

Walter Mondale and the Embrace of Deficit Reduction

One can easily score political points in the short term by attacking the opposition for being fiscally irresponsible. The notion that government budgets should be balanced holds such strong public resonance that only the most restrained politicians forgo this line of criticism when it is available to them. In the early 1980s prominent Democrats saw their opening and routinely blamed Reagan for the escalating deficits, but the Democrats' shift on the issue actually predated his tenure in office. During the 1976 campaign Jimmy Carter had criticized Gerald Ford for overseeing, during his first full year in office, deficits "larger than all the Kennedy-Johnson years combined."[18] Believing that government expenditures contributed to inflation, Carter as president attempted to keep spending in check.

Notwithstanding these antecedents in the rhetoric and policies of Carter, the Democrats' standard-bearer in the 1984 election crafted the most ambitious response to the deficit. Walter Mondale famously pledged to diminish the deficit by raising taxes, a promise widely deemed political suicide after Reagan breezed to an easy victory in November. Although Mondale's maneuver appeared foolish in retrospect, he possessed few good alternatives on which to base his campaign. By the time the Democratic nominee drew his line in the sand in the summer of 1984, Reagan's team had already signaled a campaign of "Morning in America," which would use the economic recovery to claim that America was surging forward with newfound confidence and energy. Throughout the first three years of Reagan's term, the economy ranged from average to downright abysmal, the 1982 recession being the deepest the nation had experienced since the Depression. During the election year of 1984, though, the recovery appeared robust and resilient. The timing worked to the Republicans' advantage because economic performance during an election year affects an incumbent's prospects for reelection more than do conditions during the previous three years.[19] Ironically, the depth of the downturn in 1982 made the ensuing rebound seem stronger by comparison and indirectly bolstered Reagan's chances.

Perhaps Mondale could have ignored the economy by finding other topics on which to concentrate in his speeches, advertisements, interviews, and press briefings. Yet with Reagan asserting that jobs were returning, businesses forming, and incomes rising, trying to change the subject probably would have failed. Likewise, any attempt by the former Minnesota senator and vice president to assert that the recovery was weak and fragile would have contradicted some widely recognized facts: Despite a high unemployment rate, many economic indicators showed a positive direction of change. Given that trying to shift attention away from the economy seemed unlikely to succeed, Mondale may have done better with voters—it is hard to imagine him doing worse—by avoiding the subject of tax increases and instead offering new economic programs on education, job training, industrial policy, and infrastructure development.[20] Of course, the viability of alternative campaign approaches cannot be known with certainty and can only be surmised through counterfactual reasoning.

Whether or not a different strategy would have been more effective, Mondale's gambit seemed at the time a plausible choice for attracting voters. The deficit issue stood among the few on which Reagan had violated a specific campaign promise. Mondale worked to make budget deficits a credibility test, where his own forthrightness in offering bold action would be contrasted with Reagan's delay of a much-needed response until after the election. In the most noteworthy and repeated words from his convention acceptance speech, Mondale implored the nation:

> Here is the truth about the future: We are living on borrowed money and borrowed time. These deficits hike interest rates, clobber exports, stunt investment, kill jobs, undermine growth, cheat our kids, and shrink our future.
>
> Whoever is inaugurated in January, the American people will have to pay Mr. Reagan's bills. The budget will be squeezed. Taxes will go up. And anyone who says they won't is not telling the truth.
>
> I mean business. By the end of my first term, I will cut the deficit by two-thirds.
>
> Let's tell the truth: Mr. Reagan will raise taxes, and so will I. He won't tell you. I just did.[21]

Mondale went on to vow that his tax increases would concentrate on the rich, compared with Reagan's intention to burden average Americans.

One could interpret Mondale's behavior as reflecting a sincere belief that deficits posed a looming threat to the U.S. economy. Many mainstream economists believed so then and now, and Mondale may well have found the force of their evidence compelling. Whatever his inner beliefs, he acted as though he thought the issue would help him carry the election. Had he been taking stands merely to satisfy some campaign contributors, his ideal tactics would have involved privately assuring deficit reduction but publicly focusing on the issues that would win over the electorate. Mondale's actions imply, to the contrary, that he expected his words and deeds to swing flesh-and-blood voters to his side. In speeches, advertisements, and televised debates, he regularly highlighted the deficit and the economy, a move he surely would not have taken had he anticipated no electoral payoff.[22]

Mondale's strategy, which he apparently believed could be

effective with voters, ended up failing miserably. Exit polls conducted by the *Los Angeles Times* asked respondents to choose up to two issues that were important in determining their votes. Showing a potential opening for the Democrats, the second most numerous answer was the federal budget deficit. Among those who mentioned it, though, Mondale won only a narrow 52%–48% majority. After all of Mondale's campaign themes stressing his honesty in recognizing the problem and attacking Reagan's evasiveness, the deficit worked only slightly in the challenger's favor. Among the roughly equal numbers of exit poll respondents choosing government spending as a crucial voting issue, Reagan dominated with a 69%-31% majority, and he prevailed even more strongly, by 80%–20%, among those citing taxes.[23]

Thus one piece of repositioning by Republicans—accepting deficits if that was the price for enacting tax cuts—stimulated an even greater amount of repositioning by Democrats. The repositioning began with Mondale himself, for at earlier points in his political career he had minimized the threat of deficits and actually praised them for stimulating the economy. Reagan's own reversal on the issue notwithstanding, the president used his speech accepting the Republican nomination and later the televised debates to chastise Mondale's inconsistency.[24] Raising the rhetorical ante, Reagan followed up on the campaign trail by contrasting on several occasions what he called "the old Mondale" and "the new Mondale."[25] In the president's rendition of his opponent's motivations, Mondale's recent warnings about the dangers of deficits were opportunistic and hypocritical.

Beyond the risk that a late-career conversion would undermine his credibility, Mondale's stance on fiscal responsibility meant that he could propose very little in the way of new spending. Some analysts of American politics have called him "an unreconstructed New Dealer," a common though inaccurate perception.[26] Bill Clinton later became the candidate remembered for breaking with his party's past, but the changes in the party's presidential wing—at least on budgetary matters—began eight years earlier. Mondale proposed to create a Deficit Reduction Trust Fund to which the tax increases, by law, would be directed and would be used only for that purpose. The relatively small amounts the Democratic nominee requested for new programs would be funded by cuts in other areas.

Mondale's response to the deficit thus boxed him into a corner. It forced him to propose raising taxes, never a popular move, and he did not even receive the political benefit from policies he otherwise could have offered to address problems in transportation, job training, health care, and education. Under Mondale's leadership Democrats became the party of austerity, pledging to make difficult decisions to protect the nation's future prosperity. Reagan, meanwhile, insisted that no such decisions were needed. As conventional political wisdom holds, and as Irving Kristol and *National Review* expressed in plain words, a party giving tax cuts or higher spending to the electorate gains an edge over a competitor insisting on belt-tightening. In the span of just a few years, a previously unimaginable transformation occurred: The parties switched places on who embraced fiscal restraint most tightly and thus who held the unpopular position.

Walter Mondale's repositioning of the Democrats carried through to the party's next two candidates, Michael Dukakis and Bill Clinton. All three men promised to reduce the deficit, saying that renewed fiscal discipline would restore the nation's competitiveness in international markets and boost the economy at home. Dukakis did not commit to a specific target, but Mondale and Clinton sought reductions to the deficit of two-thirds and one-half, respectively, during a four-year term. The candidates differed somewhat on taxes, with Mondale calling for tax hikes on everyone earning more than $25,000 a year (the median family income that year was $22,000), compared with Clinton's proposal of increases only for high earners, which would be combined with a tax cut for the middle class.[27] Overall, the economic programs of the three nominees were similar, and in the next section I trace the development of Clinton's actions and the fallout from the party's repositioning.

Deficit Reduction, the 1992 Campaign, and Clinton's Presidency

By 1992 the nation had witnessed a decade of large deficits punctuated by intermittent attempts to control them. The issue's continued prominence helped propel Paul Tsongas into a contender for the Democratic nomination in 1992. Initially he gained legitimacy by countering the conventional expectation of candidates who overpromise and pander to the voters, a stance summarized by his tagline "I'm not Santa Claus." The budget deficit was the leading issue for the former Massachusetts senator, and his detailed proposal to shrink it brought him news coverage filled with adjectives such as "earnest" and "sincere." Tsongas won the pivotal New Hampshire contest, along with a handful of other primaries and caucuses, before falling out of the race.

The mantle of deficit reduction then passed to the independent candidate H. Ross Perot, whose on-again, off-again campaign added excitement and unpredictability to the election. Perot's initial surge in the spring of 1992 was closely tied to his willingness to tackle the budget deficit. In the last month before Election Day, he introduced a creative dimension to modern campaigning by purchasing airtime to broadcast thirty- and sixty-minute infomercials where, using handheld charts and graphs, he explained his plan to bring the budget into balance. Confirming his message's resonance with the public, the prime-time infomercials commonly rang up higher Nielsen ratings than the programming on competing networks.[28] At certain points during the campaign, it appeared that the Texas billionaire held a realistic chance of winning the presidency.

It was in that environment that Clinton eventually clarified and strengthened his position on the deficit. His evolution can be seen in three documents he released during 1992: "A Plan for America's Future" (January); "Fighting for the Forgotten Middle Class" (March); and "Putting People First" (June).[29] The first two documents, produced during his bid to win the Democratic nomination, made no mention of the deficit. Instead, Clinton stressed his efforts to revive the economy through measures involving education, transportation, research and development, job training, and middle-class tax cuts. "A Plan for America's Future" and "Fighting for the Forgotten Middle Class" reflect Clinton's personal and political beliefs up through the primaries. Without compelling political motivations for advocating deficit reduction, one can infer, Clinton preferred a different course.

By the time the Arkansas governor released the thirty-three-page campaign manifesto "Putting People First," Perot had posed a significant challenge to both major parties.[30] Sidestepping the deficit no longer seemed politically viable, and Clinton climbed on board by assuring the nation that he would cut the deficit in half in four years. Meeting that goal required curtailing his domestic proposals, a necessity he deeply regretted at the time.[31] Shortly after the election, where Perot's vote tally of 19% exceeded that of any other third-party or independent candidate in eighty years, the wily businessman moved to turn his momentum into a permanent organization, United We Stand, to influence policy. Clinton could reasonably expect that Perot would continue to apply pressure on the federal government to reduce the deficit. It was therefore incumbent on the new president to take the issue seriously and address it squarely.

During the transition period before taking office, Clinton hosted an economic summit where he welcomed analysis and advice from a variety of business leaders and economists. Many participants pleaded the case for lowering the deficit.[32] The president-elect met with Alan Greenspan, the chairman of the Federal Reserve Board, who also urged a course of fiscal prudence. Decreasing the deficit, Greenspan reasoned, would allow the nation's central bank to take complementary actions that would stimulate the economy through a loose monetary policy. It is possible that Clinton never intended to follow through on his campaign promise but changed his mind after the summit and his meeting with Greenspan. A more plausible interpretation is that the events of the transition solidified the budgetary approach he had already publicly embraced during the campaign. The key moment came when, under threat from Perot's candidacy, Clinton made the initial pledge to cut the deficit in half.

Deficit reduction can become an appealing campaign issue under the right conditions. Despite bringing few benefits to Mondale in 1984, in 1992 the issue bolstered the candidacies of both Tsongas and Perot. Clinton's experiences, however, demonstrate the differences between sometimes-popular campaign statements and the reality of meting out the pain once in office. In 1993 the incoming president had to confront the fact that parts of his economic proposals, even in the scaled-down versions that evolved during the campaign, were inconsistent with others. To meet his deficit-reduction target, Clinton needed to restrain spending, increase taxes, or both. To make matters worse, deficit projections for future years grew throughout 1992. Shortly before taking office, the new president learned that the projected budget to be written four years later, the one on which he would campaign for reelection, was forecasted to result in a deficit $68 billion larger than the previous estimate by the Office of Management and Budget.[33]

In those early days and weeks of his presidency, Clinton and his advisers made the decisions that would define the administration for the upcoming years. One crucial choice involved health care reform, the most ambitious policy initiative of the first term. The formation of his proposal was intimately connected to the budgetary process because his steadfast position on reducing the deficit meant that the wheels of health care reform could not be greased by government spending. Instead, savings from elsewhere in the health care system would pay for subsidizing the insurance of citizens falling outside the proposed mandates for employer-provided coverage. Achieving the necessary savings required establishing a strong regulatory apparatus to control health care costs, which added greatly to the complexity of the proposal. The bureaucratic and regulatory elements of the 1,342-page behemoth of a bill then served as the focal point of opposition mounted by trade associations, think tanks, and Republican leaders of Congress.[34] It is not difficult to imagine a differently designed bill, with greater prospects of passing, had revenues from the budget been available to help finance the effort.

Even outside of health care, Clinton in his first term operated under tight limits that led him either to ignore entirely or propose in weakened form most of the economic agenda from his 1992 campaign that would enlarge the deficit. On education, the unfulfilled commitments included boosting the funding of Head Start to cover all eligible children, guaranteeing a college education for everyone willing to devote two years to national service, and establishing a national apprenticeship program. For constructing new infrastructure, the abandoned pledge was a "Rebuild America" fund with $20 billion per year.[35] The new president also left on the cutting-room floor his campaign pledge to reduce taxes on the middle class. Clinton's request for short-term spending as an economic stimulus failed in the Senate, but one of his closest advisers doubted that the small sum would have made much difference anyway.[36] Even as his early budgets offered modest increases in spending on highways, apprenticeships, Head Start, scientific research, and national service, the total allotted funding was nowhere near the levels Clinton had vowed while campaigning for the presidency.

By contrast, most of Clinton's actions that fulfilled the promises of his economic program of 1992 flowed from the imperative to cut the deficit in half in four years. These proposals either had no direct and immediate effect on the budget, and hence could be done "on the cheap," or actually helped lower the deficit. In the former category, Clinton not only pushed the North American Free Trade Agreement (NAFTA) through Congress but also backed a new installment of the General Agreement on Tariffs and Trade (GATT), U.S. entry into the World Trade Organization, and permanent most-favored-nation trading status for China. Among his enactments consistent with his goal of decreasing the deficit, Clinton signed a 1993 budget including three minor revenue sources along with higher marginal rates on corporations and high earners. The legislation raised the top marginal income tax rate on individuals to 39.6%, a change that generated the lion's share of the additional revenues in his administration.

In the end Clinton's program for job creation and economic growth featured two primary pieces: shrinking the deficit (and, in his second term, balancing the budget) and signing trade agreements. That combination proved deadly to Democratic prospects in the 1994 midterm elections. Interestingly, Clinton himself anticipated that his policies would undercut the party's congressional wing; he did not believe that issues with economic components were sideshows to social and cultural questions as determinants of election outcomes. In a meeting of administration officials early in the president's first year, he stated that Democratic members of Congress were "crazy" for thinking they could avoid an electoral backlash from the 1993 budget and the NAFTA and GATT agreements.[37] Clinton was well known during his political career for having his finger on the pulse of the public, and so his perceptions on these matters are worthy of note. According to research by political scientists, Clinton's fears were accurate: The subsequent scholarly analyses of David Brady and his colleagues indicated that supporting the president's positions greatly increased Democratic incumbents' probability of defeat, and voting for the 1993 budget resolution and the tax increase was especially likely to incite electoral opposition.[38] Of course, a comprehensive account of the 1994 elections would require additional analyses and would consider a broad range of issues and factors. Clinton's economic program did not single-handedly cause the Republican takeover of Congress, but it certainly contributed to this remarkable political event.

One of the great ironies of the early 1990s was that Clinton himself had won election in the aftermath of the last aggressive attempt to rein in the deficit. Like Clinton, George H. W. Bush steered a deficit-reduction package through Congress; and like those of Clinton, Bush Sr.'s actions largely reflected political necessity rather than deep convictions. With the Gramm-Rudman-Hollins Act in effect, the elder Bush had to choose among three undesirable alternatives: He could allow the across-the-board reductions in spending the legislation mandated, propose equally sized program cutbacks of his own, or negotiate a package of tax increases and spending cuts that required breaking his famous "no new taxes" promise from the 1988 campaign. Bush settled on the third option, with politically disastrous consequences that—as the next chapter shows in more detail—tarnished his party's economic image. Whether the other two alternatives would have proven any better for Bush Sr. is impossible to answer with any certainty, for all three options involved bringing pain to the American populace.

The challenges posed by deficits were not unique to Bush but, in fact, confront all politicians who want to maintain the public's approval during times of budgetary stress. The vast majority of federal spending funds relatively popular programs such as defense, health care, and Social Security rather than unpopular ones such as welfare and foreign aid. With the exception of defense, the former programs—along with others such as education, transportation, and environmental protection—consistently attract majorities in public opinion polls for increasing rather than decreasing spending, and those majorities do not diminish during times of large deficits. As the 1980s unfolded, for example, the level of public support for increased spending on domestic programs expanded rather than contracted.[39] That is not to say that the public prefers deficits outright. In the abstract, a situation in which government expenditures exceed revenues contrasts sharply with what most people understand, based on experiences with their own family budgets, to be responsible finance.[40] Thus when asked whether they would favor tax cuts or higher spending if either could be achieved only by creating deficits, majorities of Americans answer no for both alternatives.[41]

When large deficits already exist, the conflict between abstract principles and concrete programs becomes especially pronounced. Neither raising taxes nor cutting expensive programs such as middle-class entitlements win majority support as a means of diminishing the deficit. Political scientists find that public opinion often seems contradictory in that people desire more government services, oppose higher taxes, and dislike budget deficits.[42] Needless to say, these preferences cannot all be satisfied simultaneously. Reacting to the prevailing constraints and opportunities in public opinion, pragmatic politicians therefore criticize deficits and sometimes endorse procedural mechanisms that signal a concern with the seriousness of the problem, all while refraining from proposing or voting for the necessary tax hikes or spending cuts. Talking about reducing deficits can be popular under certain circumstances; actually doing it jeopardizes the public standing of presidents and members of Congress alike. The political advantage accrues to those who create deficits, not to those later forced to restore order by making specific decisions to increase revenues or decrease expenditures.[43] Parents have never won favor from their children by chiding them to "eat your peas," and politicians expressing the political equivalent fare no better at the hands of the electorate.

Bill Clinton, ever the astute politician, obtained in 1994 a glimpse of what his 1992 opponent must have felt: the harsh payback for a course of deficit reduction that many political elites believed to be the right thing to do. Following the 1994 election, when Republican challengers successfully campaigned by tying incumbent Democrats to his record, Clinton seemed destined for the same fate as the elder Bush before him. Meanwhile, bolstered by the idealism and discipline of congressional members first elected in 1994, the Republican party during the period of Newt Gingrich's speakership returned to its roots from earlier in the century by pressing to move all the way to a balanced budget. With the better budgetary situation brought about by the deficit reduction that Bush Sr. and Clinton engineered, the Republicans of 1995 could offer tax cuts that might ease the bitter pill of cutbacks in government spending. The congressional budgets of 1995 targeted a number of programs, including welfare, farm subsidies, Medicaid, and pensions for federal employees, but public attention gravitated to a proposed $270 billion decrease in future Medicare expenditures. Clinton, in turn, declared the Republican cuts extreme and vetoed the budget reconciliation bill. The failure of Clinton and the Republican Congress to reach an agreement culminated in two government shutdowns and stopgap measures to keep the government solvent.

Clinton's own political fortunes rebounded in 1996 with assistance from public perceptions of congressional overreach.

Whereas in early 1995 his reelection had appeared unlikely, he easily triumphed over Senator Robert Dole the next year. The difficulties posed by a Congress controlled by the opposition party, though, may have weakened the possibility of returning to some of the policies cast aside during his first term. Even as budgetary pressures lessened in the succeeding years, Clinton's record included few of his original proposals on education, worker training, transportation, and research and development. Notwithstanding his eventual delivery of the promised tax credit for children through a 1997 agreement with the Republican leadership of Congress, the core of his economic program remained fiscal responsibility and free trade.

This repositioning of the Democratic party, begun by Carter and Mondale and then carried to completion by Clinton, pushed policy to the right because it ruled out support for an extensive welfare state.[44] Earlier generations of Democrats sought to strengthen the social safety net and expand benefits for workers, policy directions now either taken off the table or, in the case of health care reform, difficult to achieve without more government spending. To make matters worse for the party, its repositioning failed to solve persistent electoral troubles—an outcome explored in more depth in the next chapter. My data in chapter 8 indicate that Clinton was fortunate to campaign for office during one of the rare moments of the last three decades when the public trusted Democrats to manage the economy more than they did Republicans. As soon as Congress began deliberating over Clinton's first budget containing tax increases and spending cuts, however, the public returned to favoring Republicans over Democrats as stewards of the economy.

Deficit Politics under George W. Bush

On broad approaches to addressing the deficit, the Republicans during George W. Bush's first term of 2001–2004 resembled the party of Reagan more than the party of Gingrich. Whereas the

Gingrich-era Republicans sought to pair tax cuts with spending cuts, Bush focused primarily on the taxation side in his opening years. In 2001 and 2003 he won enactment of broad-ranging tax cuts that exceeded Reagan's in terms of both the revenue losses and the upward distribution of the benefits. Even before September 11 and its associated spending, Bush's Office of Management and Budget projected that the president's tax cuts would soon require dipping into the Social Security Trust Fund to offset deficits elsewhere in the budget. In later years Bush differed from Reagan in reacting to deficits not by embracing some tax increases and spending reductions, as had the former president, but by proposing new tax cuts that enlarged the deficit.

With the onset of the 2004 campaign, these deficits forced John Kerry to a situation similar in some respects to that of Walter Mondale in 1984. Large deficits persuaded Kerry, like Mondale before him, to ask for tax increases that the opposition consistently attacked throughout the campaign. The Iraq war and terrorism topped the agenda in 2004, however, making economic issues less central to the candidates' rhetoric than they had been in the 1984 contest. Still, the budget deficit constrained Kerry's possibilities, and he offered, by historical standards, a limited domestic platform. The Massachusetts senator even promised that he would restrict his domestic programs further if that proved necessary to addressing the deficit. Had he won the election, the rightward trend in policy in economic areas probably would have continued, albeit at a slower pace.

Starve the Democrats, Revisited

The turn to the right in public policy from the 1970s to the present, these chapters have demonstrated, resulted from the parties' responses and counterresponses. At its core the transformation was simple and straightforward: Through reprioritizing, reframing, and repositioning, the parties departed from the policy approaches of the period from the New Deal through the Great

Society. In recent decades Republicans responded to economic insecurity largely by changing their arguments, whereas Democrats changed their positions. How this happened is a story of political, economic, and rhetorical change, of mass politics and elite politics, and of policy decisions and election results that brought important consequences to Americans' daily lives.

As my analyses have shown, the move to the right in public policy gained momentum when Ronald Reagan repositioned the Republican party to press for tax cuts first and spending cuts of corresponding size, if at all, later. Reagan's rhetoric of tying tax cuts to prosperity developed after the rise and persistence of economic insecurity and borrowed from the conservatives' invigorated intellectual infrastructure, which publicized the doctrines of supply-side economics. The resulting deficits, along with new ones in the early part of the twenty-first century, tempted Walter Mondale, Michael Dukakis, Bill Clinton, and John Kerry to critique the GOP for reckless financial management. Al Gore was so wedded to this strategy that he reacted to the large budget surpluses of 2000 not by offering bold domestic initiatives but by pledging to retire the nation's previous debt. Regardless of whether President Reagan intended it, the genius of his political and rhetorical moves lay in leading so many Democrats to believe that their newfound commitment to fiscal responsibility was both desirable on the merits and an effective stance for gaining political advantage.

Over a longer period, deficits amounted to an irresistible bait that created precisely the effects Irving Kristol had expected. Besides moving policy to the right by allowing Republican tax cuts, fiscal restraint starved the Democratic party by blocking the proposal or enactment of potential initiatives to alleviate economic insecurity, even those on which Bill Clinton had campaigned. After embracing deficit reduction as its central economic plank, the Democratic party became what Kristol called a "liberal interregnum" that dealt with the budgetary problems it inherited rather than proactively offering a popular and far-reaching agenda of its own. In one of his most important legacies, Ronald Reagan set in motion processes that would severely curtail the Democrats' maneuvering room.

A final piece of the puzzle serves to reinforce the evidence and interpretations I have presented thus far. The following chapter documents and discusses the parties' respective economic reputations and assesses their electoral implications. Those reputations, we will see, routinely bolstered the GOP's electoral appeal. Rather than representing an electoral advantage for Democrats, as many political observers assume, the economy since the 1970s usually favored Republicans.

EIGHT

The Republicans' Electoral Edge on the Economy

In the early stages of his campaign for the 2004 Democratic nomination, Howard Dean remarked: "White folks in the South who drive pickup trucks with Confederate flag decals on the back ought to be voting with us, and not [the Republicans], because their kids don't have health insurance either, and their kids need better schools too."[1] After the former Vermont governor vaulted to the status of the Democratic front-runner, he sparked a firestorm of controversy by invoking the Confederate flag once again. The explosive symbols he referenced notwithstanding, Dean was advocating a rhetorical strategy for how Democrats could triumph over Republicans based on the parties' respective electoral strengths. His "approach toward cultural issues," the *New Republic* observed, consisted of "ignoring them and trying to change the subject to economics."[2]

Dean's conclusions about which issues give each party an electoral edge are far from unique. Shortly after John Kerry's loss in 2004, longtime journalist John Judis wrote: "In the wake of almost every Democratic defeat since 1972, liberals can be found insisting that, if their candidate had adhered to the party's core economic beliefs and steered clear of social issues, he would have done much better, if not won."[3] The sentence quoted above, merely an aside in Judis's article, summarized a belief widely held by influential Democrats. The fact that the belief has so thoroughly permeated contemporary political commentary, especially on the left, is noteworthy by itself. As this chapter will show, these assumptions about which issues benefit each party miss the mark in certain key respects.

This chapter does not specifically address how the public responds to the social and cultural domains of crime, abortion, pornography, affirmative action, gun control, gay rights, and the separation of church and state. Instead, my analyses explain how the common belief that economic issues advantage Democrats obscures as much as it clarifies. If economic issues are construed expansively to cover the various components of the welfare state, then the conventional wisdom holds up reasonably well. Although surveys typically find that the public prefers Republicans on taxes, trade, and controlling government spending, majorities favor Democrats on Social Security, Medicare, education, health care, and assistance to the poor.[4] Furthermore, these are the issues Howard Dean and others have often described as the political territory on which Democrats should wage campaigns. Radically different conclusions emerge, however, if the "economic" category is defined more precisely to refer to the economy rather than to everything that contains a material dimension.

To measure public opinion on which party would be better for the economy, and thus to determine where the conventional wisdom goes astray, I conducted a broad search and identified several relevant survey questions.[5] These questions provide the observations for the main analyses of this chapter. The largest source of observations comes from a Gallup question asked at regular intervals since 1951: "Looking ahead for the next few years, which political party do you think will do a better job of keeping the country prosperous—the Republican party or the Democratic party?" Tapping the same underlying concept, several related polls administered by Gallup and other survey organizations asked respondents which party would be better for "improving the economy," "dealing with the economy," "making sure the country is prosperous," "handling the economy," "keeping the economy strong and prosperous," "keeping the economy healthy," and "keeping the economy prosperous." The various wordings are treated here as equivalent means of measuring the same concept.[6] By combining responses to the various questions, one can observe shifts in public opinion toward the parties.

Perceptions of respective proficiencies on the economy come into sharper relief when compared with the results of a second survey question, one designed to measure people's general orientations toward the parties. The Gallup organization regularly assesses people's partisan identification by asking, "In politics, as of today, do you consider yourself a Democrat, a Republican, an independent, or what?" Whereas the previous questions about the economy and prosperity focus on a particular aspect of politics, this one is pitched in general terms and is commonly called "macropartisanship" when aggregated to the level of the electorate as a whole.[7] Responses to the two questions probably maintain a mutual relationship with each other. If people increasingly think a certain party excels at such a central matter as promoting prosperity, they may feel a closer kinship with it on an ongoing basis. A growing approval of the party in the economic domain, that is, could soon create a broader and more diffuse kind of allegiance. At the same time, many reasons independent of the economy explain why people swing Republican or Democratic. If people begin to identify with a particular party for any reason, this evaluation may transfer beyond its origin and subsequently influence people's judgments in the economic arena.

An understanding of the dynamics of the relationship between these specific and general orientations lies beyond the purposes of this chapter. However, if the level of overall identification with a party is subtracted from public evaluations of it in the economic realm, a useful measure can be created. The resulting variable captures the degree to which economic images help or hurt each party at each interval, relative to everything else in the political environment. If people give a party higher evaluations on the economy than they give it overall, then economic matters—for that moment—are a net winner drawing people into the party. Should the difference be negative, then the economy is a net loser dragging the party down by comparison with everything else affecting macropartisanship.

The difference measure resembles the concept of comparative advantage often employed in studies of international trade. Although the public may favor a certain party on the economy and in general, the comparative advantage on the economy could still fall to its competitor. If a party has 55% support on the economy and 65% support overall, it would be better off directing people's attention away from economic questions and toward other issues for which its level of backing is higher. Likewise, the other party would gain votes by steering the national political conversation toward the economy, for its disadvantage is smaller in that domain than in others. The parties do not literally specialize in the production of certain goods and then trade with each other, but the metaphor of comparative advantage captures the fact that the relative benefits of the economy issue depend on each party's status on other issues.

The variables for general partisan identification and public evaluations on the economy—the two parts of comparative advantage—are measured here as the Republican share of the two-party totals.[8] Higher scores for the difference between the components, then, indicate greater favorableness for Republicans.[9] Figure 8.1 presents the quarterly measure of the extent to which economic perceptions help or hurt the Republicans vis-à-vis the Democrats. The data show that from 1951 through 1972, economic matters moved back and forth from being a comparative advantage to a comparative disadvantage for Republicans. The average during that period was almost identical to zero, meaning that the issue did not consistently benefit either party. After 1972 the figures changed dramatically and for Democrats badly. The powerful symbol of the "party of prosperity," a valuable source of political capital, became far more frequently attached to Republicans.

From 1973 to 2004, the GOP's economic image contributed significantly to the party's appeal. The Republican gains came on the measure of comparative advantage, meaning that they oc-

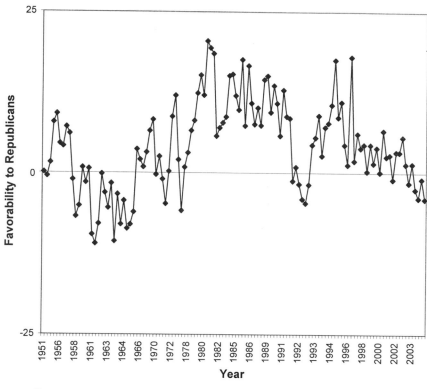

Figure 8.1. Comparative Advantage of the Parties on the Economy

curred over and above a long-term shift toward the GOP in macropartisanship. The status of the economy as a net winner for Republicans was only rarely relinquished, with the Reagan era—including the campaign year of 1980—showing particularly robust numbers. Occasionally during the 1980s and more often during the 1990s, the Democrats attracted a majority on specific questions asking respondents which party could best facilitate prosperity.[10] Those majorities were almost always smaller, however, than the majorities Democrats attained in total partisan identification. In other words, the economy remained an asset for Republicans relative to other issues.

Except in the early 1990s and the first few years of the twenty-first century, Republicans in the last three decades would have improved their standing had people chosen their party identification simply by determining which party would produce superior economic outcomes. In a related way, the Democrats normally would have fared better had questions about prosperity been taken off the table, for they continually scored worse in that area than they did in macropartisanship. Contrary to the standard assumption that people prefer Democrats on the economy, the data show that the opposite pattern usually held in recent times. The Republicans thus turned a factor that did not consistently tilt in either party's direction for the first quarter-century after World War II into a persistent advantage thereafter.

The Economy and the Republican Surge

When a fundamental component of politics shifts, scholars naturally search for the causes. One might interpret the Republican gains in comparative advantage on the economy as a reaction against the party in power when economic troubles emerged in the 1970s. Democrats had controlled Congress since 1955, but many Americans were unaware of that fact. Public opinion polls taken repeatedly over several decades indicate that the percentage of Americans correctly identifying which party held the majority in the House of Representatives averaged 63%—a figure only slightly above the 50% that would be reached if everyone chose randomly from the two major parties.[11] Most Americans who think about which party runs the federal government consider the affiliation of the president, not of Congress.

A better explanation of the patterns seen in figure 8.1 can thus be gained by examining the health of the economy under each party's presidents. The nation's economic performance during different presidential administrations offers one possible explanation for the rising public evaluations of Republicans as managers of the economy. Perhaps the more positive views of Republicans' economic competency simply reflect mass prosperity under their leadership as opposed to weaker results when Democrats were in power. Although the economic health of the nation in the 1990s under a Democratic president gives pause to anyone entertaining such a possibility, an explanation linking public opinion to what happens under a party's watch nevertheless merits a close examination. In order for differential economic performance to explain the comparative advantage achieved by Republicans, two criteria need to be met: Republicans must have presided over stronger economic outcomes than did Democrats, and the public must have adjusted its assessments of the parties accordingly.

The most common summary measure of the economy is the rate of growth of real GDP, which incorporates not only increases in the production of goods and services but also inflation. A seemingly trivial boost in the rate of growth, if sustained over time, eventually will create a major impact on the standard of living as well as on the government's finances. For example, a $7 trillion economy growing at an average rate of 2.5% over twenty-five years will become an economy with a GDP of $13 trillion. Improving the growth rate to only 3.5% over the same period will create an end point of $16.5 trillion, or a sizable 27% more in total goods and services. For this reason, even small changes in the real growth rate attract close scrutiny from politicians, policy analysts, and business leaders.

Table 8.1 shows the average annual growth rate, adjusted for inflation, for each administration in the post-1972 period. The first column simply lists what happened under each Republican and Democratic administration. The Republican figures range from a low of 2.1% during George H. W. Bush's four years in office to a high of 3.8% under the second Reagan administration, with the average being 2.8%. On the Democratic side, the Carter and two Clinton administrations yield a low of 3.2%, a high of 4.2%, and an average of 3.6%. The raw numbers obviously favor Democrats—a pattern difficult to reconcile with the usual Republican dominance in the scores capturing comparative advantage on economic prowess.

It is possible to refine the measure of the economic performance of presidents. Because policies and budgets do not take ef-

TABLE 8.1
Economic Performance under Republican and Democratic Administrations

	GDP Growth	GDP Growth, First-Year Adjustment
Republicans		
Nixon-Ford	2.6	2.3
Reagan I	3.1	3.5
Reagan II	3.8	3.6
G.H.W. Bush	2.1	1.9
G. W. Bush I	2.2	2.8
AVERAGE	**2.8**	**2.8**
Democrats		
Carter	3.3	2.8
Clinton I	3.2	3.7
Clinton II	4.2	3.2
AVERAGE	**3.6**	**3.2**

fect immediately, presidents enjoy relatively limited influence on the economy during the first year of the administration. Therefore, in the second column of table 8.1, the first year of each administration is attributed to the previous president. As one can see from the data, this alternative means of measuring performance affects the results. The outcomes under Reagan I, Clinton I, and G. W. Bush I all improve when their weak first years are grouped with the terms of their predecessors. At the same time, the records of several administrations, led by Carter and Clinton II, look less impressive. Overall, these adjustments shrink the gap between the average growth rates achieved by Republican (2.8%) and Democratic (3.2%) presidents. It remains the case, however, that the Democrats oversaw stronger economies even with these changes.[12]

The figures tilt still further toward Democrats when one considers changes in personal income rather than GDP. Families at the ninety-fifth percentile and higher of the income distribution have done equally well under both parties, but families in all other income brackets have fared much better when Democrats held the presidency.[13] The bottom line is clear: Republicans did not add to their public standing by delivering a higher level of prosperity than did the Democrats—a result that seemingly contradicts a large body of research. Many studies document how the state of the economy in modern democracies affects the public's approval of officeholders and voting choices at election time.[14] Often referred to as "economic voting," these findings are among the most widely replicated in all of political science. In the case at hand, one would expect the American public to react to the nation's economic health when each party holds office, meting out favor and disfavor as appropriate. Indeed, it would be odd if the comparative advantage on which party could better deliver prosperity did not respond to the actual state of the economy.

A straightforward extension of the existing literature would show the economy affecting public evaluations of the parties in the economic domain. To determine whether the data presented in figure 8.1 behave differently than would be predicted based on findings from other studies, one can estimate and interpret a statistical model—and that is the approach I take here. A statistical summary of the posited relationships, with the state of the economy used to explain the ups and downs of public perceptions, will yield the desired information. Measured quarterly and converted to an annual rate, the rate of growth of real GDP is the independent variable in the analysis that follows.[15] The dependent variable is the comparative advantage of Republicans as graphed in figure 8.1.[16]

Table 8.2 summarizes the results of an ordinary least squares regression that correspond with these expectations. The key coefficient in the model reaches statistical significance at the .001 level, and the parameter estimate indicates that a one-point change in real GDP growth leads to a 0.44-point change in the comparative advantage. The GOP rises in public esteem, the results indicate, when the economy strengthens during a Republican administration or falters under Democratic control. Sluggish performance under Republicans or a robust economy overseen by Democrats, by contrast, benefits the party of FDR, JFK, and LBJ. People clearly notice the fluctuations in the economy and then sanction or reward the party in power. Thus, these data confirm the well-known influence of the economy on attitudes and voting.

TABLE 8.2
Economic Growth and Comparative Advantage
on the Economy

	Unstandardized coefficients
Variables	
Constant	4.21**
	(0.62)
Real GDP growth	0.44**
	(0.13)
Diagnostics	
N	120
R^2	.09

** $p < .01$ (one-tailed)
Note: The model obervations are quarterly readings spread across the period from 1951 to 2004. Parameters are estimated with ordinary least squares. Standard errors are in parentheses. The dependent variable is public perceptions of the parties on prosperity minus overall partisan identification.

It is important to recognize, however, that the R^2 of the model is low at .09. In other words, most of the variance in comparative advantage on the economy cannot be explained by the variance in economic performance, a fact whose relevance will soon become apparent.[17] Moreover, the findings in and of themselves provide no insight into the long-term ascent of Republicans in the realm of economic perceptions. The results simply indicate that the figures on comparative advantage ebb and flow according to which party oversees economic expansions and contractions. Comprehending the *trend* favoring Republicans requires a more refined analysis.

A parallel to the world of sports helps explain the statistical procedure to be used here. Some baseball players enjoy reputations as superstars, while others are considered mediocre or inferior. The stature of certain hitters exceeds what one would predict based solely upon tallies of their singles, doubles, and home runs. Similarly, other players who rarely make the highlight reel are sometimes saddled with a public status that lags behind their concrete accomplishments. If one could subtract from the reputations of each player a measure of his success at the plate, the result would be the extent to which he is overrated or underrated. It would capture the player's performance-adjusted reputation, or the part of his reputation that stems entirely from perceptions rather than his achievements as a hitter.

The same principle applies when examining the economic reputations of political parties. We want to know how much better or worse each party fares in the public eye than one would expect by looking simply at the state of the economy as the parties alternate in office. Conceivably, the result could continually fluctuate close to zero. Such a finding would indicate that the public regularly equilibrates its opinions of the parties' economic management according to available economic indicators. When the climate for jobs and incomes under Republicans is rosy, the party's comparative advantage rises; when the economy goes sour under GOP leadership, the ratings fall. Alternatively, a party could carry a bonus or penalty by being rated systematically higher or lower than one would predict from the economy alone. Such a finding would indicate that people judge the party's economic capabilities based on something else in addition to the state of the economy.

Fortunately, there is a straightforward means of calculating whether performance-adjusted reputations hover around zero. To determine whether a party fares better or worse than expected from looking at economic performance, we can use the model summarized in table 8.2. Based on the model's results, one subtracts from the dependent variable the portion explained by the independent variable. In subtracting from each observation of comparative advantage on the economy 0.44 times real GDP growth for that period, what remains is the component of the public's economic views of the parties that is unexplained by actual economic growth.[18] By following this procedure, the economic reputation of the parties is purged of the effect from the public updating its opinions using new information on economic reality. The result is the performance-adjusted economic reputation, which represents the part of perceptions that is purely a matter of reputation rather than performance.

The measure created through this calculation is graphed in

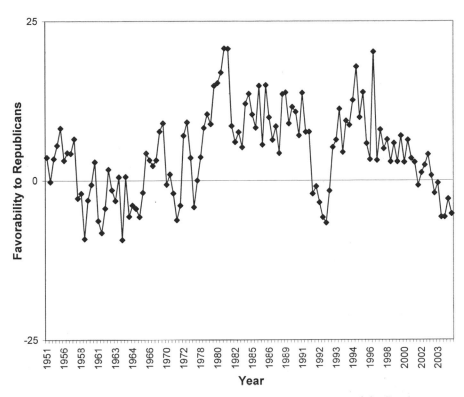

Figure 8.2. Performance-Adjusted Economic Reputation of the Parties

figure 8.2, and the data reveal some striking movements. Most important, the data essentially replicate the fluctuations already seen in figure 8.1. When one subtracts from the measure of comparative advantage on the economy the portion explained by real GDP growth, most of the original variation remains. The peaks and valleys seen in figures 8.1 and 8.2 are sometimes different, but the overall trend benefiting Republicans appears in both. In other words, the trend remains despite accounting for economic outcomes during the parties' respective tenures in office. Although the patterns depicted by the two graphs are similar, figure 8.2 is easier to interpret because one need not wonder whether a given movement simply records the public reacting to a healthy or weak economy.

As seen in figure 8.2, the period from 1951 to 1972 yields

many positive and negative data points, which combine for an average that is virtually indistinguishable from zero. The prosperity issue, in other words, was essentially a wash during that period. When the performance-adjusted economic reputation (hereafter PAER) reaches zero, the parties are perfectly credited and debited according to the objective economy. Positive data points indicate that Republicans score higher than a simple reward-and-punishment account of mass attitudes would predict. Negative data points signify the opposite, when Democrats acquire a better reputation than expected from the state of the economy when the party holds office. On average from 1951 to 1972, economic perceptions closely tracked economic realities.

A very different portrait emerges from 1973 to 2004. This period witnessed a long-term decline in economic security, with—as described in previous chapters—a complicated series of rhetorical and programmatic responses by the parties. Given that 82% of the data points measuring the PAER after 1972 are positive, the Republican strategy usually prevailed in the court of public opinion. Figure 8.2 identifies, in effect, the bonus the GOP attained that is independent of what happened in the economy. One cannot make this pattern vanish by incorporating additional economic indicators or by including lags on the variables.[19] The graph does not imply that the economy has no real effects, for the model summarized earlier in table 8.2 shows otherwise. The point, rather, is that Republicans gained even after addressing those effects. In an unpleasant twist for Democrats, their presidents must preside over a strong economy to receive the same benefits as Republicans holding office during a mediocre one.

Many observers of American politics will be surprised to discover that Republicans, not Democrats, usually enjoyed a comparative advantage on the economy. After all, that domain is frequently believed to provide an asset to Democrats, the supposed counterpoint to the Republican edge on social and cultural issues. Based on the programs and rhetoric of each party that chapters 6 and 7 described, however, it is not surprising that the GOP gained the upper hand on public evaluations regarding the economy. The Republican message of lowering taxes, eliminating regulations, and streamlining the welfare state has been clear and consistent. The Democrats, by contrast, changed their economic themes over time and offered arguments—particularly regarding the need for deficit reduction—that were difficult to convey lucidly and compellingly to the mass public. Exactly how these differences in the parties' reputations affected elections is the subject I investigate next.

The Economy, Party Perceptions, and Voting

Like profits in the realm of commerce, election victories offer the ultimate yardstick in the world of politics. Every aspiring candidate dreams of the celebratory speech, delivered before a crowd of cheering supporters, that begins with the words, "The people have spoken!" Parties and politicians that routinely stumble at the polls must eventually adapt or else vanish from the scene. The seeds of victory in the next election are sown as soon as the last one ends, for even the shrewdest campaigner will find it difficult to overcome fundamental and enduring liabilities. The questions I address below are whether, and by what degree, the parties' performance-adjusted economic reputations affect which candidates give the victory speeches and which ones return to private life.

It is well documented that the state of the economy shapes voting results, and again I do not intend to challenge this research. Instead, my analysis to follow tests whether public perceptions of the parties—their PAER—register noticeable effects *on top of* those stemming from the objective economy. I constructed a statistical model for all presidential elections from 1952 to 2004, the period in which data on economic reputations are available. The dependent variable is the Republican percentage of the two-party vote. The independent variables are the rate of growth of real GDP and the PAER of the parties, as calculated earlier and graphed in figure 8.2.[20]

Table 8.3 shows the estimates generated by an ordinary least

TABLE 8.3
Economic Growth, Economic Reputations, and Presidential Elections

	Unstandardized coefficients	Standardized coefficients
Variables		
Constant	49.16**	
	(1.32)	
Real GDP growth	0.99**	0.63
	(0.29)	
Performance-adjusted economic		
reputation of the parties	0.47**	0.47
	(0.18)	
Diagnostics		
N	14	
R²	.64	

$** p < .05$

Note: The model covers 1952–2004 and has 14 observations. Parameters are estimated with OLS. Standard errors are in parentheses. The dependent variable is the Republican percentage of the two-party vote.

squares regression. The rate of growth of real GDP, as one would expect, shows a statistically significant relationship with the vote totals. Each one-point increase in real GDP growth changes the electoral margins by 0.99 points. The state of the economy clearly exerted an effect on presidential elections throughout the half-century under study. Yet the data indicate that the PAER also matters, with a one-point change leading to a 0.47-point change in the vote tallies. The standardized coefficients are roughly similar for the two variables, 0.63 for real GDP growth and 0.47 for the PAER.

The latter variable is of greatest interest here, with its associated coefficient not only statistically significant but substantively meaningful as well. When comparing the periods before and after a long-term decline in economic security beginning in 1973, the Republican party's average level of PAER rose by 6.2 points. According to the estimates presented in table 8.3, that gain translates into an average boost of 2.9 points in presidential elections. Because presidential elections decided by three points or fewer are typically considered competitive, swings of the magnitude estimated here could reverse the results of any close election. Presidential victory margins of ten points or more—roughly the difference in the 1980 contest between Ronald Reagan and Jimmy Carter—are landslides. The Republican party's comparative advantage on the economy, these estimates indicate, brought it roughly one-third of the way toward a landslide for the average election. Perceptions, then, helped create a new reality: the transferal of political power.

Interpreting Election Outcomes

During the 1992 presidential campaign, aides to Bill Clinton posted a sign in the campaign headquarters that read:

Change vs. more of the same
The economy, stupid
Don't forget health care.[21]

Public memory of the campaign later reduced the quote to the pithy "It's the economy, stupid." Whether in the original or legendary version, the sign summarized a belief that Clinton could win by directing people's attention to the economy. Because this basic strategy was established many months before Election Day, Clinton could not know how the economy would be faring as voters trekked to the polls on November 3, 1992.

In one of the great ironies of that contest, 1992 turned out to be a better-than-average year for the economy. The growth rate of 3.3% exceeded the mean of 3.1% from 1973 to 2004. The relatively prosperous 1992, however, followed on the heels of a weak 1990 and recession-laden 1991. The economic reputation of Republicans had fallen during that period, as seen in figures 8.1 and 8.2, but a downturn in the economy did not tell the whole story. The Republicans' PAER was negative, meaning it was lower than one would expect from the economy alone. The results in table 8.3 indicate that the parties' economic reputations influenced presidential elections throughout the period under study, and the 1992 campaign offers a particularly striking example. The solid triumph of Clinton over Bush Sr. cannot be explained by the state of the economy, for growth levels during 1992 exceeded the average in recent history. It was the temporary drop in the Republicans' PAER that made the larger difference.

My analyses thus show that economic reputations complement the objective state of the economy in influencing elections. This interpretation is consistent with Clinton's approach during the campaign, for the Arkansas governor and his aides never intended to sit back contentedly and watch as a faltering economy booted the elder Bush from office. Instead, the sign at campaign headquarters reminded all representatives of the campaign to assert loudly and continually that Bush had failed in his economic management and that Clinton offered a better approach. Some of the decline in the Republicans' reputation during 1992 probably reflected media coverage, which was more negative on the economy than various economic indicators would predict.[22] Much of that media coverage, in turn, resulted from Clinton's persistence and success in hammering home his message. Thus while most of the time since 1972 the PAER benefited Republicans, 1992 was an exception.

The Democrats held an advantage on the PAER in only one more of the eight presidential elections from 1976 to 2004: the 2004 contest, when George W. Bush prevailed with 51.3% of the two-party vote. Despite carrying the election, Bush underperformed relative to the expectations many social scientists formed during the prior summer. A variety of political scientists and economists, some working in teams and others alone, offered seven different models that forecasted the 2004 election based on variables that had been shown to explain previous presidential contests. Six of the seven models predicted a Bush victory; notwithstanding the uncertainty that most citizens had about who would win, the result on November 2, 2004, matched what these social scientists expected. Almost all of the available models, however, overshot the figures for Bush's votes. The median forecast among the researchers of Bush's two-party vote was 53.7%, or 2.4% better than what he actually achieved.[23]

None of the models accounted for the variable emphasized here, the economic reputations of the parties. According to the results presented in table 8.2, those reputations subtracted 1.9% from Bush's tally, and the model developed in this chapter missed the actual vote totals by only 0.8%. Of course, other factors in the campaign—particularly the importance and framing of national security—benefited Bush.[24] Nevertheless, the results of this analysis indicate that a positive economic reputation for the Democrats, a rarity in the post-1973 period, gave Kerry a greater chance of winning than he otherwise would have had.

The analyses here also help explain the historically close election of 2000. If one had predicted the result based solely on the state of the economy, Al Gore should have won an easy victory over George W. Bush. The forecasting models of 2000, in fact, anticipated precisely that outcome because the Democrats had presided over the strongest economy in thirty years.[25] The party did not, however, lead in the performance-adjusted economic reputation. In other words, positive economic conditions were partly offset by the fact that the PAER—what remains after accounting for the state of the economy—favored Republicans. The Democrats held an edge on this measure when Clinton assumed the presidency in 1993, but it reverted to the Republicans as soon as Congress began considering his deficit-reduction package of tax increases and spending cuts. By retaining the advantage on the PAER during the rest of Clinton's two terms in office, Republicans benefited in the 2000 election.

Of course, interpretations of elections based on the effects of the PAER cannot be considered a complete explanation of Americans' voting behavior over the last half-century. A comprehensive account would require more theorizing and data analysis than is possible in any single book, this one included.[26] The evidence presented here that economic forces—both objective conditions and the parties' reputations—influence voters' decision making does not imply that the social and cultural issues that political commentators often discuss are irrelevant. Like all important phenomena, voting choices result from many causes; social and cultural issues, along with a host of other systematic and even idiosyncratic factors, can easily affect how the electorate behaves. In fact, a growing body of research documents the ways in which voters' religious identities, orientations toward moral traditionalism, and positions on social and cultural issues have shaped patterns of voting.[27] The inaccurate claim that a culture war has driven economic matters from campaigns and voting, then, should not be replaced by an equally foolish assertion that *only* economic issues matter.

A full understanding of voting also must consider the influence of foreign policy and national defense. For several years after the terrorist attacks of September 11, 2001, and especially in the midterm election of 2002 and presidential election of 2004, national security bolstered the appeal of the Republican party.[28] The realm of international affairs can be volatile, though, as George W. Bush discovered in his second term when the American death toll in Iraq mounted and sectarian strife divided the war-torn country into hardened factions. The widespread unpopularity of the Iraq war to American voters contributed mightily to the results of the midterm elections of 2006, in which Democrats captured narrow majorities in both chambers of Congress. In mid-2007 the war appeared likely to remain unpopular well into the future and to shape the dynamics of the 2008 presidential election. Clearly national security can exert strong effects on election outcomes, especially during times of war and terrorist threats.

Electoral and Nonelectoral Routes to Policy Change

This book has investigated the interplay between mass politics and elite politics that shifted the nation to the right. Now that the book's primary analyses are complete, the next few pages will summarize the themes of earlier chapters about context, rhetoric, and policy. Although new policies are commonly passed when one party increases its electoral power at the expense of the other, *repositioning in response to an altered context can produce the same re-*

sult even without electoral turnover. The fact that Democrats changed their positions as Republicans changed their arguments created important consequences for public policy and, hence, for who benefits from the actions of government. Because each party's strategy affected how it behaved in office, one need not account for the GOP's electoral strength to gain insights into the move to the right in policy.

Embracing deficit reduction, for example, consistently forced Democrats to restrain their programmatic requests, most notably when Walter Mondale asked for tax increases yet little funding for new domestic initiatives. After internalizing a belief that shrinking the deficit was the proper, statesmanlike course of action, Democratic leaders were heavily constrained in the programs they could offer the public. These constraints proved especially tight in the realm of health care, where the goal of universal coverage remained difficult if not impossible to achieve without a large infusion of government spending. Democratic proposals on job training, transportation, child care, education, and infrastructure development either collapsed or were never offered in the first place because of budgetary limitations. Bill Clinton, the only Democrat in the quarter-century following 1980 to win the presidency, began with far-reaching initiatives for public investment before scaling them back during his campaign and even more so once he took office. With Republicans aggressively promoting their agenda on taxation, deregulation, and welfare state retrenchment, and Democrats adhering to fiscal responsibility, policies linked rhetorically to the economy moved in a conservative direction. Had the electoral success of each party remained unchanged, certain areas of policy still would have turned rightward.

The nation's electoral balance did not stay constant, though, and the Republicans' ascendancy over the last few decades brought additional impetus to the conservative turn in policy. Controlling Congress, the presidency, or both over a lengthy period allowed Republicans to accomplish many of their policy goals, just as a traditional understanding of the relationship between elections and policy would expect. Explaining the evolution of the two parties' electoral fortunes therefore becomes crucial. Devising such an explanation poses a major analytical challenge, and I make no pretense of being comprehensive in this chapter; other articles and books tell part of the story.[29] The evidence offered here identifies the effects of revised public perceptions of the Republicans' economic competence that expanded the party's coalition in presidential contests. While not the only reason for the Republican resurgence, the GOP's strengthened economic reputation (or, conversely, the weakness of the Democrats' message) nevertheless was an important one that scholars, journalists, and popular writers have routinely overlooked.

Culture, Economics, and the Supposed Bait and Switch

Clues about the underpinnings of contemporary American politics can be found in a distinctive pattern: Some issues have seen momentous policy changes since the 1970s, but others have not. The evidence that I have presented in this book, summarized in the preceding section and the following one, attempts to explain the causes of these differences across issues. Other than their failure to control government spending, a glaring omission during the administration of George W. Bush, conservatives achieved the least success on their social and cultural agenda—the very agenda that attracted so much attention in popular and scholarly discourse. Religious conservatives, in particular, repeatedly failed in recent decades to restrict pornography, outlaw abortion, reinstate school prayer, or restore traditional gender relations, and they fought rearguard battles against the American public's growing tolerance of homosexuality and demands for stem-cell research.

On issues that parties and politicians associated rhetorically with the economy, by contrast, conservatives enacted many of their legislative and administrative proposals. Operating within the Madisonian institutions of the United States that normally block major initiatives, it is remarkable that policymakers could restrain the scope of government regulation, shrink some social programs, and wring much of the progressiveness out of the tax code. Although the victories on issues associated with the economy were incomplete, they still reoriented the ideological direction of government. Even if the right makes greater strides toward implementing its social and cultural desires in the 2000s and 2010s than it did in the 1980s and 1990s, those gains would come much later than its triumphs on policies that were framed in economic terms. For this reason, the discrepancy in outcomes between different kinds of issues would still call out for an explanation.

Thomas Frank offers one such explanation in his bestselling book *What's the Matter with Kansas?* Frank takes several widely believed propositions about American politics and weaves them into a lively tale filled with wit, verve, and irony. Conventional wisdom holds that social and cultural issues benefit Republicans, whereas Democrats maintain an electoral edge on economic questions. Moreover, it is commonly assumed that culture has displaced economics as the focal point of American politics, especially during elections. Frank's innovation is to argue that such an outcome arose not through impersonal and unpredictable forces but by conscious design: Republicans planned it that way. Downplaying economic matters, they focused on fighting the culture wars and thereby built electoral majorities by leading people to vote against their economic self-interest.

According to Frank, Republicans continually reneged after winning elections and gave only lip service to the cultural emphases on which the party had successfully campaigned; instead, the GOP's leaders devoted their time and energy to economic issues. Through this bait and switch, the Republican party overhauled the economic domain yet made little to no progress in reversing the policies and societal practices that galvanize its religious base. The anger of religious voters over matters such as abortion, homosexuality, feminism, the separation of church and state, and moral decadence in the entertainment media therefore remained to be mobilized during the next election season. It would be foolish for Republican politicians to pass laws that would satisfy their core constituency, Frank concludes, for that would remove the ace from their hand and force the party to campaign with weaker cards in the next election.

Frank's book found a large and enthusiastic audience in part because he articulated commonly felt sentiments about elections and policy. With most of the individual pieces of his argument shared by other writers and scholars, Frank's signal contribution was to connect the dots and push the claims to their logical conclusion. If one begins by observing that Republicans have been winning elections at both the state and federal levels, then combines that fact with an assumption about which kinds of issues benefit each party, it follows that campaigns must have revolved around culture—otherwise the GOP could not have prevailed so often. It is only a short step from that inference to Frank's assertion that Republicans knew all along what game they were playing, cynically running on culture and then governing on economics.

In a certain respect Frank's reasoning is sound: His conclusions are inescapable if one accepts the assumptions on which they are based. The problem lies with those very assumptions, beginning with the notion that economic questions have been forced to the sidelines during campaigns—and on this assumption, which is central to the supposed bait and switch, Frank is wrong. Measured by the level of prioritizing and the number of issues framed in corresponding ways, the economy is now more rather than less central to Republican rhetoric than it was during the first quarter-century after World War II. In campaign advertisements, party platforms, and legislative speeches, as I have shown in earlier chapters, the GOP has consistently prioritized its economic programs and framed issues with economic arguments.

Conservative intellectuals paved the way for this rhetoric by reinvigorating arguments supporting supply-side economics, opposing government regulation, and resisting the welfare state. During the Depression conservatives lacked a network of talented intellectuals, but after World War II visionary leaders on the right, such as Henry Regnery, Frank Chodorov, and William F. Buckley, Jr., committed themselves to creating publication outlets for like-minded writers. With vigorous efforts to form and expand think tanks in the 1970s, the right added a research capacity to its existing means of crafting and distributing analysis, commentary, and policy proposals. Through articles, reports, op-eds, and books, conservative intellectuals successfully brought their ideas to wider audiences.

Building on and drawing from the research, writing, and advocacy of these conservative intellectuals, Republican politicians reacted to the context of economic insecurity primarily by reprioritizing and reframing—in short, by updating their rhetoric. Instead of claiming that progressive taxation unfairly requires individuals to pay at unequal rates, which was the primary contention of Republican conservatives such as Barry Goldwater in the 1950s and 1960s, the party's leaders now argued that higher taxes on the wealthy decrease the incentive to work and save. Regulation of business, formerly opposed as falling outside the proper responsibilities of government, was henceforth challenged on grounds that it caused extensive job losses. Social welfare programs were targeted for cuts based in part on the rationale that they crowded out private investment. Economic means of framing these and other issues had long been present but submerged in the rhetoric of the GOP's leaders. Beginning in the early 1970s, Republican candidates increasingly justified their stands as a means of economic revival.

The bottom line of contemporary politics is clear: There was no bait and switch, at least not in the manner Frank describes.[30] In recent decades the governing emphases of Republicans followed closely what one would have predicted from the preceding campaigns. Rather than campaigning on culture and then governing on economics, the GOP highlighted its economic initiatives during both electoral contests and legislative deliberations. That fact does not imply, however, that the statements Republicans made about each policy proposal—how it would be structured, who would benefit, how much it would cost, and the like—would pass the truth test; examining those specifics would require a different kind of analysis than is possible here. My point is simply that far from hiding their ambitious economic programs, Republicans trumpeted them loudly during elections and then again once in office.

The Democrats followed suit in reprioritizing the economy in their rhetoric during campaigns and while governing. Manifestly not the exclusive property of the GOP, economically based rhetoric also rose to prominence in Democrats' speeches, platforms, and campaign advertisements. The electoral problems of Democrats stemmed not from strategic choices that emphasized the wrong issues but from the content of the party's economic programs and the repositioning that discarded old stances and adopted new ones. In the interplay of party positions and the public reaction, the Republicans gained and usually maintained a comparative advantage on which party is better for the economy. The GOP's economic reputation, my estimates in this chapter indicate, added votes to the party's tally in six of the last eight presidential elections. By linking the party's key stances clearly, directly, and repeatedly to a healthy economy, Republicans crafted a message that helped them both win elections and then construct coalitions in subsequent struggles over policy.

The book's final chapter reflects on the rhetorical revolution of the last three decades, asking whether the economy will continue to provide the focal point for domestic policies. After developing some illustrative examples that crystallize the themes of the book, I consider how past and present trends inform our thinking about the future. Recent experience indicates that unless people regain a large measure of economic security, an outcome that is increasingly unlikely, political leaders will continue framing many different policies around the purported effects on the economy. In the age-old struggle between different standards of evaluation, economic arguments will be difficult to move from the top of the rhetorical summit.

NINE

The Broad Reach and Future Prospects
of Economic Rhetoric

Like most events relating to religion, the appearance in 2000 of *The Prayer of Jabez: Breaking Through to the Blessed Life* flew under the radar screen of people with a secular orientation. In fact, many secular Americans would be lucky to pronounce *Jabez* correctly, let alone explain the significance of the book that bears the name. For observant Christians, though, the response was immediate, electric, and sustained, leading Bruce Wilkinson's short tract to sell more than ten million copies.[1] Spin-offs such as plaques, key rings, and greeting cards, plus follow-up books such as *The Prayer of Jabez for Kids*, *The Prayer of Jabez Devotional*, and *The Prayer of Jabez Journal*, netted millions more in sales. With its massive readership and brand extension, *The Prayer of Jabez* became for a time the Harry Potter of American religion.

The ancient Jew named Jabez makes his brief biblical appearance in a section of the Old Testament book 1 Chronicles that few people, Jewish or Christian, regularly read. Most of 1 Chronicles recounts the genealogy of Israel—who begat whom and with what effects—in a manner that Wilkinson calls "boring."[2] Buried within the genealogy are several lines uttered by a Jewish herdsman that Wilkinson would bring to life for a later generation. Before the Protestant teacher and writer trumpeted those words, most Christians had never heard of Jabez but could recite a different prayer from the Bible, the Lord's Prayer.[3] Coming from the lips of Jesus, who used it to explain how his disciples should pray, the Lord's Prayer has inspired and motivated Christians down through the ages.

At first glance the Prayer of Jabez seems to echo the themes of the Lord's Prayer. Jabez's request that God "would keep me from evil, that I may not cause pain" sounds like Jesus imploring his disciples to ask that God "lead us not into temptation, but deliver us from evil." Elsewhere, however, the messages of the two prayers strongly diverge. In an era when landholding was the dominant form of wealth, Jabez pleads to God: "Oh, that you would bless me indeed, and enlarge my territory."[4] Wilkinson updates the language for twenty-first-century sensibilities: "If Jabez had worked on Wall Street, he might have prayed, 'Lord, increase the value of my investment portfolios.'"[5] In the Lord's Prayer appearing in Matthew and Luke, by contrast, Jesus instructs his disciples to ask merely for their "daily bread." Whereas Wilkinson interprets the Prayer of Jabez to mean that people should ask God to shower them with prosperity, Christians articulating the Lord's Prayer appeal only for the food they need to live.

The phenomenal success of Wilkinson's book probably reflects many Christians' desires both to attain the American dream, a large component of which revolves around material prosperity, and still practice their faith. Perennially upheld as a birthright, the American dream has recently proved elusive for large segments of the population. In the midst of their desires for more and more goods, workers have faced serious economic difficulties that began in the early 1970s and continue up to the present. Recent times have ushered in more volatile incomes, downsizing during upturns as well as downturns, globalization and international competition, and colossal levels of personal debt and bankruptcy. With financial struggles a daily reality for many people, one can understand why a book recommending that followers ask God to "enlarge my territory" received such a positive reception.

Christian leaders in earlier ages did not use this obscure prayer. One reviewer commented that he "found not a single mention of it in the standard thirty-eight-volume Edinburgh edition of the Ante-Nicene, Nicene, and Post-Nicene Fathers."[6] Over the centuries since the compilation of the Christian scriptures, innumerable teachers, scribes, and clergy must have inadvertently encountered the account of Jabez found in 1 Chronicles. Considering that no documented reference to it exists, however, they apparently found spiritual sustenance in other prayers and practices. During the Middle Ages, when political, social, and religious authorities used the "Great Chain of Being" to teach generations of peasants to temper any aspirations for upward mobility, the Prayer of Jabez would not have struck such a responsive chord. Following in the footsteps of Russell Conwell and his "Acres of Diamonds" speech during the Gilded Age, Bruce Wilkinson appeared to recognize that Americans of his day yearned for greater wealth and financial security. By fusing mammon and morality into one all-encompassing message, his contribution to the contemporary "Prosperity Gospel" could solidify the faith of current believers and spread the religion to new converts.

Wilkinson's crafting of his book and the public's enthusiastic response to it show that economic means of perceiving and discussing the world transcend the political domain. Although fascinating by itself, the story of how a slim volume appealed to millions of Christians is just one example of a larger phenomenon in American society. The reaction to economic insecurity could not be confined to politics—the subject of this book—and soon spread to other areas. People became more amenable to viewing many aspects of society, including religion, in economic terms. In politics, religion, and probably elsewhere, economics has become a more central interpretive and evaluative perspective, one employed frequently by speakers and writers and grasped easily by the people who hear their messages. Economic thinking permeates the air we breathe, forming a taken-for-granted part of our everyday lives.

Will the rhetorical emphasis on many policies' economic consequences that this book has documented be long lasting? If not, what might happen to cause political participants to reorder their arguments and reduce the economic basis of policy debates?

One possible answer is an unexpected shock to the body politic that remakes the nation's political agenda—and in the first years of the new millennium, just such a shock occurred. Responding to both the terrorist attacks of September 11, 2001, and the long Iraq war, citizens, political elites, and the mass media devoted considerably more attention to national security than they had in the 1990s. In blogs, politicians' speeches, and informal conversations among friends, family, and coworkers, war and terrorism galvanized the nation's consciousness. Some observers drew parallels to the early part of the Cold War, when foreign affairs redefined the parameters of domestic political conflict.

This baseline level of similarity notwithstanding, the rhetorical landscape of the two periods contrasted sharply. During the opening decades of the global conflict with the Soviet Union, national security dominated the public sphere and also, as chapter 3 showed, served as a framing device for domestic issues with which it might seem to bear only a tenuous relationship. The more recent global war on terror brought more limited rhetorical effects than did the postwar struggle against communism, with the incidence of economically based framing largely unaltered. In the years following the outbreak of mass terrorism on American soil, federal, state, and local leaders continued to stress the economic implications of policies involving transportation, energy, labor, education, regulation, taxation, trade, and government spending. If and when more terrorist attacks occur in the future, political leaders are likely to frame a range of domestic issues in economic terms despite the prominence of national security on the public agenda. The rhetorical aftermath of the terrorist attacks of 2001 indicates that even an event of historic proportions cannot easily reshuffle the arguments through which intellectuals and parties advocate their positions on domestic issues.

Another possible route to reordering arguments would be a major change in the context of Americans' economic experiences. Should pocketbook and workplace anxieties diminish in intensity, new political strategies would then gain potency. One of the oldest political and rhetorical tactics involves shifting the grounds on which decisions rest, thereby opening opportunities for alternative outcomes. William Riker describes several examples, drawn from ancient and contemporary history, in which political leaders accomplished their goals by introducing a new dimension of an issue under discussion.[7] In a climate without pervasive economic insecurity, liberals might reverse the tide of conservative policies by making noneconomic arguments grounded in values such as compassion, justice, equality, fairness, and community. After all, those kinds of arguments helped advance liberal policies from the 1930s to the 1960s and still resonate on certain issues.[8]

A transformation of this kind, however, appears unlikely in the near future because economic insecurity is *increasing* in many key respects. With downsizing, layoffs, and outsourcing now occurring regularly in almost every major industry, the pressures of domestic and international competition continue to destabilize workplace relationships. Workers' wages are increasingly volatile from year to year, both upward and downward, leaving people uncertain about their financial futures.[9] Fringe benefits are eroding as well: Because many employers are unable or unwilling to pay for the rising costs of health insurance, the proportion of Americans without coverage continues to climb.[10] Meanwhile, many Americans carry high levels of debt, which heighten the risks of default or bankruptcy should they face job losses, recurring medical bills, or unforeseen expenses from other personal crises. Given the persistence of these trends, any political strategy that attempts to deemphasize economic standards for judging domestic policies is unlikely to achieve much success. Political actors can always try to reframe an issue, but their chances of gaining public support for their positions depend on their ability to tap into the context within which their rhetoric will be received. Political actors who ignore that context undermine their own effectiveness.

Science, Economics, and Global Warming

Global warming offers an instructive contemporary example of how political rhetoric has turned away from other evaluative standards and toward the connection of policies to the economy.

Accordingly, an investigation of this issue's evolution can illuminate some of the larger themes this book has advanced. As evidence began accumulating in the 1980s and 1990s that carbon dioxide emissions were causing global temperatures to rise, conservative intellectuals and organizations quickly mobilized in response. If global warming came to be seen as a serious problem, the federal government would probably acquire additional regulatory, taxation, and spending powers to curtail the harmful emissions. For people with a long-standing opposition to those policies, such a prospect was unwanted and unwarranted. The forces of change were far from inevitable, though; one could block the prospective policies by forestalling public acceptance of the emerging scientific consensus on climate change.

Using the tools of research and advocacy, a variety of conservative think tanks carried out this strategy. Two sociologists have analyzed the efforts through which fourteen think tanks during the 1990s produced hundreds of relevant documents including books, reports, op-eds, and press releases. Fellows from these institutes challenged the scientific legitimacy of global warming through speeches, policy forums, appearances on television programs, and testimony in congressional hearings. Whereas mainstream scientists published their findings in technical journals inaccessible to lay readers, opponents bypassed the peer-review process and took their case directly to policymakers and the public. By financing and publicizing these views, the think tanks sought to create doubts about global warming and alleviate the pressure for vigorous governmental action.[11]

The campaign to dispute the scientific basis of global warming has, so far, proven remarkably successful in influencing public policy. While the federal government has enacted minor initiatives such as funding research, it did not pass any significant legislation to reduce greenhouse gas emissions during either the 1990s or the first few years of the twenty-first century. Because the evidence documenting human-induced global warming steadily accumulates, though, denying the science probably will not work indefinitely as a political strategy. Undercutting the future prospects of a strategy based on questioning the science, a growing group of geologists, meteorologists, and oceanographers have pioneered new methodologies and tapped additional data sources that make current research far more precise and sophisticated than the studies conducted in the 1980s.[12] Some scientists have used their roles as public intellectuals to explain and dramatize the scientific consensus, thereby putting opponents back on the defensive. As disruptions to the planet's ecosystems continue or intensify, it will become progressively harder to achieve policy aims by questioning scientific conclusions.

Building on a pattern established in other policy areas, conservative intellectuals, activists, and politicians can nevertheless deploy a very different but equally persuasive form of argument, one that has proven its effectiveness many times over. Namely, they can marshal economic reasons and rhetoric to thwart the policy proposals to which they object. Throughout the 1990s conservative think tanks utterly rejected the science of climate change, devoting more attention to refuting scientific claims than to arguing that ambitious policies to address global warming would weaken the nation's economy. Despite its inclusion in conservative rhetoric, then, economics played second fiddle to science.[13] George W. Bush swiftly and forcefully reversed these emphases when, early in his first term, he formally withdrew the United States from the Kyoto treaty negotiated in 1997. Bush asserted that the treaty endangered jobs, growth, and the American standard of living: "I will explain as clearly as I can, today and every other chance I get, that we will not do anything that harms our economy."[14] Bush noted that America's competitors in the developing world, particularly China and India, stood exempt from the treaty's provisions. In the president's judgment, meeting Kyoto's emission targets would worsen the competitive position of the United States.

Shortly after Bush's decision, his spokesperson Ari Fleischer took questions from the media at his regular press briefing. When asked about global warming, Fleischer said that Bush "does not support the Kyoto treaty. It exempts the developing nations around the world, and it is not in the United States' economic best interest." Faced with a different question that encouraged Fleischer to expand on his answer, he simply repeated himself: "I know this has been the President's consistent position from the campaign forward. And the concern is that most of the world was exempt from the treaty and the treaty as it currently is written is not in the economic interests of the United States."[15] Because presidential advisers and other political figures rarely if ever "stay on message" by accident, Fleischer's answers can be understood to reflect the rhetorical strategies devised by the Bush administration—strategies that now stressed the economic threat the Kyoto treaty posed.

The administration, it should be recognized, did not abandon claims about scientific uncertainty. During a speech that summer, Bush paired his economic fears about the treaty with an argument about gaps in our scientific understanding: "We do not know how much effect natural fluctuations in climate may have had on warming. We do not know how much our climate could, or will change in the future. We do not know how fast change will occur, or even how some of our actions could impact it."[16] Having cited economic reasons when he officially rejected the Kyoto treaty, Bush made sure he reminded his listeners, viewers, and readers of the scientific case that conservatives had carefully crafted over the previous decade. A few years later, Michael Crichton's best-selling novel *State of Fear* repackaged the antiscience arguments into a highly readable form.[17]

For the purposes of this book, two lessons can be drawn from the history of the right's resistance to policies aimed at reducing greenhouse emissions. First, political actors often take the same positions over time while adapting their rhetoric to the possibilities offered by the prevailing context. Against a background of enduring and increasing economic insecurity, conservatives have slowly yet perceptibly begun to highlight the economic harms they predict would follow from government policies on global warming. Second, when one considers all the rhetorical discourse presented in different venues, political actors seldom advance only one major argument when advocating their policies. Despite the rising incidence of economically based advocacy over the last half-century, political leaders routinely defend their policies through other criteria as well. As with global warming, the rhetorical reformulation of policy usually involves changes in degree rather than kind.

The Shifting Meaning of Economic Policy

The updating of conservative rhetoric about global warming offers important clues about the meaning of terms commonly referenced by scholars, journalists, and activists. In light of the analyses of this book—represented by, though obviously not limited to, global warming—I conclude that the very lexicon of the political world needs review and possibly revision. In earlier chapters I have used phrases such as "policies associated with the economy" and "policies framed with economic rhetoric." Based on the principle that less is more when it comes to writing, such phrases may seem clumsy and overly wordy. William Strunk and E. B. White famously advised writers to "omit needless words," and some readers may wonder why my entire book, up to now, makes no mention of the succinct descriptor "economic policy."[18] After all, political observers commonly categorize the actions of government into domains such as foreign policy, social policy, morality policy, environmental policy, education policy, and economic policy. In avoiding conventional usage, I have sought to emphasize an important point: The content of what qualifies as "economic policy"—or, for that matter, any of the other areas—can radically change over time.[19]

As commonly understood by people who write about politics, "economic policy" includes budgets (aggregate taxes and government spending), the actions of the Federal Reserve Board regarding interest rates, and the rules governing international trade. Calling these areas of policy "economic," however, leads to a connotation too expansive in some periods and too narrow in others. Whether or not something should be considered part of economic policy hinges on the rhetoric through which elites articulate their positions. By either conscious intention or unconscious responses to their environments and audiences, elites search for the most persuasive rhetoric to accomplish their goals. Elected officials normally maintain strong consistency in their issue positions, but the rhetoric they express in support of those positions frequently evolves alongside the context. More specifically for this book, political figures in contemporary times can recast a long-standing position—and potentially enlarge the coalition of supporters—by tying it rhetorically to the economy.

When prosperity was spreading throughout the population during the first three decades after World War II, arguments that a policy should be adopted because it would help the economy were only marginally effective. As a result, political leaders gravitated to alternative justifications, such as freedom and national security, for their policy proposals. Politicians supporting free trade, for example, commonly asserted that countries would escape the spread of communism if they were embedded in commercial relationships with the United States through imports and exports. Meanwhile, Barry Goldwater and many authors who wrote for *National Review* invoked moral grounds for opposing progressive taxation, claiming that it violated the principle of equal treatment before the law. To be sure, conservatives kept economic arguments in their arsenal and regularly contended that government spending caused inflation. By comparison with recent times, though, they frequently advocated so-called economic policies by using noneconomic arguments.

Nowadays conservatives more often construct their rhetoric on fiscal, monetary, and trade policy around the consequences they expect for the economy. When discussing taxation, few politicians or intellectuals on the right forgo the opportunity to claim that high taxes in general, and progressive taxes in particular, jeopardize the nation's prosperity. In international trade, the connection to national security—although still present in elite rhetoric—also stands distinctly subsidiary to the linkage with the economy. When George W. Bush asked Congress to renew the president's trade promotion authority and create a free trade zone with Central America, for example, he focused primarily on economic effects. In his 2006 state-of-the-nation address Bush stated: "Keeping America competitive requires us to open more markets for all that Americans make and grow. One out of every five factory jobs in America is related to global trade, and we want people everywhere to buy American. With open markets and a level playing field, no one can out-produce or out-compete the American worker."[20]

The well-being of citizens often depends directly on the scope and content of fiscal, monetary, and trade policies. With budgets representing the lifeblood of government, fiscal policy leaves its mark on all constituencies in society. Policies on spending and taxes determine which programs are funded, which ones are abandoned, and who pays the bills. Seemingly uninteresting to many citizens, the actions of the Federal Reserve Board also hit people in the pocketbook: Individuals and businesses feel the pinch of interest rates every time they borrow money. Trade rules, too, create real consequences by determining the winners and losers of international commerce. Workers in formerly protected sectors of the economy absorb the costs associated with removing trade barriers even as those in export-oriented sectors typically benefit.

The immense importance of these policy areas notwithstanding, any reasonable conception of economic policy in contemporary politics must cover considerably more ground. The relevant category now surely includes education as a central component, for the speeches of presidents, governors, and mayors usually define the primary purposes of education to involve preparing graduates for the workforce. In the knowledge economy of the twenty-first century, the reasoning goes, we need brains more than brawn. At the elementary and secondary levels, schools must ensure that students gain the skills that will allow them to become productive workers. College and university training will then complete this occupational preparation and stimulate the higher-order thinking that professions increasingly require. In earlier periods the goals of education were often perceived differently to include not only training for employment but also civic, cultural, and personal development. Today, the dominance of economic motivations has virtually eliminated these alternative justifications for education in the rhetoric of policymakers.[21]

The reframing of education around the economy has even appeared in unexpected places. Jonathan Cole, former provost and dean of faculties at Columbia University, published a ringing endorsement of academic freedom in 2005. Reacting to the heightened scrutiny of professors' political views during the global war on terror, Cole wondered aloud whether administrations and faculties in higher education can sustain public support for the tradition of free and open scholarship. His answer demonstrates the wide reach of this book's analyses: "To do so, we must convince the public that a failure to defend dissenting voices on the campus places at risk the greatest engine for the creation of new ideas and scientific innovation the world has ever known. . . . Above all, we must show that a threat to academic freedom poses a threat as well to the welfare and prosperity of the nation." Cole then elaborated on his point: "Many of the emerging industries on which the nation depends to create new jobs and maintain its leading role in the world economy grow out of discoveries made at the American research university."[22]

To readers knowledgeable about political intrusions into the academy during the McCarthy era, it may sound jarring to hear university administrators of today making the utilitarian case that academic freedom must be protected because it strengthens the nation's economy. Once upon a time, advocates defended academic freedom exclusively in terms of, well, freedom. To be sure, that thread continues to characterize prominent writings about the topic. Still, Cole seemed to believe that he could stregthen his case by identifying the implications for people's financial livelihoods. Whether knowingly or unknowingly, political actors take the pulse of their surroundings to choose, phrase, and position their appeals in the most persuasive manner. Cole's article represents an indicator of how powerful economic arguments have become and how deeply they now penetrate discussions of many aspects of education. So long as this newly popular way of understanding the issue continues, we should expand our conception of economic policy to give education a major role.

State Governments and the Business Climate

Outside of education, the need for a broad definition of economic policy can be seen in the widespread interest in improving states' business climates—an objective that has attracted extensive commentary from those inside and outside government. Economic development now constitutes a central mission of state policymakers, one that absorbs large amounts of their time and energy. Alexander Grant & Company, a Chicago-based accounting and consulting firm later absorbed into the larger company Grant Thornton, offered to governors and state legislators a series of well-known studies comparing business climates across the nation. In 1980 the firm began publishing an index evaluating and comparing prospects for the manufacturing sector of each state. Developed to cover only manufacturing, the index nevertheless was commonly interpreted as an accurate portrait of states' overall business climates. Grant Thornton's annual reports, discontinued in 1990, drew considerable attention from journalists, academics, and policymakers.

The 1988 report, released during an election year, carried forward the central thrust of Grant Thornton's studies.[23] According to the firm's analysts, the best states for manufacturing were Nevada, New Hampshire, and Texas, and the worst ones were New York, Wisconsin, and Michigan. To reach these assessments, Grant Thornton measured and combined indicators of the states' policies and attributes. Some of these factors fell outside the control of governors and legislators, such as the average hourly wage (lower was better) and the number of available workers (the more the better). Public policy could affect most of the indicators, though, even if it could not set them in a precise way.

Some components of the index reflected nonpartisan indicators that Republicans and Democrats alike routinely sought to improve. These items included the availability of medical facilities and the effectiveness of transportation systems. Other components broke along the usual partisan divides, with the advice of Grant Thornton closely paralleling the rhetoric of the GOP. The firm recommended that states keep taxes low, restrict government spending, curtail unemployment compensation, reduce payments for workers' compensation, and prevent unionization of the workforce. In recent years other indexes attempt to measure the competitiveness of states and the prospects for sustaining a robust economy. As one would predict, conservative think tanks and advocacy organizations construct indexes premised on beliefs that a favorable business climate results from policies that limit taxes, cut spending, and eliminate regulations.[24]

On the liberal end of the political spectrum, the policies needed to attract and retain businesses differ dramatically. Liberal analysts typically see government spending as a stimulus to growth when it focuses on education, child care, job training, research and development, building transportation infrastructure, and maintaining the quality of life. Rather than representing an inherent drag on the economy, the reasoning goes, government can and must undertake specific actions to promote it. In the liberal view, public amenities such as parks, cultural events, and a clean environment spark inflows of professionals and the desirable abilities and skills they bring with them. Some analysts have even suggested that tolerance for diverse beliefs and behaviors, a value usually advocated for its own sake, facilitates an area's prosperity. Richard Florida has constructed a "gay index," finding that the same cultural openness that allows certain cities to maintain a large gay and lesbian population also attracts the talented and creative people—homosexual and heterosexual alike—who drive the most innovative sectors of the economy.[25] If a city wants to prosper in the modern economy, the index implies, it must welcome people from all walks of life.

In contrast to their disagreements on how to create the conditions for prosperity, then, liberals and conservatives share a propensity to defend particular policies through reasoning and evidence about the effects on the business climates of states and localities. The prominence of these debates, along with the large number of policies pulled into their orbit, illustrates what has happened throughout American politics in recent decades. At the federal, state, and local levels, political leaders consistently highlight the promised economic benefits of their policy initiatives. The interpretations of many political commentators notwithstanding, the economy has become more central, not less, to campaigns, policy discussions, and legislative deliberations. Far from falling off the public agenda in an age of conflicts over social and cultural issues, economic matters guide the nation's political development more fully now than they did in the immediate decades after World War II.

A potential counterargument would be that the orienting of American politics around economic interpretations of issues represents nothing new. Has it not always been the case that political actors rhetorically have constructed policies around their purported links to the economy? On one level, elected officials throughout American history have sought to implement policies that would help the nation's inhabitants steadily increase their standard of living. That goal varies across periods, however, from being paramount to being only one of many important objectives. The distinctive aspect of today's political environment is the *extent to which* policies are framed in economic terms. Political leaders increasingly advocate their positions on many different issues, this book has shown, with claims about the effects on the economy.

Based on the past and present of American politics, what might the future hold? Will the current era endure, or will we witness a world in which economic rhetoric fades from the political scene? Social scientists do not sport an impressive track record on predicting the future, and so it is with some trepidation that I venture a judgment here. Still, the theory and evidence of this book allow for an informed, albeit uncertain, projection into the future: With so many people feeling the strains of economic insecurity, a wide range of political issues will continue to be cast in economic terms. Any ideological movement or political party without a coherent and easily communicated solution to pervasive economic troubles will find it difficult to earn the lasting allegiance of citizens and voters. Should economic insecurity remain widespread, as appears likely, political actors will frame many policy initiatives around the prospects for additional jobs, higher growth, and larger incomes.

NOTES

CHAPTER ONE. INTRODUCTION

1. Wm. F. Buckley, Jr., "Publisher's Statement," *National Review*, November 19, 1955, 5.

2. Bureau of the Census, *Historical Statistics of the United States, Colonial Times to 1970*, part 1 (Washington, DC: Government Printing Office, 1975), 178.

3. On the need for principled criticism of Eisenhower, see "Welcome Back," *National Review*, November 19, 1955, 3. On Eisenhower's reelection, see the debate between James Burnham and William S. Schlamm, "Should Conservatives Vote for Eisenhower-Nixon?" *National Review*, October 20, 1956, 12–15. Buckley's thoughts on choosing the lesser of two evils can be found in Wm. F. Buckley, Jr., "Reflections on Election Eve," *National Review*, November 3, 1956, 6–7.

4. Among many positive articles on Goldwater published in 1963 and 1964, see "Reflections on California," *National Review*, June 16, 1964, 477–79.

5. A summary of Buckley's later views can be found in "10 Questions for William F. Buckley," *Time*, April 12, 2004, 8.

6. Influential works from the 1980s include Paul Gottfried and Thomas Fleming, *The Conservative Movement* (Boston: Twayne Publishers, 1988); Kenneth Hoover and Raymond Plant, *Conservative Capitalism in Britain and the United States: A Critical Appraisal* (London: Routledge, 1989); Thomas Ferguson and Joel Rogers, *Right Turn: The Decline of the Democrats and the Future of American Politics* (New York: Hill and Wang, 1986); Joseph G. Peschek, *Policy-Planning Organizations: Elite Agendas and America's Rightward Turn* (Philadelphia: Temple University Press, 1987); Michael W. Miles, *The Odyssey of the American Right* (New York: Oxford University Press, 1980); Sidney Blumenthal, *The Rise of the Counter-Establishment: From Conservative Ideology to Political Power* (New York: Times Books, 1986); and William A. Rusher, *The Rise of the Right* (New York: Morrow, 1984).

7. Jonathan Schoenwald, *A Time for Choosing: The Rise of Modern American Conservatism* (New York: Oxford University Press, 2002); Lisa McGirr, *Suburban Warriors: The Origins of the New American Right* (Princeton: Princeton University Press, 2001); Matthew Dallek, *The Right Moment: Ronald Reagan's First Victory and the Decisive Turning Point in American Politics* (New York: Free Press, 2000); Rick Perlstein, *Before the Storm: Barry Goldwater and the Unmaking of the American Consensus* (New York: Hill and Wang, 2001); Mary C. Brennan, *Turning Right in the Sixties: The Conservative Capture of the GOP* (Chapel Hill: University of North Carolina Press, 1995); Gregory L. Schneider, *Cadres for Conservatism: Young Americans for Freedom and the Rise of the Contemporary Right* (New York: New York University Press, 1999); Niels Bjerre-Poulsen, *Right Face: Organizing the American Conservative Movement, 1945–65* (Copenhagen: Museum Tusculanum, 2002); W. Wesley McDonald, *Russell Kirk and the Age of Ideology* (Columbia: University of Missouri Press, 2004).

8. Lee Edwards, *The Conservative Revolution: The Movement That Remade America* (New York: Free Press, 1999); William C. Berman, *America's Right Turn: From Nixon to Clinton* (Baltimore: Johns Hopkins University Press, 1998); Godfrey Hodgson, *The World Turned Right Side Up: A History of the Conservative Ascendancy in America* (Boston: Houghton Mifflin, 1996); Godfrey Hodgson, *More Equal Than Others: America from Nixon to the New Century* (Princeton: Princeton University Press, 2004); Thomas M. Keck, *The Most Activist Supreme Court in History: The Road to Modern Judicial Conservatism* (Chicago: University of Chicago Press, 2004); Jerome L. Himmelstein, *To the Right: The Transformation of American Conservatism* (Berkeley: University of California Press, 1990); J. Richard Piper, *Ideologies and Institutions: American Conservative and Liberal Governance Prescriptions since 1933* (Lanham, MD.: Rowman and Littlefield, 1997); Clyde Wilcox, *Onward Christian Soldiers? The Religious Right in American Politics* (Boulder, CO: Westview Press, 2000); Dan T. Carter, *From George Wallace to Newt Gingrich: Race in the Conservative Counterrevolution, 1963–1994* (Baton Rouge: Louisiana State University Press, 1996).

9. John Micklethwait and Adrian Wooldridge, *The Right Nation: Conservative Power in America* (New York: Penguin Press, 2004); Thomas Byrne Edsall and Mary D. Edsall, *Chain Reaction: The Impact of Race, Rights, and Taxes on American Politics* (New York: W. W. Norton, 1991); Dinesh D'Souza, *Ronald Reagan: How an Ordinary Man Became an Extraordinary Leader* (New York: Free Press, 1997); Amy E. Ansell, ed., *Unraveling the Right: The New Conservatism in American Thought and Politics* (Boulder, CO: Westview Press, 1998); Nina J. Easton, *Gang of Five: Leaders at the Center of the Conservative Crusade* (New York: Simon and Schuster, 2000); Sara Dimond, *Roads to Dominion: Right-Wing Movements and Political Power in the United States* (New York: Guilford Press, 1995).

10. Data provided by Russell D. Renka, ustudies.semo.edu/ui320-75/course/presandcongress.asp, accessed November 11, 2006.

11. On state and local taxes, see *Who Pays? A Distributional Analysis of the Tax Systems in All 50 States* (Washington, DC: Institute on Taxation and Economic Policy, 2003); on federal taxation, see Joseph Pechman, *Federal Tax Policy* (Washington, DC: Brookings Institution, 1987).

12. Charles Marwick, "Putting Money Where the U.S. Mouth Is," *Journal of the American Medical Association* (May 7, 1997): 1340–43.

13. Bryant Urstadt, "A Four-Year Plague," *Harper's Magazine*, May 2004, 81–88.

14. Ross Eisenbrey, "Overtime Protection in Jeopardy," *EPI Journal* (Fall 2003): 1, 9.

15. Suzanne Mettler, "The Transformed Welfare State and the Redistribution of Political Voice," in Paul Pierson and Theda Skocpol, eds., *The Transformation of the American Polity* (forthcoming).

16. Peter G. Gosselin, "If America Is Richer, Why Are Its Families So Much Less Secure?" *Los Angeles Times Magazine*, October 10, 2004.

17. Mettler, "The Transformed Welfare State."

18. Cooperative Institutional Research Program, *The American Freshman: Thirty Year Trends* (Los Angeles: Laboratory for Research in Higher Education, Graduate School of Education, University of California, 1997); Cooperative Institutional Research Program, "The American Freshman: National Norms for Fall 2000," press release, January 22, 2001.

19. W. Lance Bennett, "The Uncivic Culture: Communication, Identity, and the Rise of Lifestyle Politics," *PS: Political Science and Politics* 31 (December 1998): 741–61.

20. "Secrets of the SAT," *Frontline*, October 4, 1999. Transcript downloaded from www.pbs.org/wgbh/pages/frontline/shows/sats/etc/script.html, accessed October 22, 2004.

21. Walter Parker, *Teaching Democracy: Unity and Diversity in Public Life* (New York: Teachers College Press, 2003).

22. John I. Goodlad, *A Place Called School: Prospects for the Future* (New York: McGraw-Hill, 1984).

23. Russell Kirk, "Libertarians: The Chirping Sectaries," *Modern Age* (Fall 1981): 345.

24. Barry Goldwater, *The Conscience of a Conservative* (New York: Victor Publishing Company, 1960), 10. Emphasis in original.

25. William H. Riker, *The Art of Political Manipulation* (New Haven: Yale University Press, 1986).

26. Thomas Frank, *What's the Matter with Kansas? How Conservatives Won the Heart of America* (New York: Metropolitan Books, 2004).

27. For entry points into this literature, see Edsall and Edsall, *Chain Reaction*; and David Lublin, *The Republican South: Democratization and Partisan Change* (Princeton: Princeton University Press, 2004).

CHAPTER TWO. THE ROLE OF RHETORIC IN THE FORMATION OF POLICY

1. Landmark works in public policy include Roger W. Cobb and Charles D. Elder, *Participation in American Politics: The Dynamics of Agenda-Building*, 2nd ed. (Baltimore: Johns Hopkins University Press, 1983); John W. Kingdon, *Agendas, Alternatives, and Public Policies* (Boston: Little, Brown, 1984); and Frank R. Baumgartner and Bryan D. Jones, *Agendas and Instability in American Politics* (Chicago: University of Chicago Press, 1993).

2. Anthony Gill, "The Political Origins of Religious Liberty: A Theoretical Outline," *Interdisciplinary Journal of Research on Religion* 1, no. 1 (2005): article 1.

3. Kathryn Sikkink, *Ideas and Institutions: Developmentalism in Brazil and Argentina* (Ithaca: Cornell University Press, 1991), 18.

4. Robert Lieberman, "Ideas, Institutions, and Political Order," *American Political Science Review* 96 (December 2002): 697.

5. Sheri Berman, *The Social Democratic Moment: Ideas and Politics in the Making of Interwar Europe* (Cambridge, MA: Harvard University Press, 1998); Peter A. Hall, ed., *The Political Power of Economic Ideas: Keynesianism across Nations* (Princeton: Princeton University Press, 1989); Martha Derthick and Paul J. Quirk, *The Politics of Deregulation* (Washington, DC: Brookings Institution, 1985).

6. Stanley Feldman, "Structure and Consistency in Public Opinion: The Role of Core Beliefs and Values," *American Journal of Political Science* 32 (1988): 416–40; Stanley Feldman and John Zaller, "The Political Culture of Ambivalence: Ideological Responses to the Welfare State," *American Journal of Political Science* 36 (1992): 268–307.

7. Judith Goldstein, *Ideas, Interests, and American Trade Policy* (Ithaca: Cornell University Press, 1993).

8. Barry R. Weingast, "A Rational Choice Perspective on the Role of Ideas: Shared Belief Systems, State Sovereignty, and International Cooperation," *Politics and Society* 23 (1995): 449–64; Robert H. Bates, Rui J. de Figueiredo, Jr., and Barry R. Weingast, "The Politics of Interpretation: Rationality, Culture, and Transition," *Politics and Society* 26 (1998): 221–56.

9. John L. Campbell, "Institutional Analysis and the Role of Ideas in Political Economy," *Theory and Society* 27 (1998): 377–409; Mark Blyth, *Great Transformations: Economic Ideas and Institutional Change in the Twentieth Century* (New York: Cambridge University Press, 2002); Lieberman, "Ideas, Institutions, and Political Order"; Berman, *The Social Democratic Moment*.

10. Kenneth Burke, *A Rhetoric of Motives* (New York: Prentice-Hall, 1950); Maurice Charland, "Constitutive Rhetoric: The Case of the Peuple Québécois," *Quarterly Journal of Speech* 73 (1987): 133–50; John C. Hammerback and Richard J. Jensen, *The Rhetorical Career of César Chávez* (College Station: Texas A&M University Press, 1998).

11. Anne Schneider and Helen Ingram, "Social Construction of Target Populations: Implications for Politics and Policy," *American Political Science Re-*

view 87 (1993): 334–47; Kingdon, *Agendas, Alternatives, and Public Policies*; Deborah A. Stone, "Causal Stories and the Formation of Policy Agendas," *Political Science Quarterly* (1989): 281–300.

12. Robert D. Benford and David A. Snow, "Framing Processes and Social Movements: An Overview and Assessment," *Annual Review of Sociology* (2000): 611–39.

13. Martha Finnemore, *National Interests in International Society* (Ithaca: Cornell University Press, 1996); Jutta Weldes, *Constructing National Interests: The United States and the Cuban Missile Crisis* (Minneapolis: University of Minnesota Press, 1999).

14. Judith Goldstein and Robert O. Keohane, "Ideas and Foreign Policy: An Analytical Framework," in Judith Goldstein and Robert O. Keohane, eds., *Ideas and Foreign Policy: Beliefs, Institutions, and Political Change* (Ithaca: Cornell University Press, 1993); John Kurt Jacobsen, "Much Ado about Ideas: The Cognitive Factor in Economic Policy," *World Politics* (January 1995): 283–310; Kenneth Shepsle, "Comment on Why the Regulators Chose to Deregulate," in Roger Noll, ed., *Regulatory Policy and the Social Sciences* (Berkeley: University of California Press, 1985), 231–39.

15. John W. Kingdon, "Agendas, Ideas, and Policy Change," in Lawrence C. Dodd and Calvin Jillson, eds., *New Perspectives on American Politics* (Washington, DC: CQ Press, 1994), 215–29.

16. Lawrence R. Jacobs and Robert Y. Shapiro, *Politicians Don't Pander: Political Manipulation and the Loss of Democratic Responsiveness* (Chicago: University of Chicago Press, 2000).

17. Roderick P. Hart, *The Sound of Leadership: Presidential Communication in the Modern Age* (Chicago: University of Chicago Press, 1987); Samuel Kernell, *Going Public: New Strategies of Presidential Leadership*, 3rd ed. (Washington, DC: CQ Press, 1997).

18. William H. Riker, *The Art of Political Manipulation* (New Haven: Yale University Press, 1986); idem., *The Strategy of Rhetoric: Campaigning for the American Constitution* (New Haven: Yale University Press, 1996).

19. Although Murray Edelman takes his analysis in different directions, some of his work finds echoes in the perspective developed here. See Murray J. Edelman, *The Symbolic Uses of Politics* (Urbana: University of Illinois Press, 1964); idem., *Political Language: Words That Succeed and Policies That Fail* (New York: Academic Press, 1977).

20. Robert M. Entman, "Framing: Toward Clarification of a Fractured Paradigm," *Journal of Communication* 43 (1993): 51–67.

21. James N. Druckman, "Political Preference Formation: Competition, Deliberation, and the (IR)relevance of Framing Effects," *American Political Science Review* 98 (2004): 617–86.

22. Laura Stoker, "Political Value Judgments," in James H. Kuklinski, ed.,

Citizens and Politics: Perspectives from Political Psychology (Cambridge: Cambridge University Press, 2001), 433–68. See also Lawrence Bobo and James R. Kluegel, "Opposition to Race-Targeting: Self-Interest, Stratification Ideology, or Racial Attitudes?" *American Sociological Review* 58 (1993): 443–64; and Paul M. Sniderman and Thomas Piazza, *The Scar of Race* (Cambridge, MA: Harvard University Press, 1993).

23. John R. Zaller, *The Nature and Origins of Mass Opinion* (Cambridge: Cambridge University Press, 1992); Shanto Iyengar, *Is Anyone Responsible? How Television Frames Political Issues* (Chicago: University of Chicago Press, 1991).

24. Thomas E. Nelson and Zoe M. Oxley, "Issue Framing Effects on Belief Importance and Opinion," *The Journal of Politics* 61 (1999): 1040–67; Thomas E. Nelson, Rosalee A. Clawson, and Zoe M. Oxley, "Media Framing of a Civil Liberties Conflict and Its Effect on Tolerance," *American Political Science Review* 91 (1997): 567–83.

25. Iyengar, *Is Anyone Responsible?*

26. Donald R. Kinder and Lynn M. Sanders, *Divided by Color: Racial Politics and Democratic Ideal* (Chicago: University of Chicago Press, 1996), ch. 7; William G. Jacoby, "Issue Framing and Public Opinion on Government Spending," *American Journal of Political Science* 44 (2000): 750–67.

27. Donald R. Kinder, "Communication and Opinion," *Annual Review of Political Science* 1 (1998): 167–97.

28. Oscar H. Gandy, Jr., "Epilogue—Framing at the Horizon: A Retrospective Assessment," in Stephen D. Reese, Oscar H. Gandy, Jr., and August E. Grant, eds., *Framing Public Life: Perspectives on Media and Our Understanding of the World* (Mahwah, NJ: Lawrence Erlbaum Associates, 2001), 357.

29. Chaim Perelman, with Lucia Olbrechts-Tyteca, *The New Rhetoric: A Treatise on Argumentation*, trans. John Wilkinson and Purcell Weaver (Notre Dame: University of Notre Dame Press, 1969).

30. Herbert A. Wilchelns, "The Literary Criticism of Oratory," in Alexander M. Drummond, ed., *Studies in Rhetoric and Public Speaking in Honor of James Albert Winans, by Pupils and Colleagues* (New York: Century, 1925), 199; Lloyd F. Bitzer, "The Rhetorical Situation," *Philosophy and Rhetoric* 1 (1968): 1–14; Stephen E. Lucas, "The Renaissance of American Public Address: Text and Context in Rhetorical Criticism," *Quarterly Journal of Speech* 74 (1988): 241–60.

31. Rhetoricians working with a postmodern orientation, by contrast, begin from a different starting point that does not overlap cleanly with the foundations of this chapter.

32. Jeffrey K. Tulis, *The Rhetorical Presidency* (Princeton: Princeton University Press, 1987).

33. Kathleen Hall Jamieson, *Packaging the Presidency*, 3rd ed. (New York: Oxford University Press, 1996).

34. Robert M. Entman, *Projections of Power: Framing News, Public Opinion, and U.S. Foreign Policy* (Chicago: University of Chicago Press, 2003).

35. Erving Goffman, *Frame Analysis: An Essay on the Organization of Experience* (Cambridge, MA: Harvard University Press, 1974); William A. Gamson and Andre Modigliani, "The Changing Culture of Affirmative Action," in R. D. Braungart, ed., *Research in Political Sociology* 3 (Greenwich, CT: JAI Press, 1987), 137–76; William A. Gamson and Andre Modigliani, "Media Discourse and Public Opinion on Nuclear Power: A Constructionist Approach," *American Journal of Sociology* 95 (1989): 1–37; John L. Campbell, "Institutional Analysis and the Role of Ideas in Political Economy," *Theory and Society* 27 (1998): 377–409.

36. For an approach similar in some respects, see Teena Gabrielson, "Obstacles and Opportunities: Factors That Constrain Elected Officials' Ability to Frame Political Issues," in Karen Callaghan and Frauke Schnell, eds., *Framing American Politics* (Pittsburgh: University of Pittsburgh Press, 2005), 76–99.

37. Baumgartner and Jones, *Agendas and Instability in American Politics*.

38. Lawrence R. Jacobs and Robert Y. Shapiro, "Issues, Candidate Image, and Priming: The Use of Private Polls in Kennedy's 1960 Presidential Campaign," *American Political Science Review* 88 (September 1994): 527–40.

39. Riker, *The Art of Political Manipulation*.

40. Campbell, "Institutional Analysis"; Gamson and Modigliani, "The Changing Culture of Affirmative Action."

41. Campbell, "Institutional Analysis"; David Zarefsky, *President Johnson's War on Poverty: Rhetoric and History* (Tuscaloosa, AL: University of Alabama Press, 1986), ch. 1.

42. Timothy E. Cook, *Governing with the News: The News Media as a Political Institution* (Chicago: University of Chicago Press, 1998); Herbert J. Gans, *Deciding What's News: A Study of CBS Evening News, NBC Nightly News, Newsweek, and Time* (New York: Pantheon Books, 1979).

43. W. Lance Bennett, *News: The Politics of Illusion*, 4th ed. (New York: Longman, 2001).

44. James W. Dearing and Everett M. Rogers, *Agenda-Setting* (Thousand Oaks, CA: Sage Publications, 1996).

45. Baumgartner and Jones, *Agendas and Instability in American Politics*; Bryan D. Jones, *Reconceiving Decision-Making in Democratic Societies: Attention, Choice, and Public Policy* (Chicago: University of Chicago Press, 1994); Bryan D. Jones and Frank R. Baumgartner, *The Politics of Attention: How Government Prioritizes Problems* (Chicago: University of Chicago Press, 2005).

46. Richard F. Fenno, Jr., *Home Style: House Members in Their Districts* (Boston: Little, Brown, 1978).

47. Keith T. Poole and Howard Rosenthal, *Congress: A Political-Economic History of Roll Call Voting* (New York: Oxford University Press, 1997).

48. This need will often come when interest groups or opponents in future elections challenge particular votes or actions taken in office. See R. Douglas Arnold, *The Logic of Congressional Action* (New Haven: Yale University Press, 1990).

49. My notion of political actors' adopting new forms of rhetoric to defend their positions finds a parallel in the work of John Kingdon, who discusses how long-standing policy solutions are marshaled to address new policy problems that emerge in the public agenda. See Kingdon, *Agendas, Alternatives, and Public Policies.*

50. Maxwell E. McCombs and Donald Shaw, "The Agenda Setting Function of the Mass Media," *Public Opinion Quarterly* 36 (1972): 176–87; Cobb and Elder, *Participation in American Politics.*

51. The national exit poll contained 158 Nader voters who answered a question about what they would have done in a two-way contest between Al Gore and George W. Bush. Among those respondents, 30% would not have voted, 47% would have chosen Gore, and 22% would have chosen Bush. By reallocating the Nader voters to the categories of nonvoters, Gore supporters, and Bush supporters, Gore's nationwide edge over Bush of 0.5% would have grown to 2.4%, these estimates indicate, had Nader not entered the race. Given the thin margins of the Bush victories in Florida and New Hampshire, the absence of Nader from the race probably would have swung those two states to Gore.

52. For a related view of policy change, see the discussion of "rational anticipation" in James A. Stimson, Michael B. MacKuen, and Robert S. Erikson, "Dynamic Representation," *American Political Science Review* 89 (Sept. 1995), 543–65.

53. Bryan D. Jones, *Politics and the Architecture of Choice: Bounded Rationality and Governance* (Chicago: University of Chicago Press, 2001).

54. Kingdon, "Agendas, Ideas, and Policy Change."

55. I owe the metaphor to James A. Stimson, *Public Opinion in America: Moods, Cycles, and Swings* (Boulder, CO: Westview Press, 1991).

CHAPTER THREE. ECONOMIC INSECURITY AND ITS RHETORICAL CONSEQUENCES

1. Bush's campaign advertisements in 2004, along with those of other candidates since 1952, are addressed in more detail in chapter 7.

2. James A. Morone, *Hellfire Nation: The Politics of Sin in American History* (New Haven: Yale University Press, 2003).

3. On the flaws in the belief that Americans are deeply divided, see Morris P. Fiorina, *Culture War? The Myth of a Polarized America* (New York: Pearson Longman, 2005).

4. Bernard D. Nossiter, *Fat Years and Lean: The American Economy Since Roosevelt* (Grand Rapids, MI: Harper and Row, 1990), 38–43.

5. Robert M. Collins, *More: The Politics of Economic Growth in Postwar America* (New York: Oxford University Press, 2000), 10–16.

6. The poll was conducted by the National Opinion Research Center and

is archived at the Roper Center at the University of Connecticut, question ID USNORC.45237A, R01.

7. Angus Maddison, *Dynamic Forces in Capitalist Development: A Long-Run Comparative View* (New York: Oxford University Press, 1991), 50–53.

8. Mauro F. Guillen, *Models of Management: Work, Authority, and Organization in a Comparative Perspective* (Chicago: University of Chicago Press, 1994).

9. Adolf A. Berle, Jr., and Gardiner C. Means, *The Modern Corporation and Private Property* (New York: Commerce Clearing House, 1932); Alfred D. Chandler, Jr., *The Visible Hand: The Managerial Revolution in American Business* (Cambridge, MA: Belknap Press, 1977).

10. The income figures are based on data drawn from the Historical Income Tables, Current Population Survey, U.S. Bureau of the Census, www.census.gov. The adjustments for inflation are based on the most recent consumer price index provided by the Bureau of Labor Statistics, CPI-U-RS. On the expectations of the Roosevelt administration, see Collins, *More*, 59–61; and Herbert Stein, *Presidential Economics: The Making of Economic Policy from Roosevelt to Clinton*, 3rd ed. (Washington, DC: American Enterprise Institute, 1994), 95, 112.

11. Sanford M. Jacoby, *Modern Manors: Welfare Capitalism Since the New Deal* (Princeton: Princeton University Press, 1997), esp. 247–52.

12. Nicholas Lemann, *The Promised Land: The Great Black Migration and How It Changed America* (New York: A. A. Knopf, 1991).

13. See the Historical Income Tables, Current Population Survey, U.S. Bureau of the Census, "Gini Ratios for Families, by Race and Hispanic Origin of Householder: 1947 to 2000" and "Share of Aggregate Income Received by Each Fifth and Top 5 Percent of Families (All Races): 1947 to 2000," www.census.gov.

14. The data come from the Survey Research Center at the University of Michigan, www.sca.isr.umich.edu.

15. Frank Levy, *The New Dollars and Dreams: American Incomes and Economic Change* (New York: Russell Sage Foundation, 1998), 38–56.

16. F. M. Scherer, "Corporate Ownership and Control," in John R. Meyer and James M. Gustafson, eds., *The U.S. Business Corporation: An Institution in Transition* (Cambridge, MA: Ballinger Publishing Company, 1988), 43–46.

17. Michael Porter, "Capital Disadvantage: America's Failing Capital Investment System," *Harvard Business Review* 70 (September–October 1992): 65–82.

18. Paul Osterman, *Securing Prosperity: The American Labor Market; How It Has Changed and What to Do about It* (Princeton: Princeton University Press, 1999), 38–39.

19. Stefanie R. Schmidt, "Job Security Beliefs in the General Social Survey: Evidence on Long-Run Trends and Comparability with Other Surveys," in David Neumark, ed., *On The Job: Is Long-Term Employment a Thing of the Past?* (New York: Russell Sage Foundation, 2000), 300–34.

20. The questions read, "Would you say that you (and your family living

there) are better off or worse off financially than you were a year ago?" and "Would you say that at the present time business conditions are better or worse than they were a year ago?" See n. 14.

21. Calculated by the author.

22. The increasing connection between the personal (commonly called "pocketbook" in the literature on economic voting) and the social (dubbed "sociotropic") also appears in people's expectations of what will happen to their own families and to business conditions over the next twelve months. Quarterly responses to those two questions correlate at .64 in the 1960s, .85 in the 1970s, .91 in the 1980s, and .95 in the 1990s.

23. Calculated from data provided by the Bureau of Labor Statistics, www.stats.bls.gov.

24. Calculated from the Historical Income Tables, Current Population Survey, U.S. Bureau of the Census, "Families by Median and Mean Income: 1947 to 2000," www.census.gov.

25. Levy, *The New Dollars and Dreams*, 50–51.

26. Annette Bernhardt, Martina Morris, Mark S. Hancock, and Marc A. Scott, *Divergent Paths: Economic Mobility in the New American Labor Market* (New York: Russell Sage Foundation, 2001), 148.

27. Jacob Hacker, *The Great Risk Shift: The Assault on American Jobs, Families, Health Care, and Retirement—and How You Can Fight Back* (New York: Oxford University Press, 2006).

28. Osterman, *Securing Prosperity*, 45–47.

29. Barbara Ehrenreich, *Nickel and Dimed: On (Not) Getting by in America* (New York: Metropolitan Books, 2001).

30. Calculated from the Historical Income Tables, Current Population Survey, U.S. Bureau of the Census, "Years of School Completed—People 25 Years Old and Over by Median Income and Sex: 1958 to 1990" and "Educational Attainment—People 25 Years Old and Over by Mean Income and Sex: 1991 to 2000," www.census.gov.

31. Calculated from the Historical Income Tables, Current Population Survey, U.S. Bureau of the Census, "Share of Aggregate Income Received by Each Fifth and Top 5 Percent of Families (All Races): 1947 to 2000," www.census.gov.

32. For an entry point into these matters, see the hearing Bureau of Labor Statistics Oversight: Fixing the Consumer Price Index, conducted by the Subcommittee on Human Resources of the Committee on Government Reform and Oversight, House of Representatives, 105th Cong., 2nd sess., 1997.

33. Gregg Easterbrook, *The Progress Paradox: How Life Gets Better While People Feel Worse* (New York: Random House, 2003).

34. W. Michael Cox and Richard Alm, *Myths of Rich and Poor: Why We're Better Off Than We Think* (New York: Basic Books, 1999), 15. See also Brian Goff and Richard A. Fleisher III, *Spoiled Rotten: Affluence, Anxiety, and Social Decay in America* (Boulder, CO: Westview Press, 1999); Richard B. McKenzie, *The Paradox*

of Progress: Can Americans Regain Their Confidence in a Prosperous Future? (New York: Oxford University Press, 1997).

35. Ted Robert Gurr, *Why Men Rebel* (Princeton: Princeton University Press, 1970); James M. Olson, C. Peter Herman, and Mark P. Zanna, eds., *Relative Deprivation and Social Comparison* (Hillsdale, NJ: Lawrence Erlbaum, 1986); Faye Crosby, "A Model of Egotistical Relative Deprivation," *Psychological Review* 83 (1976): 85–113.

36. Robert J. Samuelson, *The Good Life and Its Discontents: The American Dream in the Age of Entitlement, 1945–1995* (New York: Times Books, 1995); Goff and Fleisher, *Spoiled Rotten.*

37. Juliet B. Schor, *The Overspent American: Upscaling, Downshifting, and the New Consumer* (New York: Basic Books, 1998), 15.

38. Robert D. Putnam, *Bowling Alone: The Collapse and Revival of American Community* (New York: Simon and Schuster, 2000), 272–73.

39. Schor, *The Overspent American.*

40. Robert H. Frank, *Luxury Fever: Why Money Fails to Satisfy in an Era of Excess* (New York: Free Press, 1999).

41. Putnam, *Bowling Alone.*

42. Levy, *The New Dollars and Dreams*, 49–50.

43. Calculated from Federal Reserve Board, Flow of Funds Accounts of the United States, annual historical data, www.federalreserve.gov/releases/z1/current/data.htm.

44. The poll was conducted by Widmeyer Communications from August 4 to August 9, 2004. Results are available from Public Opinion Online, the Roper Center at the University of Connecticut, question ID USWIDM.04ADREAM, R23.

45. Teresa A. Sullivan, Elizabeth Warren, and Jay Lawrence Westbrook, *The Fragile Middle Class: Americans in Debt* (New Haven: Yale University Press, 2000).

46. American Bankruptcy Institute, U.S. Bankruptcy Filing Statistics, www.abiworld.org, accessed July 23, 2005.

47. Figures on the number of bachelor's degrees awarded can be found in the *Digest of Education Statistics*, published annually by the National Center for Education Statistics at the U.S. Department of Education.

48. For historical data, see Marc Miringoff and Marque-Luisa Miringoff, *The Social Health of the Nation: How America Is Really Doing* (New York: Oxford University Press, 1999, 92–97, 198. Recent figures based on census reports are described in Debora Vrana, "Rising Premiums Threaten Job-Based Health Coverage," *Los Angeles Times*, September 15, 2005, A1.

49. Calculated from data provided by the Bureau of Labor Statistics, www.stats.bls.gov.

50. Council of Economic Advisors, *Economic Report of the President Transmitted to the Congress* (Washington, DC: Government Printing Office, 2000).

51. The poll was conducted by the Gallup Organization in October 1999.

The results are available from Public Opinion Online, Roper Center at the University of Connecticut, question ID USGALLUP.59IISR12, Q05A.

52. Av Westin, *Newswatch: How TV Decides the News* (New York: Simon and Schuster, 1982), ch. 6.

53. Doug Underwood, *When MBAs Rule the Newsroom: How the Marketers and Managers Are Reshaping Media* (New York: Columbia University Press, 1995).

54. W. Lance Bennett, *News: The Politics of Illusion*, 4th ed. (New York: Addison Wesley Longman, 2001), ch. 3.

55. See, for example, Paul M. Kellstedt, *The Mass Media and the Dynamics of American Racial Attitudes* (Cambridge: Cambridge University Press, 2003), chs. 2, 4.

56. Most of these data (1946–1994) were collected by Frank R. Baumgartner and Bryan D. Jones, with the support of National Science Foundation grant number SBR 9320922, and were distributed through the Center for American Politics and Public Policy at the University of Washington. The remaining data (1995–2004), which I compiled before Baumgartner and Jones had updated their data, reflect the front-page stories from a random sample of fifty days per year. Most aspects of the economy are covered in Baumgartner and Jones's category for macroeconomics. Some stories in their other categories, however, can be considered economic even though the content overlaps with different policy topics. In particular, stories that could be called microeconomic are included within the figures presented in this chapter. For example, stories about the prices or costs of particular goods and services such as cars, computers, gasoline, food, and college tuition fall in other categories for Baumgartner and Jones but are called economic here. Because matters of foreign trade deal with imports, exports, and jobs, I have called them economic despite their existence as a separate category for Baumgartner and Jones. Similarly, I have classified as economic most stories about strikes and labor negotiations along with some that fall within Baumgartner and Jones's topic codes of "Energy" and "Banking, Finance, and Domestic Commerce." My definition of "economic," in short, is considerably more expansive than the Baumgartner and Jones category of macroeconomics.

57. Shanto Iyengar and Donald R. Kinder, *News That Matters: Television and American Opinion* (Chicago: University of Chicago Press, 1987), ch. 4.

58. Like most of the data above on media coverage, these data were collected by Frank R. Baumgartner and Bryan D. Jones as part of the Policy Agendas Project. As with news coverage, my category for the economy includes not only unemployment, inflation, interest rates, and the overall economy, but also labor, energy production and prices, banking and commerce, and foreign trade.

59. Conducted on a regular basis, the Gallup surveys are spread roughly equally across the period. The data include 30 surveys from the period 1973–1979, 44 surveys from 1980–1989, 38 surveys from 1990–1999, and 64 surveys from 2000–2006.

60. This perspective appears, for example, in Ben J. Wattenberg, *Values*

Matter Most: How Republicans or Democrats or a Third Party Can Win and Renew the American Way of Life (New York: Free Press, 1995).

61. Thomas Frank, *What's the Matter with Kansas? How Conservatives Won the Heart of America* (New York: Metropolitan Books, 2004).

62. See Ronald Inglehart, *Culture Shift in Advanced Industrialized Societies* (Princeton: Princeton University Press, 1990), and *The Silent Revolution: Changing Values and Political Styles among Western Publics* (Princeton: Princeton University Press, 1977).

63. Ronald Inglehart, "The Silent Revolution in Europe: Intergenerational Change in Post-Industrial Societies," *American Political Science Review* 65: (December 1971): 991–1017.

64. Inglehart's thinking about what would happen if economic difficulties returned can be found in *The Silent Revolution*, 106, 114–15.

65. The extent to which, and the ways in which, public policy has contributed to economic insecurity falls outside the scope of my analysis. In this book I am primarily concerned with the consequences of economic insecurity rather than its causes.

66. Frank R. Baumgartner and Bryan D. Jones, *Agendas and Instability in American Politics* (Chicago: University of Chicago Press, 1993).

CHAPTER FOUR. THE BUILDING OF CONSERVATIVES'
INTELLECTUAL CAPACITY

1. George H. Nash, *The Conservative Intellectual Movement in America Since 1945* (Wilmington, DE: Intercollegiate Studies Institute, 1998 [1976]), xv.

2. William J. Barber, *From New Era to New Deal: Herbert Hoover, the Economists, and American Economic Policy, 1921–1933* (Cambridge: Cambridge University Press, 1985), ch. 2.

3. Nicholas Spulber, *Managing the American Economy from Roosevelt to Reagan* (Bloomington: Indiana University Press, 1989), 5–12; Barber, *From New Era to New Deal*.

4. William Trufant Foster and Waddill Catchings, *Business without a Buyer* (Boston: Houghton Mifflin, 1927), and *The Road to Plenty* (Boston: Houghton Mifflin, 1928).

5. Evelyn C. Brooks and Lee M. Brooks, "A Decade of 'Planning' Literature," *Social Forces* 12 (1934): 427–41. See also Hornell Hart, "Changing Opinions about Business Prosperity: A Consensus of Magazine Opinion in the U.S., 1929–1932," *American Journal of Sociology* 38 (1933): 665–87.

6. Milton Friedman and Anna Jacobson Schwartz, *A Monetary History of the United States, 1867–1960* (Princeton: Princeton University Press, 1963). See also Murray Rothbard, *America's Great Depression*, 2nd ed. (New York: New York University Press, 1975).

7. Jim Powell, *FDR's Folly: How Franklin D. Roosevelt and His New Deal Pro-*

longed the Depression (New York: Crown Forum, 2003); Gene Smiley, *Rethinking the Great Depression: A New View of Its Causes and Consequences* (Chicago: Ivan R. Dee, 2003).

8. Richard Vedder and Lowell Gallaway, *Out of Work: Unemployment and Government in Twentieth-Century America* (New York: Holmes and Meier, 1993), ch. 7.

9. Most of the floor debate on the old-age pensions occurred on April 19, 1935. See *Congressional Record* 74th Cong., 1st sess. (April 19, 1935), 6036–69.

10. See the debate preceding the amendment in *Congressional Record*, 74th Cong., 1st sess. (June 11, 1935), 9040–53.

11. The text of the platform is reprinted in Donald Bruce Johnson and Kirk H. Porter, *National Party Platforms, 1840–1972* (Urbana: University of Illinois Press, 1973), 365–75.

12. George Wolfskill, *The Revolt of the Conservatives: A History of the American Liberty League, 1934–1940* (Boston: Houghton Mifflin, 1962), ch. 5.

13. Robert A. Taft, Radio Address (March 18, 1939), reprinted in *Congressional Record*, 76th Cong., 1st sess., Appendix (1939), 1355–57.

14. Colin Hay, "Crisis and the Structural Transformation of the State: Interrogating the Process of Change," *British Journal of Politics and International Relations* 1 (October 1999): 317–44.

15. Mark Blyth, *Great Transformations: Economic Ideas and Institutional Change in the Twentieth Century* (New York: Cambridge University Press, 2002).

16. Nash, in *The Conservative Intellectual Movement*, describes these events in great detail.

17. Richard M. Weaver, *Ideas Have Consequences* (Chicago: University of Chicago Press, 1948).

18. As quoted in Nash, *The Conservative Intellectual Movement*, 24.

19. As quoted ibid., 129.

20. The figure incorporates all U.S.-based magazines with a national distribution whose content explicitly addressed political and social matters at least half the time. To be included, a magazine had to be openly ideological by identifying itself with a well-defined location on the political continuum for an extended period. The left, as classified here, includes not only radical orientations but also welfare or reform liberalism and rights-based perspectives; classical liberalism, or what is now called economic conservatism, is included with the right, as are publications addressing public affairs from the vantage point of traditionalist or religious conservatism. Obviously, collapsing all of these periodicals into categories of left and right loses the subtleties—there is a big difference in content, ideology, and tone between *Mother Jones* and *The American Prospect*, for example, or between *The Weekly Standard* and *Reason*—but the graph will suffice for present purposes.

21. Scholarly journals are not included unless they are written in a style

that makes them accessible to educated lay readers. The outlets on the right for the entire period are *National Review, American Spectator, Human Events, Insight, American Mercury, Intercollegiate Review, Weekly Standard, Public Interest, New Criterion, National Interest, Conservative Chronicle, New American, American Opinion, Freeman, Reason, Policy Review, City Journal, analysis, Chronicles of Culture, American Enterprise, World & I, Academic Questions, Regulation, AEI Economist, Foreign Policy and Defense Review, Southern Partisan, Plain Talk, American Renaissance, Human Life Review, Crisis, Catholicism in Crisis, Conservative Digest, Modern Age, Cato Journal,* and *First Things.* The outlets on the left are *Mother Jones, New York Review of Books, Nation, American Prospect, On the Issues, Progressive, Partisan Review, Utne Reader, New Republic, Ramparts, Washington Monthly, Boston Review, Reporter, I. F. Stone's Weekly, Dissent, Commonweal, Christianity and Crisis, Survey Midmonthly, Survey Graphic, World Watch, Liberation, Forum, Forum and Century, In These Times, The Baffler, Z Magazine, Tikkun, Sojourners, Working Papers for a New Society, Democratic Left, Multinational Monitor, Science and Society, New Leader, Progressive Populist, New Left Review, Social Policy,* and *Monthly Review. Commentary* is characterized as being on the left before 1970 and on the right thereafter. A handful of smaller periodicals on the left and right were excluded because their circulation levels were not listed in major directories. Given the large number of magazines and journals that are included, representing circulation totals of more than two million in 2000, any additional ones would not much alter the pattern in figure 4.1.

22. Very few of these reviews survived the changes over the last few decades in the public's tastes and the economics of the publishing industry. Politically oriented publications have expanded in numbers and circulation in part because they are subsidized, a point that I will revisit shortly.

23. The conservative ascent resulted from both the creation of new publications and the gains in circulation by existing ones, over and above the losses from those that ceased to exist. Additional weeklies, monthlies, and quarterlies appeared on the left as well, but their numbers and circulation levels were insufficient to offset the gains on the right.

24. For some reflections on this phenomenon, see William F. Buckley, Jr., "Can a Little Magazine Break Even?" *National Review,* October 10, 1959, 393–94, 407; Victor S. Navasky, *A Matter of Opinion* (New York: Farrar, Straus and Giroux, 2005).

25. Beth Schulman, "Foundations for a Movement: How the Right Wing Subsidizes Its Press," *EXTRA!* (March / April 1995): 12.

26. Sally Covington, *Moving a Public Policy Agenda: The Strategic Philanthropy of Conservative Foundations* (Washington, DC: National Committee for Responsive Philanthropy, 1997); Jeff Krehely, Meaghan House, and Emily Kernan, *Axis of Ideology: Conservative Foundations and Public Policy* (Washington, DC: National Committee for Responsive Philanthropy, 2004).

27. James A. Smith, *The Idea Brokers: Think Tanks and the Rise of the New Policy Elite* (New York: Free Press, 1991), chs. 3–4.

28. John K. Andrews, Jr., "So You Want to Start a Think Tank: A Battlefield Report from the States," *Policy Review* (1989): 62–65. Ownership of *Policy Review* later passed to the Hoover Institution.

29. "Mission Statement" (Indianapolis: Hudson Institute, 2004).

30. *Annual Report* (Washington, DC: Cato Institute, 2002).

31. Donald T. Crutchlow, *The Brookings Institution, 1916–1952: Expertise and the Public Interest in a Democratic Society* (DeKalb: Northern Illinois University Press, 1985).

32. James Allen Smith, *Brookings at Seventy-Five* (Washington, DC: Brookings Institution, 1991).

33. R. Kent Weaver, "The Changing World of Think Tanks," *P.S.: Political Science and Politics* 22 (July 1989): 563–79; Andrew Rich and R. Kent Weaver, "Think Tanks in the U.S. Media," *Harvard International Journal of Press/Politics* 5 (2000): 81–103.

34. Irving Kristol, *Two Cheers for Capitalism* (New York: Basic Books, 1978), 145.

35. William E. Simon, *A Time for Truth* (New York: Reader's Digest Press, 1978), 233.

36. Leonard Silk and David Vogel, *Ethics and Profits: The Crisis of Confidence in American Business* (New York: Simon and Schuster, 1976).

37. Peter H. Stone, "Conservative Brain Trust," *New York Times*, May 10, 1981, F18.

38. David Callahan, *$1 Billion for Ideas: Conservative Think Tanks in the 1990s* (Washington, DC: National Committee for Responsive Philanthropy, 1999).

39. Constructed from table 3 of Rich and Weaver, "Think Tanks in the U.S. Media."

40. Rich and Weaver, "Think Tanks in the U.S. Media," table 5. Other determinants of how often a think tank is cited are its ideological orientation and its location, with higher visibility associated with having no discernible ideology and being located in Washington, D.C.

41. Stone, "Conservative Brain Trust"; Robert C. Wood, *Whatever Possessed the President? Academic Experts and Presidential Policy, 1960–1988* (Amherst: University of Massachusetts Press, 1993); Michael Rust, "Analysis: Filling up at Think Tanks," United Press International, April 11, 2001.

42. Judith Goldstein, *Ideas, Interests, and American Trade Policy* (Ithaca: Cornell University Press, 1993); Judith Goldstein and Robert O. Keohane, "Ideas and Foreign Policy: An Analytical Framework," in *Ideas and Foreign Policy: Beliefs, Institutions, and Political Change* (Ithaca: Cornell University Press, 1993).

43. Sally Covington, *Moving a Public Policy Agenda: The Strategic Philanthropy of Conservative Foundations* (Washington, DC: National Committee for Responsive Philanthropy, 1997); Callahan, *$1 Billion for Ideas.*

44. On the greater amount of foundation giving to liberal causes than to conservative causes, see Althea K. Nagai, Robert Lerner, and Stanley Rothman, *Giving for Social Change: Foundations, Public Policy, and the American Political Agenda* (Westport, CT: Praeger, 1994); and Leslie Lenkowsky, "The Paranoid Perspective in Philanthropy," *The Chronicle of Philanthropy*, June 12, 1997, 61–62.

45. Michael H. Shuman, "Why Do Progressive Foundations Give Too Little to Too Many?" *The Nation*, January 12, 1998, 11–15; Covington, *Moving a Public Policy Agenda*.

46. Lionel Trilling, *The Liberal Imagination: Essays on Literature and Society* (New York: Viking Press, 1950), ix.

47. Mark Blyth, *Great Transformations: Economic Ideas and Institutional Change in the Twentieth Century* (New York: Cambridge University Press, 2002).

CHAPTER FIVE. THE MOVE TO ECONOMIC ARGUMENTS
BY CONSERVATIVE INTELLECTUALS

1. Stephen Moore, "How Big Government Makes America Poorer," *The Insider: A Monthly Compilation of Publication Abstracts, Events, and News* (March 2004): 3–4.

2. Ibid., 3.

3. Ibid., 4.

4. Ibid., 3.

5. Ibid.

6. Ibid., 4.

7. George H. Nash, *The Conservative Intellectual Movement in America Since 1945* (New York: Basic Books, 1976), 14–15.

8. Charles A. Beard, *An Economic Interpretation of the Constitution of the United States* (New York: Macmillan, 1935).

9. Albert Jay Nock, *Our Enemy, the State* (Caldwell, ID: Caxton Printers, 1950 [1935]), 3.

10. Ibid., 10.

11. Ibid., 12–13.

12. Ibid., 187.

13. Ibid., 7.

14. Friedrich A. Hayek, *The Road to Serfdom* (Chicago: University of Chicago Press, 1944), chs. 1–2.

15. Ibid., 32.

16. Ibid., 36.

17. Ibid., ch. 5.

18. Ibid., 62.

19. Ibid., 240.

20. Milton Friedman, *Capitalism and Freedom* (Chicago: University of Chicago Press, 1982 [1962]), 4.

21. Sales figures are provided by the University of Chicago Press.

22. Ibid., 24.

23. Ibid., 15.

24. Ibid., 7–8.

25. Ibid., 2–3, 27–28.

26. Ibid., vi.

27. Thomas Bender, "Intellectual and Cultural History," in Eric Foner, ed., *The New American History* (Philadelphia: Temple University Press, 1997); Donald R. Kelley, "Intellectual History and Cultural History: The Inside and the Outside," *History of the Human Sciences* 15 (1997): 1–19.

28. Quentin Skinner, *Visions of Politics*, vol. 1 (Cambridge: Cambridge University Press, 2002); John G. Pocock, *Virtue, Commerce, and History: Essays on Political Thought and History, Chiefly in the Eighteenth Century* (Cambridge: Cambridge University Press, 1985).

29. Deidre N. McCloskey, *The Rhetoric of Economics*, 2nd ed. (Madison: University of Wisconsin Press, 1998).

30. Martha Derthick and Paul J. Quirk, *The Politics of Deregulation* (Washington, DC: Brookings Institution, 1985); Marc Allen Eisner, *Regulatory Politics in Transition*, 2nd ed. (Baltimore: Johns Hopkins University Press, 2000).

31. Murray L. Weidenbaum, "On Estimating Regulatory Costs," *Regulation* (May/June 1978): 14–17.

32. Mark Green, "The Trouble with Murray; Weidenbaum's Figures Are 'Largely Conjectural,'" *Washington Post*, January 21, 1979, C5.

33. Murray Weidenbaum, *The Future of Business Regulation: Private Action and Public Demand* (New York: AMACOM, 1979).

34. See, for example, Charles O. Jones, *Clean Air: The Policies and Politics of Pollution Control* (Pittsburgh: University of Pittsburgh Press, 1975).

35. The other argument appearing most often in recent opposition to environmental protection involves challenging the scientific findings upon which regulatory proposals often rest.

36. The articles were located by scanning the table of contents in each issue, with further investigation undertaken when titles indicated possible coverage of the topics at hand. Not included were letters to the editor; snippets in "For the Record" and "The Week"; the arts, manners, and book sections; and regional inserts whose content varied across the country. *National Review Bulletin*, sent to subscribers biweekly from 1958 to 1979 on opposite weeks from the full *National Review*, was incorporated into the analysis because it reached a nationwide readership. Some articles focused mainly on a different topic but also discussed regulation, and they were included if they contained at least one paragraph of substantive arguments about regulatory policies. I excluded a small number of articles that did not make any explicit policy arguments, such as an article that simply reported on the current politics of a regulatory bill, taking note of who was for and against it without at least a paragraph of discus-

sion about why a certain position was merited. The purpose of the analysis was to determine the *reasons why* a certain form of social regulation should be praised or criticized; any article that did not state those reasons could not be coded.

37. My objective was to determine each author's primary argument on the desirability of social regulation in general or a specific proposal attracting attention in a legislature, a campaign, a presidential administration, or the news media. The classification did not seek to uncover the larger point of the article, which may or may not have involved advocating a position on public policy, but rather only to code that part that contained explicit arguments on the merits of a certain regulatory program, law, proposal, or action. A total of 201 articles, or about four per year, fell within the scope of the analysis.

38. William H. Peterson, "Giving the Consumer the What-for," *National Review*, June 4, 1963, 453–54.

39. John Chamberlain, "Auto Safety: The Truth of the Hokum," *National Review*, April 4, 1967, 343–46.

40. Richard Carroll, "Some Air Pollution Myths," *National Review*, November 5, 1971, 1233–34.

41. "The Continuing Decline," *National Review*, January 4, 1980, 15–16.

42. "The Environmental Thing," *National Review*, April 30, 1990, 14.

43. Eric Peters, "The Lost Bug," *National Review*, February 9, 1998, 27–30.

44. I calculated intercoder reliability for a sample of forty articles on regulation and those that follow later in the chapter on taxation. The articles were randomly selected from the full set of articles on both issues. Because the population contained far fewer *National Review* articles on regulation than taxation, the latter issue yielded a much larger share of the sample. The two coders' assessments agreed on 80% of the articles.

45. George Gilder, *Wealth and Poverty* (New York: Basic Books, 1981), 272.

46. Bruce R. Bartlett, *Reaganomics: Supply Side Economics in Action* (Westport, CT: Arlington House Publishers, 1981), ch. 1.

47. Andrew W. Mellon, *Taxation: The People's Business* (New York: Macmillan, 1924).

48. Frank Chodorov, *The Income Tax: Root of All Evil* (New York: Devin-Adair, 1959), 31–32.

49. Ibid., 32–33.

50. Charles O. Gavin, "First Lecture," in Charles O. Gavin and Boris I. Bittker, *The Income Tax: How Progressive Should It Be?* (Washington, DC: American Enterprise Institute for Public Policy Research, 1969), 18.

51. Jude Wanniski, *The Way the World Works: How Economies Fail—and Succeed* (New York: Basic Books, 1978).

52. Accounts of the development of supply-side economics can be found in Godfrey Hodgson, *The World Turned Right Side Up: A History of the Conservative Ascendancy in America* (Boston: Houghton Mifflin, 1996), ch. 8; and Sidney

Blumenthal, *The Rise of the Counter-Establishment: From Conservative Ideology to Political* Power (New York: Times Books, 1986), ch. 7.

53. Occasionally an author clearly identified the hierarchy of arguments through a statement such as "The most important reason to support this bill is . . ." More commonly, the implicit ordering had to be determined by examining how much attention was allocated to each point. Suppose that the bulk of the sentences and paragraphs advancing substantive arguments consisted of attempts to show that taxation hinders job creation, yet along the way the author also laments that taxation impinges on personal freedom. Such an article was recorded as being primarily economic. By contrast, if an article advanced a number of economic and noneconomic reasons, giving roughly equal amounts of attention to each, then it was counted as not resting primarily on economic themes. The same classification resulted if the economic consequences of taxes were not mentioned at all. This set of coding rules is identical to those used earlier for social regulation.

54. One can distinguish conceptually between an expand-the-pie argument (which I am calling economic) and a distributive concern about the size of each slice.

55. Mildred Adams McLearn, "Voluntary Taxation—A New Political Concept," *National Review*, June 14, 1958, 561–62.

56. James Jackson Kilpatrick, "Domestic Affairs," *National Review*, July 14, 1964, 586–88; "And in This Corner," *National Review*, May 18, 1965, 406.

57. "Gainsaying Gains," *National Review*, June 9, 1978, 697.

58. "Jobs," *National Review*, June 19, 1987, 18–19.

59. Alexis de Tocqueville, *Democracy in America* (Chicago: University of Chicago Press, 2002 [1835, 1840]); James Morone, *Hellfire Nation: The Politics of Sin in American History* (New Haven: Yale University Press, 2003); Rogers M. Smith, *Civil Ideals: Conflicting Visions of Citizenship in U.S. History* (New Haven: Yale University Press, 1997).

60. Although the quote comes from Herbert Hoover and the 1928 presidential campaign, the goal it describes is nearly universal among politicians.

Chapter Six. The Rhetorical Adaptations of the Republican Party

1. After choosing these cases, I acquired state-of-the-state speeches for all Republican governors serving in the relevant years. Most of the speeches are printed in the state's legislative journals, and the National Governors' Association now archives online the most recent ones. The number of Republican governors ranged from a low of fifteen in 1961 to a high of thirty-one in 1999. In a handful of instances when no state-of-the-state speech was given in a particular state, I used the inaugural address in its place. For many years it was a tradition in some New England states, for example, for the inaugural address to be

delivered to the legislature in the odd-numbered years and the state-of-the-state address, when given at all, in the even-numbered years. In other instances (11% of the total) no speech was given in the particular year, the speeches were not archived, or the speeches could not be acquired.

2. I chose the years by first compiling a list of annual real (inflation-adjusted) GDP growth rates for the nation as a whole. The years in question are defined to include the first quarter of each calendar year and the last three quarters of the previous year. With this choice, I attempted to capture the immediate context of the speeches, which are delivered in the first quarter of each calendar year but react to conditions from previous quarters that affect such pressing concerns as the revenues flowing to state government, the job situation, and the prices of important commodities. After compiling the list of real GDP growth rates, I selected the observations for analysis by examining the figures from odd-numbered years. Because many states employ two-year budgeting and policy-making cycles, the second (even-numbered) year of each legislative cycle typically has fewer policy changes than the first (odd-numbered) year. Accordingly, in the years I picked the governors had the opportunity to significantly shape their states' legislative decision-making.

3. Using national indicators of economic conditions to make the selections rests on an assumption that most of the variation involves all states moving together rather than states moving in different directions. That is, although there often exist differences in economic conditions across states, for the most part when upturns happen in the national economy, they spread to all the states, and the same applies during downturns. Available data support this assumption. From 2004 dating back to 1978, when the Bureau of Labor Statistics began compiling monthly unemployment data for each state, most of the states' annual averages correlate strongly with the national rate. Across all the states, the average correlation with the national unemployment rate is a healthy 0.81.

4. Real GDP growth rates for the four quarters up to and including the one with the speeches were 1.0, −1.0, 1.6, and 1.9, respectively, for 1949, 1961, 1983, and 2001. The figures for 1955, 1965, 1989, and 1999 were 6.0, 5.2, 4.1, and 4.2.

5. On how the identification of genres can aid in rhetorical criticism, see Karlyn Kohrs Campbell and Kathleen Hall Jamieson, eds., *Form and Genre: Shaping Rhetorical Action* (Falls Church, VA: Speech Communication Association, 1978).

6. Fractions were used when only part of the sentence covered economic goals. Speeches that did not contain a goals section (5% of the sample) are not included.

7. In the table, each cell represents the average from the pair of years falling into the respective category. For example, for the pre-1973 strong years, the initial calculation required computing the separate averages among the governors for 1955 and 1965. Those two figures were then averaged to yield the number presented in table 6.1.

8. I constructed a sample of twenty speeches to calculate intercoder reliability rates. The Pearson's correlation between the interval-level variables created by the two coders was .84.

9. Many of the addresses contain no explicit justifications and assume the desirability of improving education or of maintaining or reducing taxes without actually presenting any reasons. Those cases do not count in the calculations that follow. Most of the time, however, the governors presented some rationale for why their proposals should be adopted, thereby spelling out the principles upheld or ends furthered. I identified and coded all sentences making these justifications.

10. For education, economic arguments are those that clearly reference the economy. The most common of these is a statement that certain changes in education policy are needed to prepare students for gainful employment in the workforce or to give them skills needed to compete with workers from other states or countries. Noneconomic arguments in regard to education include preparing students to be democratic citizens, responding to the mandates of the state constitution, general improvement in quality of life, keeping kids from joining the welfare rolls or the prison population, and equalizing the funding of schools to benefit all children throughout the state. In the area of taxes, economic arguments include assertions that a particular legislative proposal would create jobs, provide incentives for business location, encourage investment, keep prices in check, and boost the standard of living. Under a loose definition of "economic," class or distributional effects would count, but they do not under the usage adopted here. Because economic arguments are those that describe the consequences of tax policies for "the economy," assertions about which citizens are benefiting, or whether tax policy tilts too heavily toward the rich or the poor, relate to fairness concerns and hence do not count as economic. Other examples of noneconomic arguments include the necessity of taxes to pay for certain programs, the importance of returning the people's money through tax cuts, or the need to fulfill a campaign promise.

11. Connecticut governor John G. Rowland, "Governor's Address," January 3, 2001, 3. Downloaded from the National Governors Association, http://www.nga.org/nga/legislativeUpdate/, accessed March 21, 2001.

12. New Hampshire governor John H. Sununu, "Inaugural address," January 6, 1983, *House Journal* (Concord, NH: House of Representatives), 18–20.

13. Oklahoma governor Frank Keating, "Governor's Address," February 5, 2001, 8. Downloaded from the National Governors Association, http://www.nga.org/nga/legislativeUpdate/, accessed March 21, 2001.

14. Illinois governor George H. Ryan, "Fiscal Year 2000 Budget, State of the State Address," February 17, 1999, 10. Downloaded from the National Governors Association, http://www.nga.org/nga/legislativeUpdate/, accessed November 3, 1999.

15. Phyllis Schlafly, "Goldwater Paved the Way for Reagan," *St. Louis Post-Dispatch*, June 2, 1998, B7; George Will, "Message of a 'Cheerful Malcontent,'" *New Orleans Times-Picayune*, June 2, 1998, B7; "Extremely Influential; a Landslide Buried Goldwater, but His Ideas Lived on," *Pittsburgh Post-Gazette*, June 1, 1998, A8.

16. Barry Goldwater, "Acceptance Speech," July 16, 1964, 1. Having been reprinted numerous times, the speech is widely available. The version used here was downloaded from http://www.washingtonpost.com/wp-srv/politics/daily/may98/goldwaterspeech.htm, accessed July 22, 2003.

17. The words were crafted by L. Brent Bozell, who relied extensively on Goldwater's earlier speeches. Like the speeches, the book expressed a clear and concise statement of Goldwater's philosophy for which both his backers and detractors acknowledged the authenticity (see note 18).

18. Barry Goldwater, *The Conscience of a Conservative* (New York: MacFadden Books, 1960), 91.

19. Ronald Reagan, "Intent to Run for President," November 13, 1979, 2. The version of the speech I used here is taken from the Reagan Foundation, www.reaganfoundation.org/reagan/speeches/intent.asp, accessed July 22, 2003.

20. Ronald Reagan, "Time to Recapture Our Destiny," July 17, 1980. The version of the speech used here is taken from the Reagan Foundation.

21. "Transcript of Reagan Speech Outlining Five-Year Economic Program for U.S.," *New York Times*, September 10, 1980, B4.

22. The texts of the advertisements were obtained from the Annenberg/Pew Archive of Presidential Campaign Discourse (CD-ROM), which acquired the source materials from the Ronald Reagan Library.

23. Goldwater, *The Conscience of a Conservative*, 14.

24. Ibid., 127.

25. Ibid., 61.

26. Ibid., 64.

27. John C. Hammerback, "Barry Goldwater's Rhetorical Legacy," *Southern Communication Journal* 64 (1989): 323–32.

28. Goldwater, "Acceptance Speech," 1–2.

29. Ibid., 7.

30. Reagan, "Time to Recapture Our Destiny," 5.

31. "Transcript of Reagan Speech."

32. Reagan, "Intent to Run for President," 2.

33. "Transcript of Reagan Speech."

34. Goldwater, *The Conscience of a Conservative*, 69. Emphasis in original.

35. On Reagan's views before becoming a candidate for office, see Amos Kiewe and Davis W. Houck, *A Shining City on a Hill: Ronald Reagan's Economic Rhetoric, 1951–1989* (New York: Praeger, 1991), 12–19.

36. "Transcript of Reagan Address Reporting on the State of the Nation's Economy," *New York Times*, February 6, 1981, A12.

37. "Transcript of State of the Union Message on Economic Recovery," *New York Times*, February 19, 1981, B1.

38. "Transcript of Reagan Speech to Houses of Congress," *New York Times*, April 29, 1981, A3.

39. Darrell West, *Congress and Economic Policymaking* (Pittsburgh: University of Pittsburgh Press, 1987), 41.

40. The 77% figure comes from West, *Congress and Economic Policymaking*, 54.

41. "Transcript of Reagan Speech to Houses of Congress," *New York Times*, April 29, 1981, A22.

42. "Transcript of Reagan Address Reporting on the State of the Nation's Economy," *New York Times*, February 6, 1981, A12.

43. R. Douglas Arnold, *The Logic of Congressional Action* (New Haven: Yale University Press, 1990), 177–81.

44. Full texts of the platforms can be found in Donald Bruce Johnson and Kirk H. Porter, eds., *National Party Platforms, 1840–1972* (Urbana: University of Illinois Press, 1973).

45. Robert M. Collins, *More: The Politics of Economic Growth in Postwar America* (New York: Oxford University Press, 2000), 112.

46. Allen J. Matusow, *Nixon's Economy: Booms, Busts, Dollars, and Votes* (Lawrence: University of Kansas Press, 1998), 16.

47. The 1976 platform was obtained from *Congressional Quarterly Almanac XXXII* (1976): 902–18; the 1980 platform comes from Donald Bruce Johnson, ed., *National Party Platforms of 1980* (Urbana: University of Illinois Press, 1982); the 1984 platform comes from *Congressional Quarterly Almanac XL* (1984): 73B–106B; the 1988, 1992, and 1996 platforms come from www.cnn.com/POLITICS, accessed September 28, 2001; and the 2000 platform comes from www.rnc.org, accessed November 11, 2001. Unlike the others, the 1980 platform was not organized into sections and could not be easily classified. Nevertheless, the economic focus appeared early in the text and hence fits into the pattern reported here.

48. George W. Bush, "Acceptance Speech," August 3, 2000. Downloaded from http://www.cnn.com/ELECTION/2000/conventions/republican/transcripts/bush.html, accessed August 25, 2004.

49. President George W. Bush, "Radio Address by the President to the Nation," February 3, 2001. Downloaded from www.whitehouse.gov/news/radio/20010203.html, accessed August 25, 2004.

50. I calculated the figure by reading the transcript of the floor debate published in *Congressional Record*, 107th Cong., 1st sess. (March 8, 2001).

51. On the close correspondence between the package on which Bush campaigned and what he submitted to Congress, see John D. McKinnon, "The Bush Tax Plan: Bush Turns Election Vow into Tax Package," *Wall Street Journal*, February 8, 2001, A2.

52. Thomas Frank, *What's the Matter with Kansas? How Conservatives Won the Heart of America* (New York: Metropolitian Books, 2004). See also Everett Carll Ladd, Jr., with Charles D. Hadley, *Transformations of the American Party System: Political Coalitions from the New Deal to the 1970s* (New York: W. W. Norton, 1975).

53. Larry M. Bartels, "What's the Matter with *What's the Matter with Kansas*," *Quarterly Journal of Political Science* 1 (2006): 201–26. See also Bartels's earlier paper, "What's the Matter with *What's the Matter with Kansas*," paper presented at the annual meeting of the American Political Science Association, September 1–4, 2005.

54. Jeffrey M. Stonecash, *Class and Party in American Politics* (Boulder, CO: Westview Press, 2000); Nolan McCarty, Keith T. Poole, and Howard Rosenthal, *Polarized America: The Dance of Ideology and Unequal Riches* (Cambridge, MA: MIT Press, 2006).

CHAPTER SEVEN. DEMOCRATS AND THE LONG SHADOW
OF DEFICIT POLITICS

1. The platform can be found online at www.democrats.org/pdfs/2000platform.pdf.

2. Andrea Campbell, "Parties, Electoral Participation, and Shifting Voting Blocs," paper presented at the conference on the Transformation of American Politics, Harvard University, December 10–11, 2004. The bulk of Campbell's essay, it should be noted, focuses on other themes. In the quotations here, she is summarizing the conventional wisdom rather than reporting the findings of her own research.

3. Media coverage of campaigns, by comparison, flows from the imperatives and norms of the journalistic enterprise, meaning that candidates can affect but cannot control how the news portrays them. When their rhetoric and positions are refracted through opposing parties, interest groups, and commentators, the amount of control shrinks still further.

4. With the exception of those from Barry Goldwater, all of the ads for 1952–1996 were acquired from the Annenberg/Pew Archive of Presidential Campaign Discourse (CD-ROM). Goldwater's ads (with some missing) were acquired from the Living Room Candidate, http://livingroomcandidate.movingimage.us/index.php, accessed July 20, 2005. A partial collection of the ads of Al Gore and George W. Bush in 2000 was acquired from the Living Room Candidate, http://livingroomcandidate.movingimage.us/index.php, accessed February 3, 2005, and from the Stanford University Political Communication Lab, http://pcl.stanford.edu/campaigns/index.html, accessed February 3, 2005. The full set of John Kerry's ads in 2004 were acquired from his campaign Web site, http://www.johnkerry.com/tv/, accessed February 7, 2005; George W. Bush's ads in 2004 come from the *Houston Chronicle*, http://www.chron.com/

content/chronicle/electioncentral/2004/adsarchive.ssi, accessed March 22, 2005.

5. Descriptions of candidates' backgrounds and vague appeals to families, children, the future, or the middle class fall outside the coding system, but linkages to specific issues—say, a program promoting child nutrition—are included. Statements that cut across two issue areas are classified in both; for example, a proposal for "tax cuts to help parents pay for college" goes under taxes and education.

6. A second coder classified the advertisements of six candidates (the Democrats in 1952, 1968, and 2000 and the Republicans in 1964, 1980, and 2004) to determine intercoder reliability. The average Pearson's correlation coefficient between the two coders' assessments of each candidate was .89.

7. Robert Alan Goldberg, *Barry Goldwater* (New Haven: Yale University Press, 1995), 105, 120.

8. Goldwater made the remark on the floor of the Senate. See *Congressional Record*, 87th Cong., 1st sess. (June 27, 1961): 11471.

9. Barry Goldwater, *The Conscience of a Conservative* (New York: MacFadden Books, 1960), 65.

10. "Transcript of Reagan Speech Outlining Five-Year Economic Program for U.S.," *New York Times*, September 10, 1980, B4.

11. Ibid.

12. David Stockman, *The Triumph of Politics: How the Reagan Revolution Failed* (New York: Harper and Row, 1986), 124–25.

13. Goldberg, *Barry Goldwater*, 315.

14. For a similar interpretation, see Robert M. Collins, *More: The Politics of Economic Growth in Postwar America* (New York: Oxford University Press, 2000), 204–10.

15. Amos Kiewe and Davis W. Houck, *A Shining City on a Hill: Ronald Reagan's Economic Rhetoric, 1951–1989* (New York: Praeger, 1991), 12–19.

16. "Kemp-Reagan vs. Simon-Reagan?" *National Review*, April 4, 1980, 392–93.

17. Irving Kristol, "The Battle for Reagan's Soul," *Wall Street Journal*, May 16, 1980, A22.

18. As cited in James D. Savage, *Balanced Budgets and American Politics* (Ithaca: Cornell University Press, 1988), 190.

19. Christopher H. Achen and Larry M. Bartels, "Musical Chairs: Pocketbook Voting and the Limits of Democratic Accountability," paper presented at the Annual Meeting of the American Political Science Association, Chicago, 2004.

20. For discussion about this alternative strategy, see Thomas Ferguson and Joel Rogers, *Right Turn: The Decline of the Democrats and the Future of American Politics* (New York: Hill and Wang, 1986).

21. Walter Mondale, acceptance speech before the Democratic National

Convention, San Francisco, California, July 19, 1984; Annenberg/Pew Archive of Presidential Campaign Discourse.

22. See, for example, Walter Mondale, transcript of debate with Ronald Reagan at the Kentucky Center for the Arts, Louisville, Kentucky, October 7, 1984; Annenberg/Pew Archive of Presidential Campaign Discourse.

23. Scott Keeter, "Public Opinion in 1984," in Gerald M. Pomper, ed., *The Election of 1984: Reports and Interpretations* (Chatham, NJ: Chatham House Publishers, 1985), 91–111.

24. Ronald Reagan, acceptance speech before the Republican National Convention, Dallas, Texas, August 23, 1984; Annenberg/Pew Archive of Presidential Campaign Discourse; Ronald Reagan, transcript of debate with Walter Mondale at the Kentucky Center for the Arts, Louisville, Kentucky, October 7, 1984.

25. Ronald Reagan, speeches delivered in Deshler, Ohio, October 12, 1984; in Tuscaloosa, Alabama, October 15, 1984; and in Portland, Oregon, October 23, 1984; Annenberg/Pew Archive of Presidential Campaign Discourse.

26. The phrase "unreconstructed New Dealer" is offered by John Micklethwait and Adrian Wooldridge, *The Right Nation: Conservative Power in America* (New York: Penguin Press, 2004), 97.

27. The income figure for 1984 comes from U.S. Census Bureau, Historical Income Tables—Households, "Table H-6. Regions—All Races by Median and Mean Income: 1975 to 2003"; http://www.census.gov/hhes/income/histinc/h06ar.html, accessed February 13, 2005.

28. "Perot Outscores Regular Shows," *New York Times*, October 20, 1992, A18.

29. Clinton for President Committee, "A Plan for America's Future," January 1992, Little Rock, Arkansas; "Fighting for the Forgotten Middle Class," March 1992, Little Rock, Arkansas; "Putting People First," June 1992, Little Rock, Arkansas.

30. Clinton's campaign later expanded "Putting People First" into a full-length book.

31. Bob Woodward, *The Agenda: Inside the Clinton White House* (New York: Simon and Schuster, 1994), 42.

32. *President Clinton's New Beginning: The Complete Text, with Illustrations, of the Historic Clinton-Gore Economic Conference, Little Rock, Arkansas, December 14–15, 1992* (New York: D. I. Fine, 1993).

33. "Bush Leaves Clinton a Budget Surprise," *Congresssional Quarterly Almanac*, 103rd Congr., 1st sess. 49 (1994): 82–84.

34. Theda Skocpol, *Boomerang: Health Care Reform and the Turn against Government* (New York: W. W. Norton, 1997).

35. The phrase "Rebuild America" is from Clinton for President Committee, "Fighting for the Forgotten Middle Class."

36. Robert B. Reich, *Locked in the Cabinet* (New York: Alfred A. Knopf, 1997), 64.

37. Woodward, *The Agenda*, 165.

38. David W. Brady, John F. Cogan, Brian J. Gaines, and Douglas Rivers, "The Perils of Presidential Support: How the Republicans Took the House in the 1994 Midterm Elections," *Political Behavior* 18 (1996): 345–67.

39. Benjamin I. Page and Robert Y. Shapiro, *The Rational Public: Fifty Years of Trends in Americans' Policy Preferences* (Chicago: University of Chicago Press, 1992).

40. Savage, *Balanced Budgets*.

41. Andre Modigliani and Franco Modigliani, "The Growth of the Federal Deficit and the Role of Public Attitudes," *Public Opinion Quarterly* 51 (Winter 1987): 459–80.

42. David O. Sears and Jack Citrin, *Tax Revolt: Something for Nothing in California* (Cambridge, MA: Harvard University Press, 1982).

43. James M. Buchanan, *Liberty, Market, and State: Political Economy in the 1980s* (New York: New York University Press, 1985).

44. For additional discussion on this point, see Mark Blyth, *Great Transformations: Economic Ideas and Institutional Change in the Twentieth Century* (New York: Cambridge University Press, 2002), ch. 6.

CHAPTER EIGHT. THE REPUBLICANS' ELECTORAL EDGE ON THE ECONOMY

1. "Dems Battle over Confederate Flag," CNN.com, November 2, 2003, http://www.cnn.com/2003/ALLPOLITICS/11/01/elec04.prez.dean.confederate.flag/, accessed February 5, 2005.

2. "Scream 2," *New Republic*, December 13, 2004, 9.

3. John Judis, "Structural Flaw," *New Republic*, February 28, 2005, 20.

4. John R. Petrocik, "Issue Ownership in Presidential Elections, with a 1980 Case Study," *American Journal of Political Science* 40 (1996): 825–50; Byron E. Shafer and William J. M. Claggett, *The Two Majorities: The Issue Context of Modern American Politics* (Baltimore: Johns Hopkins University Press, 1995); Byron E. Shafer, *The Two Majorities and the Puzzle of Modern American Politics* (Lawrence: University of Kansas Press, 2003).

5. The questions must be asked more than once over time so that changes can be assessed. Questions about particular candidates or those that focused only on Congress are not included here; the intention was to identify public opinion specifically about the *parties*. Public Opinion Online, the archive of public opinion marginals maintained by the Roper Center for Public Opinion Research, was invaluable for locating the relevant material.

6. Although question-wording effects are prevalent in public opinion polls, the close similarity in the wording of the questions used here makes any systematic biases unlikely.

7. See Robert S. Erikson, Michael B. MacKuen, and James A. Stimson, *The Macro Polity* (Cambridge: Cambridge University Press, 2002).

8. Following Erikson, MacKuen, and Stimson, I apply a correction of 3.12 points to account for the greater number of Republicans that emerged when Gallup switched from using in-person to telephone surveys. Without the correction, an immediate Republican gain in partisan support of 3.12 points appears, which can be shown to simply reflect a method artifact. Measures of perceptions of the parties on prosperity and macropartisanship both receive this adjustment when they are based upon polls conducted by Gallup. See Erikson, MacKuen, and Stimson, *The Macro Polity,* 121.

9. When two or more observations per quarter were available for a sample of the national adult population, they were averaged together; in many cases, however, no data at all could be gathered for the prosperity question. In total, 120 of the 216 quarters from 1951 to 2004 and 46 of the 54 years yield usable observations.

10. Political scientists often study the raw numbers—which party people prefer on the economy—whereas the data here focus on comparative advantage, or how much the economy benefits the Democrats or Republicans by comparison with everything else affecting people's party identifications. For example, an edge for the Democrats on the raw numbers in 2000 is documented in Richard Johnston, Michael G. Hagen, and Kathleen Hall Jamieson, *The 2000 Presidential Election and the Foundations of Party Politics* (Cambridge: Cambridge University Press, 2004), ch. 5. The difference between their interpretation and mine, then, is that they are reporting the raw numbers that favored Democrats whereas I show here that the comparative advantage favored Republicans.

11. Michael X. Delli Carpini and Scott Keeter, *What Americans Know about Politics and Why It Matters* (New Haven: Yale University Press, 1996), 316.

12. Incidentally, the same differences in economic performance appear in more robust form during the post–World War II years before 1972. The Democrats (Truman, Kennedy-Johnson, and Johnson) had an average real GDP growth rate of 4.9%, or 5.4% when allocating the first year of each administration to the previous president. The Republicans (Eisenhower I, Eisenhower II, and Nixon I) registered much lower average raw and adjusted growth rates, 3.0% and 3.0% respectively.

13. Larry M. Bartels, "Partisan Politics and the U.S. Income Distribution" (working paper, Princeton University, 2004).

14. For an overview, see Michael S. Lewis-Beck and Mary Stegmaier, "Economic Determinants of Electoral Outcomes," *Annual Review of Political Science* 3 (2000): 183–219.

15. The coefficient on the independent variable should be positive when Republicans hold the presidency, meaning that the public's economic preferences move toward the GOP in the presence of concrete proof of the party's bona fides. When the president is a Democrat, though, it is lower growth that should bolster the comparative advantage of Republicans—an expectation built into the model by multiplying the GDP variable by −1 when Democrats

occupy the White House. By the same logic, either fast growth under Democrats or slow growth under Republicans should shift the public's judgments toward Democrats and away from Republicans. After a recoding of the independent variable, the hypothesized relationships imply a positive coefficient on real GDP growth.

16. The variables are measured contemporaneously with each other, but missing data on economic assessments of the parties force the sample size down to 120.

17. The relationship between the state of the economy and the figures on comparative advantage, although clearly present, is weaker than typical findings in published research on how much the economy influences election outcomes. One possible explanation for this discrepancy is that the model estimated here requires the public to transfer its evaluations beyond the incumbent president and to the person's party, where some slippage is possible. In the analyses within most of the existing research, voters can simply reward or punish the incumbent or a designated proxy appearing on the ballot, such as the vice president, without making the transition to crediting or blaming the president's entire party as well.

18. The resulting measure is conceptually similar but not identical to the residuals, which can be calculated by subtracting from the dependent variable the effects not only of the independent variable but also the constant. The residuals always carry a mean of zero by definition, whereas the measure desired for this chapter has no predetermined average.

19. Conceivably the economy affects economic perceptions of the parties in ways that the model summarized in table 8.2 has failed to capture. To address this possibility, I reestimated the model while including a wider array of economic variables as explanatory factors. More specifically, I included as measures of the economy not only real GDP growth but also the unemployment rate, the inflation rate, and the growth rates of the index of lagging indicators and the index of coincident indicators. All variables were recoded (as before) by multiplying them by −1 during periods when Democrats held the presidency. The coefficient on real GDP growth is the only one that reaches statistical significance at the .05 level. I also estimated a model with a full year's worth of data for each indicator, using lag 0 (the current quarter) as well as the first three lags. The purpose of this procedure is to attempt intentionally to "overfit" the model. To show that important variation remains unexplained by the state of the economy, one must give the economy every chance to explain the movements in economic perceptions of the parties. This approach borrows heavily from Suzanna DeBoef and Paul M. Kellstedt, "The Political (and Economic) Origins of Consumer Confidence," *American Journal of Political Science* 48 (October 2004): 633–49. In this additional analysis, none of the individual coefficients are statistically significant, which would be expected because of the massive collinearity when including four lags of each economic indicator. More relevant, then, is the joint

statistical significance of the lags on each variable. F-tests show that the variables' four lags are not statistically significant as a group. Thus, the best model is the one reported in table 8.2, which includes only real GDP growth, measured contemporaneously.

20. Real GDP growth is recoded (as before) by multiplying it by -1 for elections in which the incumbent administration is Democratic. To permit an apples-to-apples comparison, the two independent variables are measured over the same intervals by averaging them across all quarters from the election year in which data for both variables are available. Similarly, to ensure proper time-ordering—the independent variables occurring before the dependent variable—real GDP growth and the PAER do not include any observations from the quarter of the election year (the fourth) when elections take place.

21. Bob Woodward, *The Agenda: Inside the Clinton White House* (New York: Simon and Schuster, 1994), 54.

22. Marc J. Hetherington, "The Media's Role in Forming Voters' National Economic Evaluations in 1992," *American Journal of Political Science* 40 (1996): 372–95. See also DeBoef and Kellstedt, "The Political (and Economic) Origins of Consumer Confidence," who report that "irrational pessimism" peaked in 1992.

23. James E. Campbell, "Introduction: The 2004 Presidential Election Forecasts," *PS: Political Science and Politics* 37 (2004): 733–35.

24. Barry C. Burden, "An Alternative Account of the 2004 Presidential Election," *The Forum: A Journal of Applied Research in Contemporary Politics* 2, no. 4 (November 15, 2004): article 2.

25. See the symposium in *PS: Political Science and Politics* 34 (2001): 8–48.

26. The closest approximation to a comprehensive explanation contained within two covers can be found in Warren E. Miller and J. Merrill Shanks, *The New American Voter* (Cambridge, MA: Harvard University Press, 1996).

27. See, for example, Geoffrey C. Layman, "Religion and Political Behavior in the United States: The Impact of Beliefs, Affiliations, and Commitment from 1980 to 1994," *Public Opinion Quarterly* 61 (1997): 288–316; Herbert Weisberg, "The Structure and Effects of Moral Predispositions in Contemporary American Politics," *The Journal of Politics* 67 (2005): 646–68; Jonathan Knuckey, "A New Front in the Culture War? Moral Traditionalism and Voting Behavior in U.S. House Elections," *American Politics Research* 33 (2005): 645–71; John Kenneth White, *The Values Divide: American Politics and Culture in Transition* (New York: Chatham House Publishers, 2003).

28. Burden, "An Alternative Account of the 2004 Presidential Election"; Andrew J. Taylor, *Elephant's Edge: The Republicans as a Ruling Party* (Westport, CT: Praeger, 2005), ch. 5.

29. See, for example, David Lublin, *The Republican South: Democratization and Partisan Change* (Princeton: Princeton University Press, 2004); Jacob S. Hacker and Paul Pierson, *Off Center: The Republican Revolution and the Erosion of American Democracy* (New Haven: Yale University Press, 2005); Taylor, *Elephant's*

Edge; Thomas Byrne Edsall with Mary D. Edsall, *Chain Reaction: The Impact of Race, Rights, and Taxes on American Politics* (New York: W. W. Norton, 1991).

30. Besides the supposed bait and switch, *What's the Matter with Kansas* makes other, related arguments not directly tested here. In particular, Frank contends that the Republican party has increasingly induced the white working class to vote against its self-interests. For evidence that undermines his claim on that score, see Larry M. Bartels, "What's the Matter with *What's the Matter with Kansas*," *Quarterly Journal of Political Science* 1 (2006): 201–26; Jeffrey M. Stonecash, *Class and Party in American Politics* (Boulder, CO: Westview Press, 2000); and Nolan McCarty, Keith T. Poole, and Howard Rosenthal, *Polarized America: The Dance of Ideology and Unequal Riches* (Cambridge, MA: MIT Press, 2006).

CHAPTER NINE. THE BROAD REACH AND FUTURE PROSPECTS OF ECONOMIC RHETORIC

1. Angie Kiesling, "'Jabez' Enlarges Multnomah's 'Territory,'" *Publisher's Weekly*, April 1, 2002, 17. With sales of 9.2 million in its first two years, the book surpassed 10 million copies shortly thereafter.

2. Bruce Wilkinson, *The Prayer of Jabez: Breaking Through to the Blessed Life* (Sisters, OR: Multnomah Publishers, 2000), 13.

3. The Lord's Prayer appears in Matthew 6:9–13 and Luke 11:2–4.

4. 1 Chronicles 4:10. Wilkinson uses the New King James Version of the Bible.

5. Wilkinson, *The Prayer of Jabez*, 31.

6. Philip Zaleski, "In Defense of Jabez," *First Things: A Monthly Journal of Religion and Public Life* (October 2001): 10–12.

7. William H. Riker, *The Art of Political Manipulation* (New Haven: Yale University Press, 1986).

8. On how mass prosperity facilitates progressive political change, see Benjamin M. Friedman, *The Moral Consequences of Economic Growth* (New York: Knopf, 2005).

9. Jacob S. Hacker, *The Great Risk Shift: Assault on American Jobs, Families, Health Care, and Retirement—and How You Can Fight Back* (New York: Oxford University Press, 2006); Diego Comin, Erica L. Groshen, and Bess Rabin, "Turbulent Firms, Turbulent Wages?" (working paper no. 12032, National Bureau of Economic Research, February 2006).

10. Debora Vrana, "Rising Premiums Threaten Job-Based Health Coverage," *Los Angeles Times*, September 15, 2005, A1.

11. Aaron M. McCright and Riley E. Dunlap, "Challenging Global Warming as a Social Problem: An Analysis of the Conservative Movement's Counter-Claims," *Social Problems* 47 (November 2000): 499–522.

12. Naomi Oreskes, "Beyond the Ivory Tower: The Scientific Consensus on Climate Change," *Science* 306 (December 2004): 1686.

13. McCright and Dunlap, "Challenging Global Warming as a Social Problem."

14. George W. Bush, "Press Conference," March 29, 2001. Downloaded from www.whitehouse.gov/news/releases/2001/03/20010329.html, accessed February 18, 2005.

15. Ari Fleischer, "Press Briefing," March 28, 2001. Downloaded from www.whitehouse.gov/news/briefings, accessed August 23, 2004.

16. George W. Bush, "President Bush Discusses Global Climate Change," June 11, 2001. Downloaded from http://www.whitehouse.gov/news/releases/2001/06/20010611-2.html, accessed February 18, 2005.

17. Michael Crichton, *State of Fear: A Novel* (New York: HarperCollins, 2004).

18. William Strunk, Jr., with E. B. White, *The Elements of Style*, 3rd ed. (New York: Macmillan, 1979).

19. For a similar view, see Frank R. Baumgartner and Bryan D. Jones, *Agendas and Instability in American Politics* (Chicago: University of Chicago Press, 1993).

20. George W. Bush, "State of the Union Address," January 31, 2006. Downloaded from http://www.whitehouse.gov/stateoftheunion/2006/, accessed March 23, 2006.

21. W. Norton Grubb and Marvin Lazerson, *The Educational Gospel: The Economic Power of Schooling* (Cambridge, MA: Harvard University Press, 2004).

22. Jonathan Cole, "Academic Freedom Under Fire," *Daedalus* 135 (Spring 2005): 2.

23. *Ninth Annual Grant Thornton Manufacturing Climates Study* (Chicago: Grant Thornton, 1988).

24. The Cato Institute, the Tax Foundation, and the Small Business & Entrepreneurship Council are among the organizations constructing the state-by-state rankings.

25. Richard Florida, *The Rise of the Creative Class: And How It's Transforming Work, Leisure, Community and Everyday Life* (New York: Basic Books, 2002).

ACKNOWLEDGMENTS

I began working on this project five years ago believing that economic ideas and arguments were central to the flow of American politics, but I was uncertain about the specific ways in which they mattered. During my subsequent reading and research, I discovered the connections between my interests and a range of interdisciplinary literatures in rhetoric and communication, policy studies, political sociology, public opinion, and intellectual history. Now that the book is complete, I am surprised by how much it has evolved since I began.

I am grateful to the reviewers for Princeton University Press and to friends and colleagues who read and commented on the entire manuscript in one of its drafts: Graeme Boushey, Laura Evans, John Gastil, Talal Hattar, Bryan Jones, and Jeff Wolf. All helped diagnose problems with the manuscript and encouraged me to rethink important parts of its theory and evidence. I also benefited from the insights of those who read parts of the book, especially Jeff Hornstein, Paul Kellstedt, Dave Peterson, Paul Pierson, Gary Segura, and Steve Teles. Research is a communal enterprise, perhaps never more so than when scholars give each other a fair and honest critique that allows the author to tighten the argument and address its shortcomings.

The University of Washington contributed to the manuscript through both a faculty leave and a grant from its Royalty Research Fund. I received valuable research assistance from Rose

Ernst, Seth Greenfest, and Trevor Zimmerman. The staff of Princeton University Press, especially Chuck Myers and Linny Schenck, skillfully carried the book to publication, and Dalia Geffen provided excellent copy editing. Parts of chapters 5 and 8 were published earlier in *Studies in American Political Development* (2006) and *The Transformation of the American Polity* (2007), edited by Paul Pierson and Theda Skocpol. I appreciate the publishers' permission to include a revised version of the material.

Among my family, John Hammerback went far above and beyond a father-in-law's call of duty by carefully reading and editing two versions of the manuscript. In addition to clarifying and enlivening my prose, he continually used his keen judgment and scholarly acumen to push my thinking to the next level. My wife, Kristen Hammerback, cheerfully served as the sounding board for all of my work in progress and pointed out the instances where my ideas were half baked. Julie and Ali, my energetic and loving daughters, kept my spirits high and my life balanced.

INDEX